Psychology Without Foundations

Psychology Without Foundations

History, Philosophy and Psychosocial Theory

Steven D. Brown and Paul Stenner

Los Angeles | London | New Delhi
Singapore | Washington DC

SAGE Publications Ltd
1 Oliver's Yard
55 City Road
London EC1Y 1SP

SAGE Publications Inc.
2455 Teller Road
Thousand Oaks, California 91320

SAGE Publications India Pvt Ltd
B 1/I 1 Mohan Cooperative Industrial Area
Mathura Road, Post Bag 7
New Delhi 110 044

SAGE Publications Asia-Pacific Pte Ltd
33 Pekin Street #02-01
Far East Square
Singapore 048763

Library of Congress Control Number: 2008938915

British Library Cataloguing in Publication data

A catalogue record for this book is available
from the British Library

ISBN 978-0-7619-7226-6
ISBN 978-0-7619-7227-3 (pbk)

Typeset by C&M Digitals (P) Ltd, Chennai, India
Printed in India at Replika Press Pvt Ltd
Printed on paper from sustainable resources

We dedicate this book to Ailbhe, Ezra, Kittie and Anna: XoX

Contents

Preface

Psychology Without Foundations offers a range of philosophical and theoretical resources that contribute to a vision of psychology as a transdiscipline. The guiding theme is that we need to rethink our relationship to foundations and to affirm the paradox that foundations must be continually self-constructed. A case is made for a 'reflexive' or 'creative' (non)foundationalism that might give rise to a 'psychology of the second order'. The psychological resists any easy determination. We must seek an 'image of the psychological' as it appears across the most diverse of terrains. To this end the book assembles a range of thinkers who share an orientation to reality as multiply mediated *process* or *becoming*.

Following an introductory chapter, the philosophies of Alfred North Whitehead and Michel Serres are drawn upon to introduce these twin concepts of process and mediation. Each of the subsequent six chapters takes a key thinker as a guide to an important psychological topic. These include Niklas Luhmann (on communication); Antonin Artaud (on embodiment); Baruch Spinoza (on affect); Henri Bergson (on memory); Michel Foucault (on subjectivity) and Gilles Deleuze (on life). A final chapter proposes a concept of experience based on the relations between power (or affect), image (or percept), proposition (or concept) and enunciation (or discourse) in order to make the arts of existence or the art of living the central object of psychology. The book is envisaged as a work of assemblage rather than systematisation and as an intervention into the current impasse between critical psychology and the 'mainstream'.

Acknowledgements

This book has been long in preparation. In fact, since we began working on it a series of events has flowed under the bridge. We have moved through four jobs (Paul from the University of Bath to University College London and then to the University of Brighton, Steve from Keele University to Loughborough University to the University of Leicester); moved house four times; had three children (two for Paul and one for Steve); and both of us have turned 40... We therefore have more people to thank than we could possibly acknowledge here, including various employees of Sage Publications who have patiently fielded our various requests for extensions (special thanks to Michael Carmichael and Sophie Hine).

Thanks also to those who kindly read through drafts of various chapters or who otherwise offered support, inspiration and criticism (including Matt Allien, Casper Bruun Jensen, Mark Egan, Ros Gill, Lewis Goodings, Monica Greco, Paul Hanna, Paula Reavey, Carlos Silva, Derek Stenner)

Paul would like to thank Günther Teubner, the Alexander von Humboldt Foundation, and the Leverhulme Trust for enabling a year in Frankfurt that challenged him to engage with some of the more philosophical aspects of psychology, and also Axel Honneth, Tilman Habermas, Ute Osterkamp and Dimitris Papadopoulos for your unexpected hospitality and thought-food.

Steve would like to thank his former colleagues across the way in Social Sciences at Loughborough for their good training, especially Malcolm Ashmore who finds himself included here; his new colleagues at Leicester for their support and loveliness; SPEDO survivors John Cromby, Darren Ellis, Lewis Goodings, Harriet Gross, Abi Locke, Johanna Motzkau, Ian Tucker; and especially Dave Middleton, Hugo Letiche and Paula Reavey for support, friendship and more.

Chapter 2 includes elements of Stenner, P. (2007). Non-foundational criticality? On the need for a process ontology of the psychosocial. *Outlines, Critical Social Studies*, 9(2), 44–55; and Stenner, P. (2008). A.N. Whitehead and subjectivity, *Subjectivity*, 22, 90–109.

Chapter 3 includes elements of Stenner, P. (2006). An outline of an autopoietic systems approach to emotion. *Cybernetics and Human Knowing, 12*(4), 8–22; Stenner, P. (2007). The adventure of psychosocial studies: re-visioning the space between the psychic and the social. Inaugural Lecture, Brighton: http://www.brighton.ac.uk/sass/contact/staffprofiles/stenner/inaugural_lecture.pdf; Brown, S.D. (2002). Michel Serres: science, translation and the logic of the parasite. *Theory, Culture & Society, 19*(3), 1–27; and Brown, S.D. (2004). Parasite logic. *Journal of Organisational Change Management, 17*(4), 383–395.

Chapter 5 includes elements of Brown, S.D. (2007). After power: Artaud and the theatre of cruelty. In C. Jones & R. ten Bos (Eds.), *Philosophy and organization* (pp. 201–223). London: Routledge; and Brown, S.D. (2005). Collective emotions: Artaud's nerves. *Culture & Organization, 11*(4), 235–246.

Chapter 6 includes elements of Brown, S.D. & Stenner. P. (2001). Being affected: Spinoza and the psychology of emotion. *International Journal of Group Tensions, 30*(1), 81–105.

Chapter 7 includes elements of Ashmore, M., Brown, S.D., & MacMillan, K. (2005). Lost in the mall with Mesmer and Wundt: demarcation and demonstration in the psychologies. *Science, Technology & Human Values, 30*(1), 76–110; and Middleton, D. & Brown, S.D. (2005). *The social psychology of experience: studies in remembering and forgetting.* London: Sage.

Publisher's Acknowledgements

The authors and publishers wish to thank the following for permission to use copyright material:

We thank the Department of Psychology at the University of Copenhagen and the University Press of Southern Denmark for permission to reproduce elements of Stenner, P. (2007). Non-foundational criticality? On the need for a process ontology of the psychosocial. *Outlines, Critical Social Studies*, 9(2): 44–55.

We thank Elsevier for permission to reproduce the opening quotation to Chapter 4. Reprinted from Ashmore, M., MacMillan, K., & Brown, S. D. (2004). It's a scream: professional hearing and tape fetishism. *Journal of Pragmatics*, 36(2): 349–374.

We thank Emerald for permission to reproduce elements of Brown, S.D. (2004). Parasite logic. *Journal of Organisational Change Management*, 17(4): 383–395.

We thank Imprint Academic for permission to reproduce elements of Stenner, P. (2006). An outline of an autopoietic systems approach to emotion. *Cybernetics and Human Knowing*, 12(4): 8–22.

We thank Palgrave Macmillan for permission to reproduce elements of Stenner, P. (2008). A.N. Whitehead and subjectivity. *Subjectivity*, 22: 90–109.

We thank SAGE Publications for permission to reproduce the following:

Elements of Ashmore, M., Brown, S.D., & MacMillan, K. (2005). Lost in the mall with Mesmer and Wundt: demarcation and demonstration in the psychologies. *Science, Technology & Human Values*, 30(1): 76–110.

Elements of Brown, S.D. (2002). Michel Serres: science, translation and the logic of the parasite. *Theory, Culture & Society*, 19(3): 1–27.

Elements of Middleton, D. & Brown, S.D. (2005). *The social psychology of experience: studies in remembering and forgetting*. London: Sage.

We thank Springer Science and Business Media for permission to reproduce elements of Brown, S.D. & Stenner, P. (2001). Being affected: Spinoza and the psychology of emotion. *International Journal of Group Tensions*, *30*(1): 81–105.

We thank The Johns Hopkins University Press for permission to reproduce Serres, M. *The parasite*. Figure, pg 4. © 1982 The Johns Hopkins University Press. Reprinted with permission of the John Hopkins University Press.

We thank Taylor and Francis for permission to reproduce the following:

Elements of Brown, S. D. (2007). After power: Artaud and the theatre of cruelty. In C. Jones and R. ten Bos (Eds). *Philosophy and organization* (pp. 201–223). London: Routledge.

Elements of Brown, S.D. (2005). Collective emotions: Artaud's nerves. *Culture & Organization*, *11*(4): 235–246 (http://www.informaworld.com).

We thank the University of Michigan Press for permission to reproduce an extract from Serres, M. (1995). *Conversations on science, culture, and time* (R. Lapidus, Trans.). Ann Arbor: University of Michigan Press.

ONE

The First Word or: in the Beginning is the Middle

> For an instant, the tranced boat's crew stood still; then turned. 'The ship? Great God, where is the ship?' Soon they through dim, bewildering mediums saw her sidelong fading phantom, as in the gaseous Fata Morgana; only the uppermost masts out of water; while fixed by infatuation, or fidelity, or fate, to their once lofty perches, the pagan harpooneers still maintained their sinking look-outs on the sea. And now, concentric circles seized the lone boat itself, and all its crew, and each floating oar, and every lancepole, and spinning, animate and inanimate, all round and round in one vortex, carried the smallest chip of the Pequod out of sight. (*Moby-Dick*, ch. 135)

We start at the end, at the famous scene in Herman Melville's novel where the whaling ship *Pequod*, having finally engaged the great white whale, is crushed by Moby-Dick and slips slowly into the waters. The tiresome journey, driven forward by the obsession of Captain Ahab, is finished. But not for all. There is a survivor, Ishmael, who floats in the shark-infested waters, orphaned, awaiting his eventual rescue. What does Ishmael think as he bobs on the ocean and considers his miraculous fate? Does he actually consider himself saved? Would he not have preferred to have followed Ahab and the *Pequod* to the very end of their mission? Does he consider how to begin again, is he already dreaming of resuming the search for Moby-Dick? Or does his future lead elsewhere, away from the whale and the sea?

Melville's classic is a novel which dwells at great length on ambitions, obsessions, on the drive to accomplish projects that seem perpetually just out of reach. As such, it is a psychological novel, a work that grapples with what it means to be a person. Ahab's search for the white whale is an exemplary demonstration of human endeavour, of the desire to have done with something, to have finished off and realised a goal. Melville suggests that such ambitions contain within them something fateful and portentous. The search for Moby-Dick will end in tragedy. It is destined to go unresolved. At the very end of the novel the whale itself – which has in any case only existed as, at best, a wave on the surface of the water, and, at worst, the object of Ahab's fevered vengeance – disappears entirely. Ahab, along with Starbuck, Queequeq, Tashtego and the entire crew are drawn towards the end of their long, wearisome search. Except for the sole survivor, belched back to the surface of the water from the sinking wreck. Call me Ishmael…

This is a book about what it means to think psychologically. About what it might mean, what it could mean to be a social psychologist. It is a book, we hope, befitting the times. To write on these themes 50 years, maybe even 30 years, ago would mean starting in a very different way. We would perhaps begin with the departure of the *Pequod* as it sets sail, determined in its search. We would seek to write from the perspective not of Ishmael but of Ahab, with his dogged conviction that the whale is within his reach. In other words that it is possible to be entirely clear about precisely what it means to study the psychological, and that, moreover, the project of a social psychology is both clearly mapped and entirely realisable. From our historical perspective, we are less sure.

What separates Ishmael and Ahab is the shipwreck. What separates twenty-first-century from twentieth-century social psychology is not quite as dramatic, but every bit as eventful. It is the so-called 'crisis' experienced by the discipline in the 1970s. This comprised an intense set of debates about the nature of doing social psychology (see Gergen, 1973, 1982/1994; Harre & Secord, 1972; Israel & Tajfel, 1972), followed by a prolonged period of acrimony and reflection amongst the various participants. If before the crisis it was possible unproblematically to proclaim social psychology as a discipline with a bold vision and intellectual project, after the crisis such claims could only be made cautiously, argumentatively, and with a great many caveats. Ahab knows what to do. He will hunt the whale no matter what stands in his way, he will track down and have done with Moby-Dick. Ishmael does not. He is confronted with choices: Should the project be begun anew? Should it be revised and entirely rethought? Should it simply be abandoned?

But why did the crisis come about in the first place? Why is it so difficult to adequately theorise the psychological? If a novelist like Melville can so brilliantly explicate the nature of obsession and vengeance, why can these same psychological processes not be unravelled in the laboratory, or at the very least be properly named and characterised by social psychologists? We will return throughout the book to the philosophical and methodological problems which psychologists face when attempting to do so. At the most general level the answer is that such attempts to fix and provide once-and-for-all explanations actually impedes rather than enhances our understanding. Because such explanations drag the phenomenon kicking and screaming from its rightful place in the complex weave of human affairs and make it stand on its own, as something to be characterised, dissected and classified outside of the places and times where it has any meaning. If psychology kills its subject matter in the course of taking hold of it, then novelists like Melville bring it back to life precisely because they approach the psychological indirectly, off-to-the-side (so to speak), by exploring how it unfolds when set loose in a particular context (How far will Ahab go? Where will this journey lead?).

Our contention is that all post-crisis writing in social psychology necessarily begins from the perspective of Ishmael rather than Ahab. It begins within the shadow of a calamity, of a disruption to the project. As such, it confronts uncertainty and indecision. The question is how to go on. For some writers, the answer is to return to previous convictions, to re-launch the project of social psychology and redouble our efforts to secure clarity and knowledge. For others, the project needs rethinking, a questioning of ambitions and goals and of the techniques needed to accomplish these ends. For others still the project is no longer worth pursuing, and the search for the white whale of the psychological needs to be replaced with other tangible pursuits (perhaps a search for the biological or for the discursive as foundations).

Whatever option is chosen, it seems that what is required is a new form of clarity. This involves a new start to the project, a clear sense of beginning again, or a new project altogether. Our argument in this book is that we do not need to consider the grounding of psychology as a practice in this way. That is to say that if it is correct to speak of psychology as having 'foundations' then we need to rid ourselves of the idea that these resemble the physical foundations of a house, or the financial act of commitment which establishes a charitable foundation. The foundations of psychology are, we want to argue, more akin to the ways in which biological cells and organisms continuously rebuild themselves whilst retaining their intrinsic identity over time. Or if psychology is akin to a building or an institution, it is closer to the model of the Shinto temple described by David Lowenthal (1985) which is systematically dismantled and rebuilt every twenty years without apparently disrupting its status. This is what we might call foundation through displacement, or, as we will describe later, as *creative* and *reflexive foundationalism*.

To begin to speak of foundations in this way is to run several risks. We are not suggesting that psychology ought to be founded anew in biology, and on the basis of the insights of the modern bio-sciences on the nature and processes of life. But we do want to rethink the relationship psychology has to biology and to the established ways we have of apportioning subject matter between 'nature' and 'society'. We are not claiming that what is required is a new, once-and-for-all grounding of psychology in a clearly defined set of assumptions about how the worlds (physical, organic, personal and social) that we inhabit are organised. This would be to echo the call for 'new foundations' that is so routinely and tiresomely heard across the discipline. But we are proposing that such assumptions need to be continuously invoked and explored as an ongoing and integral part of what it means to be a psychologist. Finally, we are most certainly not calling for the demolition of all foundations whatsoever. Such a call is, of course, a foundational gesture in itself, albeit of a most peculiar and regressive nature.

What we seek to do in this book is proceed from the troublesome relationship we have to that which grounds us, which includes the desire to have done with grounding altogether. We will argue throughout that we can neither settle nor dispense with this relationship, and that attempts to do so merely push the problem into more complex and immediate forms (such as the complex recursive relationships that model builders discover when they need to relate their terms or variables). What needs to be done instead, we want to demonstrate, is to hold the relationship close and to continuously examine how foundations are constructed and reconstructed as a live feature of the phenomena we study.

We want then, to start from the perspective of Ishmael, confronted in a very literal way with the question of how to go on, and the means through which to persevere. We are not claiming that we are alone in this position, nor that we have the hubris to see ourselves as sole witnesses to a great disaster that has befallen the discipline. Rather, Ishmael denotes a particular way of seeing psychology that is available to any psychologist. We could call this, following the terminology of Michel Foucault, an 'Ishmael-function' (see Foucault, 1978). This would stand in contrast to the 'Ahab-function' of choosing to see psychology as a clearly defined project that is getting ever closer to making firm statements about the nature of psychological processes, despite their frustrating tendency to continually recede at precisely those moments when they seem just in reach.

As a discipline, psychology has tended towards the Ahab-function. It seeks answers to fundamental questions about thinking, about being a person. However, it attempts to do so by rigidly posing very narrowly defined questions which concern very specific facets of personhood that can be made to show up in laboratory settings or in the transcribed record of a tape-recorded interaction. In some sense, psychology ends up killing – or at the very least simplifying – the phenomena of which it desires to speak, in the same way that Ahab's search for Moby-Dick strives to finish it off for good. But the psychological is no less elusive than the great white whale. Attempts to pin down the exact nature of psychological processes are notorious for their tendency to excise precisely that which is felt to be most essential. In this way psychology typically falls far short of providing a convincing account of the rich diversity of human experience – the psychological slips away from what psychologists try to do.

How might we even begin to address this tendency? We can first of all observe that the psychological is to be found way beyond the laboratories and transcripts of the discipline of psychology. The psychological is quite literally everywhere – it is being worked out and worked through as a live concern in all aspects of human activity. Moreover, there are a great many disciplines and practices which seek to articulate the psychological. We find fine and subtle accounts of the psychological in art, literature, music, theatre, and in journalism, broadcasting, political commentary and public debate. What it means to be a person, to think psychologically, is being addressed and engaged in these realms. So it makes sense to say that not only ought we, as psychologists, to engage with these realms (such as the nineteenth-century North American literature of Melville), but we also have a kind of obligation to try to follow attempts to articulate the psychological wherever they lead us, which will be way beyond the safe confines of the psychology department. We need to do so not least because there is a reciprocal relationship, or interdependency, between academic psychology and these other realms of psychological enquiry. For example, the nineteenth-century psychology of someone like William James is most certainly influenced by the literary traditions of the time, not least that represented by his brother Henry James. Correspondingly, the work of a modern novelist such as Sarah Waters is shaped by shifting kinds of sexual identity and forms of experience that can be indexed to very particular historical and cultural moments, which include the versions of 'the psychological' offered by the professional psychology of the time. We might then say that 'psychology' – broadly defined as the study of what it is to be a person – is everywhere.

We propose something like a kind of 'second-order psychology' which attempts to pursue the psychological across the complex cultural and material forms that it takes. If 'first-order psychology' is the attempt to replicate and reproduce the psychological under narrow, laboratory-like conditions with the ambition of putting the mechanisms of human action 'under the microscope', so to speak, then 'second-order psychology' is all about following human experience through the myriad of forms that it takes, including the forms mediated by scientific psychology itself. At every point, and with respect to the concrete form of experience we are studying, we should take guidance from those commentators and experts on experience who seem most relevant – here it may be literature, there it may be molecular biology, sometimes sociology, at other times art. If first-order psychology is governed by the Ahab-function ('find and have done with the whale') then second-order psychology is governed by the Ishmael-function ('follow the whale, wherever it takes us, endlessly').

Second-order psychology, however, must have another dimension to it that would chime with von Foerster's (1993) notion of 'second order cybernetics' as a cybernetics of cybernetics. This dimension goes beyond the affirmation that psychology must 'observe' beings that are themselves 'observers' (a situation which necessitates what Luhmann [1998b] refers to as 'second-order observation' or the observation of observation). Thus, second-order psychology must also be a 'meta' or 'reflexive' psychology to the extent that it recognises the need to study the scientific discipline as well as the subject matter (and the relations between the two). The psychological as subject matter is ultimately not separable from the forms of knowledge that take it as their object, and these forms of knowledge are in turn inseparable from the forms of social order in which they are implicated. The purpose of this book is to assemble some of the theoretical resources necessary for such a second-order psychology. We want to lay out a very different 'image of the psychological' alongside sets of terms, concepts and relations that enable its thought.

It should be clear from the above that we are not in the business of merely peddling one more postmodern story urging that we dispense with foundations in favour of continuing the job of deconstructing each and every claim to truth in the name of resistance to power. We are not 'anti-foundationalist' in this sense. Rather, we wish to explore the paradoxical sense in which we must continually create our foundations, precisely because we lack them. This is no small distinction. Anti-foundationalism proceeds negatively, smashing claims to truth, relativising notions of value, and ironising ideals of progress. Our reflexive or creative foundationalism, by contrast, risks the proposition that we must create our realities and live out values, that we are doing this already (whether we know it and like it or not), and that the art of living is always in the process of either progressing or regressing. Our environments, our bodies, our minds, our relationships, our societies are never static or singular, and can never be dissociated from 'value'. This means that we must take care. It does not mean, however, that human beings are somehow autonomous and God-like creators, inventing our worlds out of nothing but acts of will. On the contrary, we are ourselves creatures of a creative process that exceeds our own limited existence. Anti-foundationalism, for the most part, thrives on a premature distinction between natural and social sciences, or between the natural and the social and cultural more generally. Reflexive or creative foundationalism refuses this distinction and insists that we are hybrid creatures with multiple forms of heritage: creatures of biochemistry, creatures of consciousness, creatures of communication.

Following this introductory chapter, we have organised the book into eight core chapters and a conclusion. Each of the core chapters serves a double function. On the one hand, each deals with a key thinker in the development of reflexively foundational modes of thought and practice. On the other hand, each chapter homes in on a subject matter of psychological relevance. We use the key thinker as our 'guide' or mediator to shed light on the topic or subject matter. We also read each thinker selectively. Although we hope each chapter is wide-ranging enough to serve as an introduction, we will admit that we adopt a reading strategy that emphasises connections and juxtapositions between thinkers rather than offering a 'purist' view of each in particular.

The eight core chapters divide into two sections. Chapters 4 to 9 deal with specific topics: communication (Luhmann), embodied experience (Artaud), affect (Spinoza), memory (Bergson), subjectivity (Foucault) and the stylisation of life (Deleuze). To set the scene for this run of six chapters, however, we considered it necessary to include two chapters dealing with much more general concepts that are indispensable to our project. We enlist Alfred North Whitehead as our guide to a concept of *process*, and Michel Serres as our guide to a concept of *mediation*. The accounts of communication, embodiment, affect, memory, selfhood and life-style that follow presuppose and put to work these more general notions of process and mediation. We are uncomfortably aware of the fact that our thinkers are all white, European males and that, with the exception of Michel Serres, all are dead. This selection rather obviously reflects our peculiar intellectual paths and our particular interests and desires. Equally obviously it should not be taken as suggesting that these are the only thinkers worth engaging with, or that scholarship prior to the era of TV was inherently superior (although sometimes we think this latter point may be true!).

Our aim throughout the book has been – to borrow a phrase from Isabelle Stengers (2002) – to 'think with' our key authors. More specifically, we have tried to put the concepts to work in order to open up what are hopefully fresh insights into psychological phenemona and issues. We have not attempted to speculate on what psychology might look like when considered solely from the perspective of each thinker – a 'Bergsonian Psychology', a 'Spinozist Psychology', and so on. We have instead followed Deleuze's strategy in asking what particular 'image' of the psychological can be discerned through an engagement with the work of each thinker in turn. For this reason, we have also envisaged each chapter as an 'intervention' into a key debate or controversy within psychology. The chapter on Luhmann, for instance, constitutes an intervention into the current debate around what might be called the 'linguistic imperialism' of some forms of discourse analytical and discursive psychology. This debate lies paralysed in front of a bifurcation of paths that resulted from two answers to the question of where the 'psychological' is to be 'located'. For the cognitivists and phenomenologists who inherit the Cartesian and Kantian tradition, the answer is that the psychological is 'inside'. For strict behaviourists and discursive psychologists who inherit the tradition of pragmatism, speech act philosophy and Wittgenstein, the answer is that it is 'outside'. Luhmann would agree with Whitehead that the answer should be 'both'. As Whitehead puts it, language has two functions: 'It is converse with another, and it is converse with oneself' (1938/1966, p. 32). The psychological is not thinkable without linguistic mediation, and yet neither is it reducible to language. The chapter on Bergson, to give a second example, intervenes in the 'memory wars' debate that was stirred up around the notions of 'recovered memory' and 'false memory syndrome'. Again, rather than polarise the debate into a choice between memories either being 'true' or being 'false', we use Bergson to 'loosen' proceedings and to explore the ethics of articulated memories as gifts of mediation that are passed from oneself in the past to oneself in the present.

Since our intention has been to 'think with' our thinkers, we have not tried to unify the various concepts at play, but to keep them quite specific. We wish to allow Luhmannian terminology to resonate alongside Whiteheadian, for instance, and to allow Artaud's 'mômo thought' to reverberate with the memory of Bergson. To put it somewhat differently, this book does a job of *assemblage* rather than *systematisation* (Whitehead, 1938/1966, pp. 1–3). We do not reject the goal of systematisation, but consider it premature. Systematisation must start from presuppositions that we do not think have been adequately clarified. Psychology has long suffered from a premature systematisation that embodies an impoverished view of human capacities and hence of the human being. If we are to avoid dismissing relevant forms of experience in the interest of system we must first concern ourselves with the task of assemblage. In this book, we assemble these things on the table before you, and we thereby invite the reader to think about Luhmannian systems theory next to Serres' notion of parasitism, and Bergsonian duration next to Foucaultian subjectivity. In doing so, we are not unaware of the differences and discontinuities between such approaches. We are not unaware, for instance, that Luhmann begins with the proposition 'systems there are!', whilst Serres doubts that there has ever been a system and suggests that what we call systems are actually spaces of transformation. In their own spaces, we think that both thinkers are right. The premature application of a mode of systematisation that construes this as a 'contradiction' would be fruitless and potentially damaging.

We thus consider the juxtapositions and contrasts to be important ingredients rather than waste product to be eliminated, and we consider it a virtue to adopt a different theoretical vocabulary with each different subject matter. In Chapter 4 we selected Luhmann as our guide to communication because he draws upon autopoietic systems theory to rethink social systems. Autopoietic systems theory, as we will describe, is a mode of thought derived from biology that approaches the problem of the nature of organic life by beginning with a paradoxical principle of self (auto) creation or production (poeisis). In applying this notion to systems that operate in the element of communication, Luhmann gives us an account of the social and the psychological based upon a form of reflexively creative foundationalism compatible, but not identical, with the philosophies of Whitehead and Serres.

But this does not mean that Luhmann has somehow 'got it right', or that his approach adequately covers all relevant aspects of experience. On the contrary, Luhmann's thinking remains rather 'cognitive', 'orderly' and 'disembodied' in orientation. As a critical contrast to this, however, Chapter 5 brings to life the highly visceral, counter-normative and tormented life-work of Antonin Artaud. Where Luhmann stresses the autonomy and self-referentiality of communication, Artaud revels in the shrieks and howls of its physicality and embodiment. In this contrast, it might be said that science confronts art. Art cannot be avoided by a reflexively foundational psychology. Language can be used to write scientific papers, but it is also the medium of song, theatre and poetry. We speak with the intimate vitals of our bodies. The lungs and throat come into play, the heart and the gut respond and reverberate. Our intimate organic existence is thus stirred by speech and excited by song. The visceral engagements of Artaud are the very experiences excluded by the Luhmannian systematisation, and Artaud refuses to be 'processed' in a Luhmannian system. If Artaud the artist can experience what most of us refuse, then surely the contrast between Luhmann and Artaud can be experienced without being rejected.

Artaud draws our attention to the mixed pleasures and pains involved in the perpetual problem of 'ordering' our lives and being 'ordered'. This theme is taken up in Chapter 6 where we focus upon Spinoza's account of the affects. For Spinoza, affects are inseparable from the ongoing ethical task of living as well as possible. Psychology as a discipline badly needs to reconnect with this ethical dimension, and hence we take issue with current tendencies in neuro-science (notably the work of Antonio Damasio) to deploy 'Spinozism' in a way which arguably detracts from this. In a similar way, in Chapter 7 Bergson offers us a way beyond the narrow psychological notion of memory as a device for squirrelling away instants of past experience so that they can be retrieved at some future point and towards a notion of psychological life as itself a mobile continuity implicated in an uncertain ethical process of creative evolution. For Bergson, memory is less a mechanical device for storing and retrieving representational traces of experience than a 'burden' that we perpetually drag behind us and that grows heavier as we age. Our past is always with us, informing our present moment of experience, and sometimes – as the video for Radiohead's 'Karma Police' eerily illustrates – it catches up with us.

A key concern of Chapter 8 is to 'rescue' Foucault's work on subjectivity from a predominantly Anglophone interpretation which entirely misses the sense in which Foucault's work resonates with reflexive foundationalism. Although this Anglophone interpretation recognises Foucault's point that power is productive, it still construes that productivity in a monolithically neg-ative sense, and hence notions of norm, normalisation and normativity take on only the static and negative meaning of the correspondence of an entity to an already given norm. In fact, as authors such as Greco (2004) have made clear, Foucault was influenced by, amongst many other things, Canguilhem's dis-tinction between normalisation and normativity. Normativity is the opposite of being 'normed' since it is the capacity to *invent* norms, and for Canguilhem, this is a defining feature of health as such. On this reading, Foucault's later work on the care of the self was as much about experimenting with and pursuing forms of normativity as about avoiding normalisation.

The chapter on Deleuze develops this notion of the challenge to enhance one's capacity for normativity. The problem we face in psychology, it is argued, is less the problem of 'the subject' and of our own individual 'selves' or 'iden-tities' than the problem of 'life' and living. Life is the prior term and the source of more complex and self-conscious subjective modes, and it is perfectly possible that our 'selves' can become obstacles to our normativity. If we follow Deleuze we are led to a re-invention of the psychological in relation, not to static qualities of personhood, but to *forces*: becomings, flows, motions, events, e-motions, and to the patterns of mediation that bring this flux to life.

At the end, of course, we begin again. The final chapter offers a simple mnemonic device that we hope will serve to condense some of our hot air into a memorable droplet. A key take-home message from all of our thinkers is that psychology must attend to experience. The components of experience are infinitely various, but, as put by Whitehead (1933/1935, p. 291):

> Nothing can be omitted, experience drunk and experience sober, experience sleeping and experience waking, experience drowsy and experience wide-awake, experience self-conscious and experience self-forgetful, experience intellectual and experience physical, experience religious and experience sceptical, experience anxious and experience care-free, experience anticipatory and experience retrospective, experience happy and experience grieving, experience dominated by emotion and experience under self-restraint, experience in the light and experience in the dark, experience normal and experience abnormal.

In the final chapter we suggest that the infinite components of experience can be usefully gathered together under the four headers of *power, image, proposition* and *enunciation* which together give us a process-oriented synthesis of the whole psyche stuffed into the mnemonic of a PIPE. We explicate this mnemonic using Magritte's famous artwork on the pipe theme. Power, image, proposition and enunciation are envisaged not as self-contained essences but as mutually mediating connective nodes or links in unfurling chains of process and becoming. Each is thus double-sided, with one side oriented to experience (which receives the gift of its inheritance from the past) and the other to expression (which transmits that gift to future experience). Life is this constant *pulse* of experience and expression which affords mediated connectivity with the wider universe. In this conception it could be noted that the psyche is rendered as a heart of sorts (see Dumoncel, 2003, p. 118, whose expression of Whitehead's 'faculty psychology' in a 'nutshell' gave inspiration for our pipe proposition). Experience is the moment of dilation associated with the diastole in which the heart fills with the blood of the world, and expression is the systolic contraction by which the blood of experience is driven back out into the world through the mediating arteries. In making this analogy we are being consistent with what was most important to that most austere of behavioural psychologists, J.B. Watson, albeit J.B. Watson in a mode of experience that was excluded from his formal psychology:

> Every cell I have is yours, individually
>
> And collectively.
>
> My total reactions are positive
>
> And towards you.
>
> So likewise each and every heart reaction...
>
> (J.B. Watson to Rosalie Reyner, April 1920, cited in Buckley, 1989: 12)

TWO

Whitehead and Process

Whereas physiological psychology assumes that experiences are the outcome of physiological events (physiology comes first), psychological physiology assumes that physiological events are the outcomes of experiences (psychology comes first).

(George Wolf, 1981, p. 274)

The question of experience is central to psychology, and yet hardly ever is it raised as such. The fact that we are organic, embodied beings seems to accord a primacy to the biological. It is simply commonsense to reason that experience must be derived from the very particular neurological, physiological and biochemical composition of our bodies. George Wolf's (1981) counter-argument is striking because it seems so counter-intuitive. How can it be possible for psychology, for experience to come first? The very idea seems vaguely spiritual, mystical even, suggesting an immaterial consciousness which somehow governs the body. Wolf's argument makes no such claims. It proposes, drawing on the philosophy of Alfred North Whitehead, to see experience as neither divorced from reality nor considered as an epiphenomenal 'projection', but quite literally as the *becoming* of objective reality.

A.N. Whitehead was born in the UK in 1861 and died in the USA in 1947. He was a mathematician and physicist by training, and worked in these fields at the Universities of Cambridge and London. His early work included an alternative version of relativity theory and, with Bertrand Russell, the three-volume *Principia mathematica* (published in the years 1910–1913), which built on the *Grundgesetze I* of Frege and revolutionised the foundations of mathematics (and provoked Gödel's famous theorem). His work has also influenced some prominent natural scientists (including the physicist David Bohm, the biologist Conrad Waddington, and the chemist Ilya Prigogine). His move to Harvard in 1924 was also a formal move into philosophy, and from this date until his death at the age of 86, he wrote a number of important works including *Science and the modern world* (1926), *Process and reality*

(1927–1928), *Adventures in ideas* (1933) and *Modes of thought* (1938). This corpus of philosophical work, after long neglect, has in recent years received serious attention from radical social theorists such as Donna Haraway (1991) and Isabelle Stengers (2002), and was a key influence on Gilles Deleuze (cf. Deleuze and Parnet, 1987). In the 'What is an event?' chapter of the book on Leibniz, Deleuze describes Whitehead as 'the successor' or *diadoche*, and as the 'last great Anglo-American philosopher before Wittgenstein's disciples spread their misty confusion' (1993, p. 76). In the preface to *Process and reality* Whitehead announces a large debt to Henri Bergson and to William James and John Dewey and describes one of his preoccupations as being to 'rescue their type of thought from the charge of anti-intellectualism' (1927–8/1985, p. xii).

Whitehead has also long exerted a slow but steady influence within psychology, particularly, but not exclusively, at the theoretical and biological ends of the discipline. Perhaps the earliest example is Charles Hartshorne's (1934) *The philosophy and psychology of sensation*, which develops the broadly Whiteheadian notion of an *affective continuum* which underlies and unifies otherwise distinct types of sensation (visual, auditory, etc.). A.H. Johnson's (1945) *The psychology of Alfred North Whitehead* usefully summarises Whitehead's discussions of psychological issues, and Susanne Langer's work, beginning in the early 1960s, systematically develops a broadly Whiteheadian account of feeling which largely pre-empts the currently popular work of figures such as Damasio (e.g. Langer, 1988). Some of the implications of Whitehead's thought for psychology are developed in the 2003 volume edited by Franz Riffert and Michel Weber.

We have chosen to encounter Whitehead in this chapter because he offers a far-reaching cosmology that, if critically adopted, has radical implications for how we might conceive the problem of foundations in psychology. His work has acquired renewed significance in recent years in a context where psychologists and social scientists concerned with the psychological dimension are once again coming to recognise the need to reflect deeply on their epistemological and ontological commitments. There is, for example, a perceived need for modes of thought that do not bifurcate nature into irreconcilable subjective and objective aspects. More generally, there is a need for modes of thought which embrace process, affirm creativity, foreground value, incorporate the affective dimension, and work with multiplicity and difference. Whitehead provides some rigorous insights of relevance to each of these issues.

In short, Whiteheadian philosophy offers a relational process ontology that promises a profound version of constructivism which does not reduce the universe to 'discourse' or 'subjective meaning', and a deepened empiricism which does not reduce nature to meaningless materiality (for further discussion of 'deep empiricism' see Stenner, 2008). There are two core principles of this ontology which correspond to the radicalisation of space and time that coalesced in mathematics and physics in the early twentieth century. First, things (whether physical, biological, psychological or cultural) are *definable* as their *relevance* to other things and in terms of the way other things are relevant to them. Things, in other words, have *relational essences*. Secondly, things do not exist independently of time but are *constituted* by the history of their specific and situated encounters (their *process*). Every actual thing is 'something by reason of its activity' (Whitehead, 1927–8/1985, p. 26). For this reason we write of a *relational process* approach.

The Bifurcation of Nature

When we ask whether experience or physiology comes first we are already dividing nature up along distinctly modern lines. Whitehead characterises this division in the following way:

> The two great preoccupations of modern philosophy now lie clearly before us. The study of mind divides into psychology, or the study of mental functionings as considered in themselves and in their mutual relations, and into epistemology, or the theory of the knowledge of a common objective world. In other words, there is the study of the cogitations, *quâ* passions of the mind, and their study *quâ* leading to an inspection (*intuition*) of an objective world. This is a very uneasy division, giving rise to a host of perplexities whose consideration has occupied the intervening centuries. (Whitehead, 1926/1985, p. 182)

The two great preoccupations of modern philosophy are highly *subjective* in nature. This means that they concern the *subject* as recipient and organiser of experience. This tinge of subjectivism in fact characterises many aspects of 'modernity'. In the sphere of art, for instance, one sees from the Renaissance onwards a decisive trend towards concern with the subjectivity of the subject matter, artist and audience alike. In the sphere of law, to give a second example, the concept of legal right was connected during antiquity and the middle ages to the objectivity of a given social order. Rights followed from objective membership of specific social groups and were not attached to individuals as such. They concerned the extensive coordination of the groups that made up the entire social structure. The transition from the middle ages to modernity, however, brought with it a concept of *subjective rights* 'that have legal quality, because they are due to a subject and therefore need no further foundation' (Luhmann, 1981, p. 45; see also Verschraegen, 2002; Stenner, 2004). In the sphere of politics, one sees the gradual growth of forms of political legitimation based upon the subjective happiness or wellbeing of citizens (or at least a rhetoric to this effect) rather than a divinely inspired objective order. Descartes begins modern philosophy with the gesture of a *subject receiving experience*. With respect to religion, to give a final example, the protestant reformation emphasised the individual experiences of believers and made legitimacy dependent upon such experience. As Whitehead puts it: 'Luther asked, "How am I justified"; modern philosophers have asked, "How do I have knowledge?"' (1926/1985, p. 174).

In sum, whether in law, art, politics, religion or philosophy, one sees a modern preoccupation with the individual subject of experience gradually taking over from a prior concern with 'the total drama of all reality' (Whitehead, 1926/1985, p. 174). The modern period cannot be adequately comprehended without recognition of the seemingly infinite value it accords, in such instances, to the individual human psyche. The *psychological*, we might say, acquires an increasingly profound *social life* in the law, politics, art, religion and philosophy of the modern period: it acquires decisive importance in the practical realities of social organisation and communication. But 'the psychological' is not yet 'Psychology', understood as a specific scientific discipline. The emergence of that discipline was, however, intimately and inevitably related to its newly extensive and intensive 'social life' (Danziger, 1990; Richards, 1996; Rose, 1996; Stenner, 2003).

But there is, of course, another side to this story. The same geniuses who secured the bases of modern philosophy also established the principles of modern science. The 'flip-side' to the growing modern subjectivism was the stark objectivism of the forms of scientific materialism that came to dominate as the true understanding of the foundational nature of the universe. Figures such as Descartes and Newton lent an authoritative seal of approval to a commonsense doctrine which 'even today is the common doctrine of ordinary life because in some sense it is true' (Whitehead, 1934: 17). The basic assumptions of this doctrine are rarely explicitly posed. Rather, they are unconsciously presupposed or 'taken for granted'. 'Such assumptions appear so obvious that people do not know what they are assuming because no other way of putting things has ever occurred to them' (1926/1985, p. 61). Whitehead summarises the doctrine as follows:

> There are bits of matter, enduring self-identically in space which is otherwise empty. Each bit of matter occupies a definite limited region. Each such particle of matter has its own private qualifications – such as its shape, its motion, its mass, its colour, its scent. Some of these qualifications change, others are persistent. The essential relationship between bits of matter is purely spatial. Space itself is eternally unchanging, always including in itself this capacity for the relationship of bits of matter. Geometry is the science which investigates this spatial capacity for imposing relationship upon matter. Locomotion of matter involves change in spatial relationship ... Matter involves nothing more than spatiality, and the passive support of qualifications. (Whitehead, 1934, p. 18)

According to the doctrine of scientific materialism the ultimate and fundamental reality is a 'succession of instantaneous configurations of matter' (Whitehead, 1926/1985, p. 63). The foundational assumption is that nature is ultimately composed of brute stuff, matter or material, and the laws that govern that material. That is to say, it is composed of that which has the property of *simple location:* it belongs to a specifiable point in time and a specifiable point in space.

This doctrine, of course, was (and still is) in a process of continual evolution and refinement. Already in the seventeenth century, the transmission theories for light and sound dealt a significant blow to the fine detail of the taken-for-granted foundational doctrine outlined by Whitehead in the quotation above. That is to say, these theories challenged the idea that each bit of matter has its 'own private qualifications – such as its shape, its motion, its mass, its colour, its scent'. This challenge directly prompted the famous seventeenth-century distinction between primary and secondary qualities. This distinction served to separate off so-called 'secondary' qualities such as colour, tone and scent from the 'primary' qualities of mass and spatial relation. Secondary qualifications, it was argued, are not in fact part of nature itself but are instead merely mental reactions on the part of the observer. Sensations such as the redness and scent of a rose came to be conceived through this distinction as projections of the subjective mind which clothe external bodies which in nature have no such qualities. Secondary qualities were thus conceived as the offspring of mind and have nothing to do with real, fundamental reality. Nature itself is confined to mere bits of matter qualified only by mass and spatial relations.

This notable modification to the commonsense notion of fundamental reality described above thus did not resolve the distinction between observing subject and observed object but rather served to intensify and re-entrench it. It deepened what Whitehead calls the 'bifurcation of nature' into mind and matter in which the latter is cast as the real, underlying foundation. Questions of value, of creativity, of purpose and of feeling were quickly assigned to the 'mind' side of the dichotomy, leaving the matter of nature to appear as 'a dull affair, soundless, scentless, colourless; merely the hurrying of material, endlessly, meaninglessly (ibid., p. 69).

To briefly recap: on the one hand we have in the modern period a new social and practical importance conferred upon the *subject* of experience (and hence a valorisation of the perceiving, suffering and reasoning mind); on the other hand we have a profoundly influential account of the true nature of reality as *matter*: simple and meaningless location in time and space. This, as Whitehead points out, is a very uneasy division. Issues of aim, value, motive and purpose which are fundamental to social organisation and coordination (and are hence unlikely to disappear from the practical realities of projects such as law, politics, art and religion) are excluded from the category of nature and granted an ethereal existence as disconnected ghostly projections. In this context, it becomes the height of anthropomorphism to imagine that animals might have feelings, aims or intentions. The unease that this bifurcation generates can be thought of as a kind of affective motive force underlying subsequent intellectual activity. That is to say, the debates that it has given rise to ever since can be thought of as efforts at temporary *settlements* (or unsettlements) of this unease. There were bold attempts either to put mind into matter (as with materialist monism) or to put matter into mind (as in Bishop Berkeley's famous idealist monism), for instance. Dualism, by contrast, is a settlement that accords equal value to the subject and the object as distinctive realms. This is not merely an 'intellectual' issue, however, but also a practical social matter of the coordination of efforts. Hence, in specifying the statutes of the Royal Society in 1663, Thomas Hooke presented its mission as 'to improve the knowledge of naturall things, and all useful Arts, Manufactures, Mechanick practises, Engynes and Inventions by Experiments'. In so doing, however, he added that this would not involve 'medling with Divinity, Metaphysics, Moralls, Politicks, Grammar, Rhetoricks or Logick' (Lyons, 1968, p. 20).

The dualistic 'management' of the 'unease' thus became inscribed within influential institutions. The intellectual settlement thus found its way into more stable and enduring forms of practical social reality. Whitehead, for example, notes the 'astounding efficiency' of scientific materialism 'as a system of concepts for the organisation of scientific research. In this respect, it is fully worthy of the genius of the century which produced it. It has held its own as the guiding principle of scientific studies ever since. It is still reigning. Every university in the world organises itself in accordance with it. No alternative system of organising the pursuit of scientific truth has been suggested. It is not only reigning, but it is without a rival' (Whitehead, 1926/1985, p. 69).

When Whitehead writes of the organisation of scientific research within the institutional form of the university he is talking of the revitalisation of the university from the late eighteenth century onwards. For about two centuries prior to this point, universities had become rather moribund institutions (Wallerstein et al., 1996, p. 6). Their intimate association with the business of theology during a long period of vicious religious strife had ensured their declining relevance to the power brokers of the new nation states as locations for the creation of knowledge. Meanwhile, what would come to be called the 'natural sciences' had set up their own institutional forms (such as the Royal Society and the various Academies) outside of the university, and could make plausible claims of socially potent results. In the nineteenth century, the universities – particularly those in the UK, France, Germany and the USA – were revitalised and transformed. This transformation included institutional specialisation into the pattern of modern disciplines and increased levels of professionalisation of knowledge production.

In the early stages of this process, according to Wallerstein et al. (1996, p. 8) it was historians, classicists, scholars of national literatures and others from the arts and humanities who put the main effort into gaining state support for this revitalisation. In so doing, however, they 'pulled the natural scientists into the burgeoning university structures, thereby profiting from the positive profile of the natural scientists'. In this sense, Whitehead's bifurcated nature found institutional expression in what C.P. Snow (1959/2003) would later call the 'two cultures' (arts/humanities and natural science) of the education system. This, however, was only the beginning. The end of the eighteenth century was not just the beginning of a new phase for the university, it was the age of the political revolution (notably the American and the French revolutions) and the industrial revolution, and their combination entailed social transformation on a vast scale. Such social, political, economic and technological change, many argued, called out for systematic study, organisation, planning and rationalisation. There was a perceived requirement for an understanding of the general laws of the social world that would permit active intervention in the shaping and steering of social systems. Indeed, this very perception was widely seen to be part of what distinguished the modern period from its unenlightened past and from its unenlightened global contemporaries.

The birth of the social sciences as institutionalised scientific disciplines in the nineteenth-century university was viewed very much as part of the triumph of science over the 'speculations' of philosophy, not to mention theology. These new social sciences thus constituted a 'third' culture distinct from the natural sciences (in so far as they took social processes as their subject matter) and from the arts and humanities (in so far as they modelled themselves on natural scientific practice). Early influential arguments for modelling such new sciences upon the successes of Newtonian astronomy were made by Auguste Comte in France and John Stuart Mill in the UK. Arguably, it was the adoption of a 'positivistic' doctrine of science that enabled a 'fudging' of the material status of social scientific objects. For positivists, a scientific law is nothing more than a *description*: it is an observed persistence of pattern throughout a series of comparative observations. This effectively eliminated the need for metaphysical statements, and hence a materialist ontology could still be vaguely presupposed, but did not need to enter directly into the process of legitimating scientific practice. So long as there are distinct 'observables' whose regularities can be described, one need not concern oneself with broader questions about where these observables come from, why they exist or where they are going. Newton's law of gravitation proved exemplary in this respect, since the statement that any two particles of matter attract each other in direct proportion to the product of their mass and in inverse proportion to the square of their distance merely expresses observed correlations between the observed facts of mass and mutual spatial relations (this is why Newton insisted that he was neither speculating nor explaining, but observing and describing). Although the social sciences have never even approximated the precision of this law, they have been perfectly able to accumulate observations (e.g. population statistics) and to correlate them. The perceived social requirement for such knowledge, its symbolic association with the progress of 'the modern', and its promissory claim to youthful status were more than sufficient ingredients to distract from ontological quibbles and to persuade most people to turn a blind eye to any lack of precision. In addition, much as the quantitative/qualitative distinction functions today, since there was an 'ideographic' alternative waiting where 'nomothetic' approaches failed, social scientists had the option of converting the failures of one scientific mode into the successes of another. According to Wallerstein et al., between 1850 and 1914 multiple social science disciplines were proposed and tested (notably in France, Germany, the UK and the USA), resulting in the consensual organisation of at least five social sciences: history, economics, sociology, political science and anthropology.

Scientific materialism and the foundational paradox of psychological science

The discipline of psychology acquired its institutional niche as an experimental science in the modern university late in the nineteenth century. Like its siblings in the social sciences, it emerged for the most part from out of faculties of philosophy. Compared to the social sciences, however, it was more difficult for psychology to avoid the 'unease' of the inherited settlement of a mind/nature bifurcation. In fact, psychology was caught in something of a paradoxical double-bind with respect to this bifurcation. As we discussed above, scientific reasoning since the seventeenth century had been 'completely dominated by the presup-position that mental functionings are not properly part of nature' (Whitehead, 1938/1966, p. 156). The experience of colour or of the scent of a rose were considered as subjective *additions* to nature: they have no objective existence since they lack the materiality that had come to define the objective reality of nature. Thanks to the successes of natural science, the 'psychological' had become identified with an illusory 'projective' content whose removal is precisely the condition of possibility for genuine scientific knowledge.

Psychology could thus be perceived not just as lacking a real scientific subject matter, but as *being* the 'lack' whose exclusion constitutes the unity of scientific truth (Stenner, 2007). We will refer to this as the *foundational paradox* of psychology. If what was decisive about science was its ability to go 'outside' the mind, then a science *of* the mind is, if we accept the materialistic definition, an *anti-science*. That is to say, in a gesture of *foundation by exclusion*, modern natural science had founded itself upon the exclusion of 'first causes', 'final' or 'teleological causes', 'ends', 'aims', 'purposes', 'subjectivity' and so forth as a matter of methodological course. It was this exclusion that had enabled natural processes to be approached as a realm of purely public, external, objective facts. Auguste Comte (1903, p. 21) called for a mimicking of this gesture on the part of the social sciences when he stated that 'our researches … in every branch of knowledge, if they are to be positive, must be confined to the study of real facts without seeking to know their first causes or final purpose'. But even Comte hesitated at the prospect of a scientific psychology since, as he himself had put it, 'the eye cannot look at itself'.

Psychology hence came to be associated less with the social sciences than with medicine and biology, and, since then, one has been more likely to find psychology departments in faculties of natural science than social science. Since its inception, the discipline of psychology has struggled in various ways with its foundational paradox. Indeed, this paradox might be viewed as the motivating force for the history of perpetual revolutions and transformations that psychology has gone through in its career as a science. Often, for example, efforts were made to *identify* its subject matter with material biological processes. Earlier in the nineteenth century, for example, forerunners of modern experimental psychology had offered new physiological definitions of 'the emotions' (Dixon, 2004). This trajectory was greatly enabled by growing knowledge of the central nervous system and by the increasing interest in Darwinian evolutionary theory, which was a great influence on Galton and the subsequent British psychometric tradition, and on North American pragmatism. Others, by contrast, founded psychology in an attempt to correlate objective stimuli with subjective experiences (as with the tradition of psychophysics that influenced German psychology). Others still carved out a space for psychology as a branch of medicine (as in the French tradition of clinical experimentation with 'hysterics' and 'somnambulists' inaugurated by figures such as Binet). Despite important forays into the social sciences (especially by founding fathers such as Wilhelm Wundt), psychologists increasingly sought their legitimacy in moves 'beyond' social science and into natural science and medicine. Its history since then has been a story of constant unease prompted by its grounding paradox as an anti-science, which it has never squarely faced up to. The paradox, when it is confronted, results in paralysis – or an inability to 'go on'. The ability of the discipline to go on is then proportional to its ability to evade its paradox, or to find ways around it that keep it (however temporarily) 'out of sight'.

This 'unease', as we have suggested, is borne witness to by the multiplicity at the very origin of scientific psychology. Some, like Wundt in Germany, attempted to base a science upon the subjective stone that the builders of objective science had discarded, and strove to use systematic introspection to discover the laws of *psychic causality* which might complement the physical causality of the physical sciences. As Danziger (1990) discusses, this resulted in a research scenario in which the research participant or 'subject' was granted considerably more power and status than the researcher. The paradox was grappled with on another plane by the French clinical tradition (with which Freud was in contact), since here one was dealing for the most part with conditions excluded by the medical system due precisely to the absence of a specifiable organic and hence material cause. Others, like Galton in the UK, attempted to base psychological science on the statistical analysis of aggregate data sets of various measures of *performance*. In this way, the problem of gaining access to 'objective' data was thus 'got around' via the generation of notions of comparative performance on standardised scales (which were typically then attributed to biological functioning). As Danziger (1990) discusses in some detail, there were thus at least three different versions of scientific psychology at the end of the nineteenth century, each with a rather distinct idea of what the psychological might be, and how it might be squared with the natural scientific requirement for a materially 'real' subject matter. All of these influences fed into North American psychology, which – due to a clearly perceived social need for the assessment and social engineering of human behaviour – quickly became the most powerful force (particularly after the devastation of Europe during the second world war).

It should be no surprise, therefore, that the history of psychology has been pervaded by almost perpetual internal and external criticism of its foundations. That is to say, it has been pervaded by criticism of the very basis upon which it projects itself as a scientific project. North American founding father William James (James, 1926, pp. 393–394), for example, referred retrospectively to his own *Principles of Psychology* as a 'loathsome, distended, tumefied, bloated, dropsical mass, testifying … that there is no such thing as a *science* of psychology'. Likewise, reflecting on the development of the discipline, John Dewey wrote to a friend that 'Psychology got so frightfully off in trying to be scientific (Thorndike et all) I quit – it was a mistake.' Whilst James and Dewey appear to express despair and resignation, most of the formal critique has been what might be called 're-foundational' critique, since the critique is undertaken in the name of the effort to establish more adequate scientific foundations (Stenner, 2007a).

The Thorndike mentioned by Dewey, for example, was a key figure in the 'revolution' through which a new foundation for psychology was articulated around the themes of learning and behaviour. This entailed a critique of 'introspection' (associated with the Wundtian school and its offshoots) and the suggestion of a new basic category for scientific observation ('behaviour' and its contingencies). This shift enabled psychologists to temporarily 'get around' their foundational paradox, since behaviour has the virtue of appearing to be publicly observable. A science of behaviour, however, is clearly a very different science from a science of psychical causation (made observable via the intermediary of introspection), or, for that matter, a science of the distribution of 'traits' in a population (made observable via the outcomes of various tests). Indeed, for some the label 'behavioural science' was preferred over 'psychology'. Another example of re-foundationalist critique is provided by the so-called 'cognitive revolution' which, emboldened by the metaphor of the digital computer as a foundational construct, critiqued the anti-mentalistic tendencies of behaviourism and set about studying the operations hypothesised to mediate perceptual input and behavioural output. Here again, there was a tendency to ditch the title 'psychology', this time for the more prestigious sounding 'cognitive science'. More recently still, thanks to technological developments that permit real-time access to brain functioning, neuroscientists have begun to critique the ontological basis of cognitive approaches and have offered re-foundational arguments for the primacy of their own key terms and metaphors.

Rethinking Foundations

'Re-foundationalist' calls for new and more solid foundations for psychology thus appear to have been a permanent feature of the discipline. It has suffered, it could be argued, from a 'metaphysical compulsion' to seek out stable foundations that might restore a long-lost sense of certitude to the discipline. But what does it mean to talk about the foundations of something like psychology? According to the *Shorter Oxford English Dictionary* (1978), a foundation is 'the solid ground, basis or principle, on which anything … is founded'. It is 'that upon which any structure is built up'. Or, once again, the 'establishing of an institution, together with provision for its perpetual maintenance.' In talking of the foundations of psychology, then, we are talking about the grounds and principles upon which the discipline, as an institution of sorts, is based, and we are talking about the grounds and principles which provide for its perpetual maintenance. This emphasis on perpetual maintenance is important. Good foundations are important since they permit whatever is founded upon them to continue its existence in time: to *endure*. Perpetual in this context does not need to imply existence for eternity. It means, to use an English word that became extinct in the nineteenth century, that the entity or being is *perpetuable*. Namely, that it can perpetuate itself in time and therefore, unlike the word 'perpetuable', preserve itself from oblivion and extinction. A foundation is thus a beginning or inauguration which permits the endurance of whatever form is begun.

The metaphor of foundations, however, lures us towards the fallacy of misplaced concreteness. It lures us into adopting highly spatial and material metaphors: a solid platform of concrete that can support a large structure over many years. For sure, such solid matters are not irrelevant to the foundation of the discipline of psychology. Wundt is credited with establishing scientific psychology in large part because he was able to acquire physical laboratory space in the built environment of Leipzig University. Nevertheless, it is clear that the discipline of psychology is more than a set of buildings on a set of university campuses. It is, one might argue, the specific and distinct set of thoughts, acts and communications that 'haunt', as it were, that material architecture. It is a distinct yet evolving set of thoughts, acts and communications that circulate in an enduringly recognisable manner. Not only does psychology haunt architecture, we might also say that it haunts the physical bodies, the brains, for example, of those psychologists who carry it on through time, passing it from one year to the next and from one generation to another. These 'material' bodies are not the foundation of psychology, however. They are conditions of its possibility – it could not exist without them – but they do not establish it or provide for its perpetual maintenance. The same buildings and the same human bodies could just as well form a department of chemistry, for instance. They are essential aspects of its environment, we might say, but they are not *it*.

We need ways of thinking about foundations that shift us away from the commonsense metaphor of a truly-real-because-independently-substantial material base and a psychic or discursive superstructure located spatially above this base. This metaphor lures us into thinking of endurance as if it were some kind of fight that concrete spatiality might win against time. The 'perpetuability' of a concrete slab (i.e. its ability to endure in time) appears to most of us to be thanks to its static and robust material qualities. Time does not seem to be 'internally' relevant to its material character. The slab endures because it resists movement and time. If, however, we were to take a simple spinning top as our image of endurance we get a rather different and perhaps more interesting picture. A spinning top in motion achieves a degree of temporary stability precisely through the constant spinning motion of rotation. It stays the same only in so far as it keeps moving. Time appears to us to be internally relevant to this mode of endurance. A spinning top, however, clearly requires some occasional input from a child to keep it spinning. This does not apply to a third image of endurance that is supplied by a living organism. Human-made artefacts and machines are allopoietic in that they are produced and maintained by something else – i.e. people, and not by themselves. *Autopoiesis*, on the other hand, literally means 'self-production'. It is a term that was coined by the Chilean biologists Maturana and Varela (1975). It names the way in which self-referential systems reproduce themselves from out of their own elements. A cell, for instance, can be seen as a complex production system. As Zeleny (1981) discusses, the macromolecular population of a cell is renewed about 10^4 times during its lifetime. Through this staggering turnover of matter the cell maintains its unity as a cell. That is to say, although it produces lots of components, more fundamentally, *it produces itself.* We will return to the idea of self-production throughout this book.

In a way that can be at least compared to an organism, a discipline of psychology must continuously maintain its unity as a form of discourse and practice. It is a network of communications – teachings, research practices, journal articles, and so on – that recursively produces itself. To understand its mode of endurance we must move away from spatial metaphors of stacked substances and towards metaphors of ongoing processes of self-creation. We need to understand that the foundations of psychology are not anything material. Rather, there is a sense in which the discipline of psychology grounds itself in the abstract conceptions of the psychological that its practices make available. Its foundations – like those of a living cell – are thoroughly self-referential. Thanks to its foundational paradox, these conceptions have been far from stable and it has been forced to continually revise and question its foundations, shifting from psychic causality to behaviour to information processing, and so forth. Through such shifts in paradigm the discipline undergoes mutations through which it *becomes* something new and different. Psychology thus grounds itself in the 'psychological', but only in so far as the 'psychological' is grasped and managed through the concepts and techniques of psychology (e.g. the psychological *as* behaviour; the psychological *as* aggregate test results; the psychological *as* observable brain activity, etc.).

In this last respect there is nothing exceptional about psychology. Physics, chemistry and biology must also ground themselves as disciplines by way of their evolving conceptions of the physical, the chemical and the biological. Physics grounds itself not in the physical world 'as such' but in the abstract conceptions of the physical world that its practices make available. We have seen that for about 200 years physics operated with an extraordinarily powerful conception based on the notion of matter, with its simple location in space and time. To this notion of brute materialism was superadded a perceiving, experiencing subject. But this notion of ultimate reality as material (which has served as such a powerful foundation for all the sciences) is in fact a conceptual abstraction, albeit a highly efficacious one in certain contexts. It is not 'reality'.

In fact, this notion of enduring bits of matter with simple location in otherwise empty space has been completely abandoned by physics for a long while now. In the nineteenth century the commonsense foundational notion of empty space was eliminated and replaced with an idea of the spatial universe as a field of force or incessant *activity*. Early twentieth-century developments associated with the concepts of relativity and the quantum theory accelerated this process of the denial of commonsense foundationalism. The notion of a passive substratum of self-contained enduring bits of matter has been replaced with the identification of matter with sheer activity or *energy*. The idea of simple location presupposed by the old notion of localised substance has given way to the concept that the 'group of agitations' we call matter is 'fused into its environment' (Whitehead, 1934, p. 31) such that there 'is no possibility of a detached, self contained local existence. The environment enters into the nature of each thing' (ibid., p. 31). In short, by the early twentieth century the entire commonsense doctrine expressing the fundamental features in terms of which the universe should be interpreted lay in tatters. It was replaced by a radically different view which emphasised 'activity' and 'process' as fundamental concepts.

Anti-foundationalism

We mentioned earlier that psychology as a discipline parted company early on from the social sciences (sociology, history, economics, anthropology, political science) and founded itself, for the most part, as a natural and experimental science, albeit a deeply troubled one thanks to its foundational paradox. A notable exception to this was the 'interdiscipline' of social psychology, which tended to be located either within departments of psychology, or within sociology, and as a result tended to have more contact with developments within the social sciences. As twentieth-century social science (particularly sociology and anthropology) began to shed its positivistic self-conception and adopt more interpretivist and interactionist approaches, so social psychologists began to challenge the experimental paradigms that had come to dominate its theory and practice (the famous 'crisis' in social psychology discussed in our introductory chapter). These developments were associated with the tendency to draw clear boundaries between the natural and the social in a way which strongly reinforced, rather than challenged, what Whitehead called the 'bifurcation of nature'. The social sciences, it was argued, dealt with 'meaning' whilst the natural sciences dealt with brute matter. The social sciences were thus required to 'understand' and 'interpret' whilst the natural sciences must 'explain' and 'predict'. In this way, the expectation of contact and dialogue between the social and the natural sciences was minimised. This social scientific distancing from natural science brought them more into contact with the arts and humanities, which also dealt with the products of human construction via concepts like 'narrative' and 'discourse'. These developments created some of the conditions in which some psychologists called, not for new scientific foundations (re-foundationalism) but for the absence of natural scientific foundations altogether (anti-foundationalism).

Anti-foundationalism in psychology can thus be construed as an attempt to ground psychology within the collective of *social* sciences and humanities that has its own issues with foundations (Silverman, 1993). Associated with the 'textual turn', this anti-foundationalism has been central to some of the most thoroughgoing critiques of psychology (Gergen, 1982/1994; Edwards & Potter, 1992). It draws, for instance, on a fundamental distinction between the natural and the social sciences which in turn draws, amongst other things, upon Wilhelm Dilthey's (1883/1989) observations concerning the distinct *Verfahrungsweisen* of the *Geisteswissenschaften* and the *Naturwissenschaften*. The critical question of the appropriateness or not of a 'scientific methodology' is, and always has been, a principal problem of the social sciences, and their own issues with foundations are not unrelated to this question (Curt, 1994). This troubled relationship has been particularly acute for psychology, since, as Dilthey was well aware, our discipline straddles his distinction. Subsequent reformulations of the distinction, such as that between the ideographic and the nomothetic (Windelband, 1894/1998) were also formulated with the peculiarities of psychology very much in mind.

This long historical predicament informs the recent tendency amongst psychologists critical of the foundational assumptions of the mainstream to adopt an anti-scientific stance. For example, this tendency manifests itself as a series of polemics that focus on phenomena that have been taken as natural, only to reveal them as social, cultural, historical and political in nature (cf. Hacking, 2000). This procedure, however necessary it may be, entails the reiteration of a staged polarisation of natural and social scientific issues in which the former is associated with negative images (all that is static, mechanistic and essentialist). Although this approach to deconstruction has some obvious virtues, it can lead to a paradoxically formulaic criticality: arguments for nature are bad, for culture are good. Deconstruction comes to appear simply as an assertion of 'the discursive construction of' whatever phenomenon is under scrutiny.

Whitehead's Alternative to Materialistic Foundationalism: Groupings of Actual Occasions

In sum, previous 're-foundational' efforts share with 'anti-foundationalism' a problematic acceptance of the old spatially oriented notions of substantial foundation that have long been discarded by physicists. They thus respond to the foundational paradox of psychology by inventing and recycling foundational concepts that re-duplicate and reinforce the bifurcation of nature that followed from the now abandoned abstractions of seventeenth-century cosmology. The often heard rhetoric about the need to abandon 'Cartesian dualism' typically boils down to either the effort to reduce all to the discursive (as with the 'nature is a discourse and scientific knowledge a social construct' school of thought), or to the familiar totalitarian monism of materialism ('when it comes down to it, we are all materialists, are we not?').

It is one thing to diagnose a problem, quite another to propose a viable solution. We have suggested that it is not enough to continue with a notion of scientific psychology based upon the residual tatters of a defective foundationalist ontology, and neither is it enough to argue for a fundamental distinction between explanation and understanding, fact and meaning, constructionism and realism, that tacitly assumes that social and psychological phenomena belong to the 'secondary' side of a bifurcated nature. It is not enough to blindly pursue an empirical agenda in the name of promissory pragmatic outcomes, and neither is it enough simply to cynically pile criticism upon criticism. The solution is as simple as it is daunting. A positive agenda is required based upon a cosmology adequate to our knowledge of the universe. The fact that this is an impossible task is no reason to abandon it. Throughout his career Whitehead was engaged in a radical rethinking of scientific cosmology. He was aware that if materialism is to be succeeded as a foundational doctrine, then an alternative account of fundamentals is required. This alternative account, if subjectivity is not to be excluded from nature, must be consistent both with what we know about the natural world and what we know about the psychological and social worlds. In a work published in 1920 entitled *The concept of nature*, he put the matter in the following terms: 'If we are to look for substance anywhere, I should find it in events which are in some sense the ultimate substance of nature' (Whitehead, 1920/2004, p. 19).

We wish to dwell on this astonishing statement. An event is not a substance but an *activity of realisation*. Through the course of his writings, Whitehead uses many terms that are more or less synonymous with the concept of event, including 'occasions of experience' (*Adventures in ideas, Modes of thought*), 'actual occurrences' (*Science and the modern world*), 'immediate occasions' (*Nature and life*), 'epochal occasions' (*Religion in the making*) and 'actual events' (*Science and the modern world*). It is important not to get misled by arbitrary terminology. It is the *concept* that is decisive, not whether it goes under the label of actual 'event', 'occasion', 'experience' or whatever else. In *Science and the modern world* (1926) and then *Process and reality* (1927–8) he develops a cosmology grounded in the notion of the *actual occasion* or, as he sometimes says, *actual entity*. He states that 'a theory of science which discards materialism must answer the question as to the character of ... primary entities. There can be only one answer on this basis. We must start with the event as the ultimate unit of natural occurrence ... accordingly, a non-materialistic philosophy of nature will identify a primary organism as being the emergence of some particular pattern as grasped in the unity of an event' (1926/1985, pp. 129–130). By 1929 his terminology had more or less shifted from the notion of an actual event to that of actual occasion/entities. The positive doctrine of *Process and reality*, for instance, 'is concerned with the becoming, the being, and the relatedness of "actual entities." "Actual entities" – also termed "actual occasions" – are the final real things of which the world is made up. There is no going behind actual entities to find anything more real' (1927–8/1985, p. 18).

The final real things out of which the world is made up are thus *occasions* – 'drops of experience, complex and interdependent' – and not the inert bits of stuff typical of atomic cosmologies. The actual world is conceived as, at bottom, a process rather than a realm of extended materiality or a timeless substratum of mentality. Process does not simply mean 'change' or 'flow' but the 'expansion of the universe in respect to actual things' (1927–8/1985, p. 215). Process is defined as the *becoming of actual occasions*. Whitehead devotes *Process and reality* to the task of elucidating the nature and relations of actual occasions. However, it must be stressed that, as a metaphysician, he was aiming at a generic description that would be applicable to *all* actual occasions at *all* times. That is to say, he aims for a general level of description that will be as applicable to the occasions constituting an electron as to those constituting the personal being of the reader of this text. The result is a form of argument pitched at an extremely high level of abstraction. However, the general abstractions should be applicable to *any* more specific particulars. The historical emergence of the social form of the discipline of psychology should be analysable in terms of its constitutive actual occasions no less than the subject matter that it takes as its object, for example. This level of abstraction permits the avoidance of the bifurcation of nature, and this has enormous implications for the discipline of psychology. The following list (based on Stenner, 2008, p. 99–100), gives a provisional sketch of 14 of the features that all such Whiteheadian actual occasions might share in common. Some of these will be further developed at the end of this chapter.

1   Consistent with the fundamental concepts of physics, an actual occasion is not a substance or material but an *activity of realisation*.

2   The concepts of realisation and activity require the concept of process. Process is defined as *the becoming of actual occasions*. An ontology of *process* thus replaces an ontology of state or substance (Stengers, 1997, p. 67): 'At an instant there is nothing. Each instant is only a way of grouping matters of fact. Thus there are no instants, conceived as simple primary entities ... Thus all the interrelations of matters of fact must involve transition in their essence' (Whitehead, 1934, p. 48).

3   The word 'actual' in actual occasions requires a distinction between the actual and the potential. Actuality is the realisation of potential in a particular concrete form. An actual occasion – in which a subject concerns its objects – is this process of actualisation.

4   The realisation of potential into actual form is called the process of concrescence in the sense of becoming concrete. Potential, when actualised in a given occasion, concretises in a radically specific concrete form (*this* actuality and not *that* one).

5   Through concrescence many things (objects, data) are grasped or *prehended* through a process (i.e. through the becoming of an actual occasion) into a new unity. The many become one.

6   This process of unification effects a reduction in the complexity of the prior potential. Actuality is thus a *decision* (in the sense of a 'cutting off') amid potentiality. The exclusion of aspects of potentiality that are not selected for actualisation in a given occasion is called 'negative prehension'.

7   The inclusion of aspects of potential that are actualised is called positive prehension or *feeling*. A feeling is the operation of passing from the objectivity of an object to the subjectivity of an actual occasion. The concrescence of an actual occasion is thus effected by feelings through which objects enter into the real internal constitution of a subject.

8   An actual occasion is thus a *pattern* grasped into the unity of an event or a selective *patterning* of the many into one. In other words, an actual occasion is a passage from a state of *disjunctive diversity* to a state of *conjunctive unity*.

9   Creativity is central to this process of *conjunctive synthesis*. Something new is added to the universe by the actual occasion (e.g. the pattern itself is added). '[T]he many become one and are increased by one' (Whitehead, 1927–8/1985, p. 21).

10 This principle of creativity stresses the potential novelty of any particular instance of actualisation. Potentialities, by definition, can be actualised in various different ways. The way an actual occasion does in fact actualise its potentials into concrete form is a matter of that occasion's perspective on the many and its 'subjective aim'. Its specific manner of feeling the many is its 'subjective form'.

11 The subject with its perspective does not pre-exist its feelings but creates itself through them. Ultimately an actual occasion is a creature that creates itself. What modern biologists would call *autopoiesis*, Whitehead identifies as the *category of subjective unity* (Whitehead, 1927–8/1985, p. 222).

12 One must thus distinguish the process of self-realisation from its product. To do this, Whitehead distinguishes the subject from the superject. The subject is the process of self-realisation considered in terms of its own novel internal constitution or in terms of the immediacy of its self-enjoyment. It is the internal self-becoming of the actual occasion. The superject, by contrast, is the objective *product* of these experiences – the creature of its creative process. An actual occasion is thus always di-polar, involving the subjective process of feeling and its objective product (Whitehead, 1927–8/1985, p. 29).

13 As subject, the actual occasion is the becoming unity of conjunctive synthesis. As superject it takes its place as one more amongst the many in disjunctive diversity. In short, the experience of the subject is expressed by way of the superject as an object.

14 Finally, we return to process by way of the principle of relativity which holds that 'it belongs to the nature of every "being" that it is a potential for every "becoming" (Whitehead, 1927–8/1985, p. 45). Once an actual occasion becomes a determinate superject, then it can play the role of one of the many objects that are the concern of another actual occasion with its process of creative conjunctive synthesis. The subject becomes the superject which in turn becomes the object for a new subject.

The concept of the actual occasion requires a supplementary concept. This is because a Whiteheadian actual occasion is not something that can endure over time and, as we have discussed, foundations are all about 'perpetuability'. An occasion is something which *occurs* rather than something which *endures*. As a pure occurrence – a pure actuality – an occasion has no history and is not something that changes. It is something which becomes and then perishes. Your experience of having just read this line of text becomes and then perishes. It will never happen again in exactly that way. To re-read it is to have another unique experience which becomes and then perishes. This is a paradoxical 'ultimate foundation' indeed: the 'completely real things' do not endure in time and space. How then to account for our routine experiences of continuity and endurance on the basis of this 'atomic' theory?

Whitehead states that the enduring things that we routinely encounter (mountains, chairs, trees, animals, conversations, institutions, etc.) are not actual occasions. The things that endure, change and have histories (including ourselves) are in fact groupings of actual occasions, arranged spatially (as contemporaries) and temporally (in an unfolding sequence). Whitehead thus talks of a *nexus* of occasions which can spread itself both spatially and temporally. A nexus, by definition, is divisible into the actual occasions out of which it is composed, but these occasions themselves are 'atomic' in that they are not further divisible. When a nexus has a specific type of self-sustaining order, it may be referred to as a *society*. A society is thus a specialised nexus which is self-organising and self-referential. A biological system, for example, is a society of spatially and temporally coordinated actual occasions. The occasions that compose the society share a common character which they mutually impose on the other occasions of that society. Each 'microcosmic' actual occasion repeats 'what the universe is in macrocosm'. In this way the 'environment enters into the nature of each thing' (1934, p. 31).

The actual occasion thus functions to explain atomicity whilst the concepts of nexus and society function to explain continuity. Combining the atomic and continuity aspects suggests how we might entertain the idea of the relevance of actual occasions to all kinds of entities whilst still grasping that there might be vast differences in the quality and detail of such occasions, and hence the quality and detail of the things we find in the universe. In other words, it enables us to recognise continuities between, say, human, animal, vegetable and mineral forms of existence (all are groupings of actual occasions) but without denying important qualitative differences between them. A rock is not more real than a conversation or a fleeting feeling. Likewise, a tree, no less than a philosopher, is composed of multiple occasions in which potentialities are actualised into concrete 'experiences' (although it is important to recognise that experience does not necessarily entail consciousness – which is a component only in high-grade occasions).

More specifically, Whiteheadian cosmology suggests that, instead of bifurcating nature into subject and object, we think in terms of different types or grades of actual occasion operating at a variety of levels of complexity expressed through differing forms of assemblage or composition. Psychology might then acquire a genuine subject matter, but not one divorced from 'reality' and not one reduced to brute materiality: 'An occasion of experience which includes a human mentality is an extreme instance, at one end of the scale, of those happenings which constitute nature. ... any doctrine which refuses to place human experience outside nature, must find in descriptions of human experience factors which also enter into the descriptions of less specialized natural occurrences' (Whitehead, 1933/1935, p. 237).

Whitehead offers six such grades of actual occasion, stressing that the boundaries between them are always fuzzy. These are:

1 human existence, body and mind
2 all other animal life
3 all vegetable life
4 single living cells
5 all large-scale inorganic aggregates
6 all happenings on the infinitesimal scale disclosed by modern physics.

These diverse kinds of occasions are produced within diverse modes of organisation or forms of assemblage. The more complex and specialised the grade of occasion, the more enhanced is its 'subjective' aspect, and, as a result, it is capable of higher degrees of novelty and creativity. Thus although there is continuity between the modes, there are also important differences. The occasions that compose living cells, for example, are considerably more specialised than those that occur in large-scale inorganic aggregates (a mountain range, for example). Such inorganic aggregates are characterised by the forms of repetition and conformity that give rise to the laws of physical nature (although at the infinitesimal scale of level six the infra-molecular activity has 'lost all trace' of this passivity [Whitehead, 1938/1966, p. 157]). They are dominated by the average and the subjective and self-determining aspect of each occasion is negligible. The actual occasions involved are thus 'conformal' in nature. In the temporal dimension one gives rise to another very much like it, and in the spatial dimension, one contemporary is largely indistinguishable from its neighbours. A unicellular organism, by contrast, can be thought of as an isolated pocket of nature within which comparatively idiosyncratic coordination takes place. The specialised events that occur in a cell do not and could not occur in a rock. For Whitehead, something is alive if it is a region of nature 'which is itself the primary field of the expressions issuing from each of its parts' (Whitehead, 1938/1966, p. 22).

This self-referential internal coordination of a region of nature is even more specialised when it comes to vegetable life and animal life. Both vegetables and animals are 'composed of various centres of experience imposing the expression of themselves on each other' (ibid., p. 23). The actual occasions are thus grouped into complex societies and each occasion derives its characteristics by virtue of its involvement in that society. When we compare animal to vegetable life, however, we find that animal life is comparatively more centralised. Of the numerous centres of experience, one or more tends to dominate and to receive as its data expressions from numerous other more specialist centres. If this dominant 'central' activity is lost, the animal dies because the whole coordination collapses. This higher-order coordination affords an extension of the difference between the actual and the possible and hence a deepening of the repertoire of possible occasions (as experiences and expressions). A vegetable, by contrast, is more like a democracy (ibid., p. 24). Its bodily organisation lacks a centre of experience operating at a higher level of complexity. This makes it more robust (a piece can often survive independently of the whole, for example), but less innovative. Compared to an animal, a vegetable lacks the capacity to respond in novel ways to novel situations. All is relative, however, since compared to large-scale inorganic aggregates, a vegetable displays considerable novelty at the cost of a robust ability to endure.

The human body, like all societies, has recognisable boundaries, but – as the coordinated functioning of billions of molecules – it is also part and parcel of the larger field of nature. It is thus both continuous with wider nature, and distinct from other natural forms. It is forever gaining molecules and losing molecules, and a clear-cut distinction between it and its wider environment is never strictly possible. The human body, then, is a *region* of the wider world and universe. It is that region of nature which is the 'primary field of human expression' (ibid., p. 22). But compared to other life forms it is an even more highly coordinated region that is therefore capable of actual occasions that are considerably more idiosyncratic, specialised, novel and organised. Its occasions of experience are thus qualitatively distinct, not just from those that occur at purely physical levels, but also from those that occur in other life forms, since they are the product of this extensive and intensive coordination. As with other animals, numerous parts of the body are coordinated into the unity of a definite system, and that system both coordinates its own responses and responds to itself. However, with our species the specialised centralisation of bodily control into a high-grade brain appears to have crossed a threshold which distinguishes us from other organisms. As Whitehead (1933/1935, p. 243) puts it, the human body is a 'set of occasions miraculously co-ordinated so as to pour its inheritance into various regions within the brain'.

At each level in the nested hierarchy the actual occasions that occur at a higher grade of coordination can presuppose, abstract from and build upon those that are occurring at a more basic level. As Whitehead puts it in drawing an analogy with Spinoza, 'his one substance is for me the one underlying activity of realization, individualizing itself in an interlocked plurality of modes'

(1926/1985, p. 87). Instead of a materialistic cosmology bent on reducing complexity down to more and more basic elements that are more and more real (irreducibly material), emphasis is placed on a process of 'bottom up' creative evolution. Fortunately, the form that is our planet, thanks to its particular relation to our sun (not too near, not too far) could afford the creation of oceans and of an atmosphere that could afford the emergence of basic life forms that could afford the creation of a biosphere hospitable to the slow and gradual development of the flora and fauna that eventually afforded the evolution of human societies that developed technics that would spread across the face of the earth and become visible from cameras installed on satellites. Each nexus of systems grows out of an environment that was previously a nexus of systems growing out of its environment. The fate of each nexus of systems is to become an environment that can be presupposed by a new nexus of systems. The events that occur in human consciousness include features that do not occur in less specialised environments such as the body of a jellyfish. These events cannot be explained by way of laws that may nevertheless apply perfectly well to jellyfish. The events that occur in the body of a jellyfish include features that do not occur in the trunk of a tree, and these latter events in turn include features that do not occur in a chunk of granite. But granite, too, is a complex and structured nexus of occasions. Different laws apply in each case because different emergent realities are at play: something new comes into being under the sun.

In this way the actual occasions of that living assemblage we call the brain generate an inheritance that is poured into a yet more abstracted grade of actual occasion that historically has gone by the name of the 'soul' to distinguish it from the 'body'. The occasions that compose what Whitehead calls a 'personal' society are obviously dependent upon the neural occasions of the brain, just as these are in turn dependent upon the occasions of the body more generally and the various nexuses and societies that make up its wider environment. Nevertheless, the actual occasions of the brain are, for Whitehead, not to be identified with the 'presiding occasions' of personal experience that occur in a personal society. 'There is no necessary connection between "life" and "personality". A "personal" society need not be "living", in the general sense of the term; and a "living" society need not be "personal"' (Whitehead, 1933/1935, p. 264). A human being is thus always more than its particular personal society of actual occasions of experience, since any 'stream of consciousness' presides over, as it were, a broader matrix of living occasions from which it abstracts itself. The consequence of a cosmology of 'one underlying activity of realization, individualizing itself in an interlocked plurality of modes' is that the psyche – as a specific individualised mode – is never disembodied, and the body – as another such mode – is never de-worlded.

In short, Whiteheadian cosmology suggests that psychic existence is both distinct from and continuous with wider nature. As a distinct mode, it entails the composition of a specialised grade of actual occasion, but as one mode amongst others, it is indistinguishable from an underlying activity of realisation. The everyday sense of a coordinated stream of personal experience associated with concepts such as 'the psyche' and 'subjectivity' is thus, for Whitehead, yet another instance of a society of actual occasions. Each occasion of experience is a self-realising event that becomes and then perishes. Each occasion has its direct 'inheritance' from its immediate past and its anticipation of what it will become in the future. Each occasion is a concrescence of many data into the unity of subjective form.

There is, however, something that is very distinctive about the manner in which the occasions of a 'personal' society are grouped. Namely, the assemblage that makes up the society is purely temporal with no spatial dimension in evidence. There are, in other words, no contemporaries, but purely a matter of one occasion of experience following another and giving rise to yet another, and so forth in a temporal chain. The occasions have become maximally abstract and, lacking a spatial dimension, they have no visible or sensible aspect. Whitehead calls the occasions of a purely temporal personal society 'presiding occasions'. The subjective and creative element of presiding occasions is at a maximum, and the difference between potential and actual is skewed heavily towards the former. Thus the human being is capable of what Whitehead calls 'outrageous novelty'. Not only are such high-grade occasions capable of novelty, they also thrive on novelty, and would be reduced without it.

Foundations Revisited: Key Concepts for a Reflexively Critical *Creative* Foundationalism

In the course of this chapter we have introduced the notions of 're-foundationalism' and 'anti-foundationalism'. We wish to suggest that a relational process ontology provides us with a 'reflexively critical foundationalism' (a *creative* foundationalism) which responds directly to the foundational paradox of psychology and works with the fact that we have a *troubled relationship to the question of what grounds us*. We must relinquish the false certainty of objective access to timeless facts (which yields continual 'revolutions' in search of this certainty) but without flipping over to a position that holds that scientific knowledge has no access to what is external to it (and hence that knowledge speaks only of its authors and their cultural and political predicaments). The latter denies any possibility of a relationship to what grounds us, whilst the former operates with a delusory relation of dominance-based ownership. Both overlook the fact that we need foundations precisely because we lack them. In other words, foundations are the product of *creative effort*. Whether we are talking about the nature of our souls or the nature of the discipline which studies them, the question concerning foundations should always be an issue for us. It cannot be finally settled but must be a cause for ongoing concern. The principle of creativity ('by which the many, which are the universe disjunctively, become the one actual occasion, which is the universe conjunctively') is thus central to this radical shift in perspective. Creativity, for Whitehead, is 'the universal of universals characterizing ultimate matter of fact' (1927–8/1985, p. 20).

This chapter also suggested some different metaphors for thinking about endurance and its relationship to occurrence or change (notably the concrete slab, the spinning top and the cell). Once again, the bifurcation of nature was based upon a prioritising of permanence over transition and of stasis over process. This reflects a longstanding philosophical preoccupation with an 'unchanging subject of change' which might serve as an absolute foundation, and hence a prioritising of endurance over occurrence. For some, 'objectivity' supplied that unchanging subject of change, and a materialist doctrine resulted. For others, 'subjectivity' played that role (leading to idealism). For Whitehead, process rather than stasis is the key term. In effect, this reverses the relationship between things that occur (happenings, events, occasions) and things that endure (substance, continuity). The things that occur (actual occasions) are the atomic 'foundation' of the things that endure, and not the other way around. This simple formulation betrays a rather radical change of perspective and of guiding metaphor. As Stenner (2007a, p. 51) puts it:

> Thus the spatial 'stack' foundation metaphor of a static substance with its predicated qualities must be replaced with a notion that affirms the rootedness of being in time. Not an image of one brick placed on top of another, but an intuition of an immediate present conforming to the actualities of its immediate past and thus supplying potential for the immediate future in process of becoming. In jettisoning the spatial notion of foundation we do not thereby announce a libertarian scenario in which 'anything goes', since the future can only arise from its creative engagement with the stubborn facts of past actualities. The 'self-creation' of autopoiesis – to the extent that it occurs in a non-negligible manner – is always already conditioned and occasioned by what is inherited as stubborn fact.

From a process perspective, the inherited concrete actualities of the past are no simple foundation. On the one hand, looking backwards, they are themselves the outcome of a creative process of concrescence that has resulted in one specific actualisation of potential. On the other hand, looking forwards, they are no 'finished product' but rather one of the many 'potential' ingredients that will play a role in the actualisations of the future. A realist might be forgiven for dwelling on the brute fact of concrete actuality, whilst a relativist has their eye on future possibilities (the pessimist takes a dim view of these possibilities whilst the optimist looks to an improved future). The actualities of the present, states Whitehead, 'are deriving their characters from the process, and are bestowing their characters upon the future. Immediacy is the realization of the potentialities of the past, and is the storehouse of the potentialities of the future' (1938/1966, p. 99). This is why Whitehead is difficult to place on the realism/relativism binary. On the one hand, he is the first to insist on brute facts, since a given actual occasion concretises its potential in only *this* way, and then it is no more. On the other hand, his *principle of relativity* states quite emphatically that 'it belongs to the nature of every "being" that it is a potential for every "becoming"' (1927–8/1985, p. 45). For Whitehead, in other words, process *is* the reality. The fallacy of misplaced concreteness that we inherited from seventeenth-century physics lured us into thinking of process as some irrelevant epiphenomenon to be explained away, and staked its claim on a cosmology grounded in the idea of a brute material reality existing with its 'simple location' in the immediate present and enduring through time. For Whitehead, this fallacy is a mere abstraction of thought. In actual fact, there is *nothing* that exists in-and-of-itself in a given instant of time, since each instant is only a way of assembling the ingredients of the world (1934, p. 48).

Rethinking the relationship between occurrence and endurance thus links directly to the principle of creativity. The things that occur – the 'ultimate realities' are self-creating and self-realising. For Whitehead, the transformation of potentiality into actuality in an actual occasion is nothing less than the self-creation of that actual occasion. The many potentialities of the concrete past are integrated into a unified moment of actuality. Through concrescence the 'many' are lent a novel quality of 'unity' that the actual world may previously have lacked. This process of creative unification is the process of self-realisation. That self-creative activity (the transformation of the potential into the actual), as we have seen, is, of course, highly *conditioned*. It must 'conform' to the actualities of the past. The past is not the foundation for the present and future, but it does supply the 'given' to be worked with: 'Thus the immediate present has to conform to what the past is for it … whatever is settled and actual must in due measure be conformed to by the self-creative activity' (Whitehead, 1927, p. 36). Nevertheless, each actual entity, and each society, 'is self-sustaining; in other words, that it is its own reason' (1927–8/1985, p. 89).

Conclusion: Subject/Object Revisited

With respect to the principle of creativity and self-realisation, it should be noted that the concept of subjectivity acquires a key position in relational process ontology. Indeed, Whitehead refers to the process of self-creative creativity in terms of the *category of subjective unity*. Subjective unity 'has to do with self-realization. Self-realization is the ultimate fact of facts. An actuality is self-realizing, and whatever is self-realizing is an actuality. An actual entity is at once the subject of self-realization, and the superject which is self-realized' (1927–8/1985, p. 222). Whitehead thus does not do away with the subject/object distinction. Rather, he refuses to bifurcate the world into a realm of essentially meaningless matter (from which subjectivity has been expelled) and a realm of subjectivity that is effectively restricted to the highgrade experiences of a human 'knower'. He refuses, in short, to evacuate subjectivity from nature and to concentrate it in the human domain of knowledge and culture. It is thus the *splitting* of the subject/object distinction into 'knower' from 'known' that concerns Whitehead. What he offers is a form of *deep empiricism* that radically extends and refines the domain of subjectivity, but refuses to 'detach' it from objects. In this manner, neither 'subject' nor 'object' play the role of first term or primary substance. The 'first term' is always, as we have seen, an actual occasion, and an actual occasion is always a fusion of subject and object in the unified event of an experience. In an actual occasion, the subject *concerns* its objects and comes into being through this concern. Each actual occasion is thus a di-polar fusion of subject and object. Subjectivity (which, we have stressed, may or not involve consciousness and other cognition) is that which belongs to the subject of self-realisation: it is a concept that is used when an actual occasion is considered in terms of its novel internal constitution, i.e. in terms of its own real process of concrescent creativity (or the immediacy of its self-enjoyment). The subject of self-realisation is the *experience* of concrescence, and that is why Whitehead defines actual occasions as 'drops of experience'. In this sense, the actual occasion is a subject 'presiding over its own immediacy of becoming' (1927–8/1985, p. 45). Whitehead puts this succinctly in *Nature and life* (1934, p. 60) when he says that the 'process of self-creation is the transformation of the potential into the actual, and the fact of such transformation includes the immediacy of self-enjoyment'. This immediacy is a moment of 'sheer individuality, bounded on either side by essential relativity'.

But an actual occasion can also be considered as the *product* of its experiences, i.e. as the creature of its creative process. To express the latter Whitehead coined the term *superject*. A superject is thus an 'atomic creature' that has become a being. An actual entity 'is subject–superject, and neither half of this description can for a moment be lost sight of' (1927–8/1985, p. 29). In the first place the actual occasion is the becoming unity of conjunctive synthesis, in the second it takes its place as one more amongst the many in disjunctive diversity. In the first place one is dealing with the conversion of the merely real into determinate actuality, in the second with the transition from attained actuality to actuality in attainment. In short, the 'subject' is the actual process of becoming (the creative and self-creating concrescence) considered from its own unique ('private') perspective. Once this process is satisfied and it has become a determinate 'public' being it is 'superject' – the self-created product of its own process. The superject is thus the creature of its own creative process, and that process considered from its own perspective, is the subject. The subject actualises the potentials of the past, and the superject takes its place as one of many matters of public fact that will become an ingredient in future subjects. In this sense, an actual occasion, as superject, achieves a state of objective immortality: in becoming objective and determinate it becomes available as part (datum) of a process that continues in a new concrescence after its own subjective moment of concrescence has passed. In the relay race of process, the baton of potentiality is passed on and on via quantum events of actuality. Subjectivity gives rise to objectivity which is absorbed once more into novel subjectivity, and hence, to return to our opening theme, experience is the *becoming* of objective reality.

THREE

Serres and Mediation

Have you noticed the popularity among scientists of the word *interface* – which supposes that the junction between two sciences or two concepts is perfectly under control? On the contrary, I believe that these spaces *between* are more complicated than one thinks. This is why I have compared them to the Northwest Passage ... with shores, islands, and fractal ice floes. Between the hard sciences and the so-called human sciences the passage resembles a jagged shore, sprinkled with ice, and variable ... It's more fractal than simple. Less a juncture under control than an adventure to be had. (Serres with Latour, 1995, p. 70)

In Chapter 2 we drew upon Whitehead to articulate a relational process ontology and a corresponding 'deep empiricism'. We also suggested some of the ways in which this permits a radical rethinking of psychology's foundations. This ontology replaces a long discredited but ever-lingering mechanistic materialism (and its solipsistic subjectivist flip side). There are two main presuppositions of mechanistic thinking that we will briefly recap here; one is to do with space, the other is to do with time (or to put it another way, one is to do with relationality, the other is to do with process).

1   Things are what they are independently of their relevance to other things, and independently of the way others things are relevant to them. This is the idea of simple self-contained spatial location.
2   Things are what they are independently of what they were in the past and independently of what they will become in the future. This the idea of simple self-contained temporal occurrence.

A viable non-mechanistic process ontology reverses these related presuppositions. It stresses precisely that no thing in the universe, whether a chemical reaction, an emotional experience, or a conversation, can be abstracted from its broader scheme of relationality and process if it is to be understood rigorously. There is no such thing as a simple self-contained temporal occurrence in a self-contained spatial location. We thus raise two alternative propositions:

1 Things do not exist independently of their relevance to other things, and independently of the way other things are relevant to them. Rather, things are *definable* as their relevance to other things and in terms of the way other things are relevant to them.
2 Things do not exist independently of temporality and process, rather things are *constituted* by events that occurred in the immediate past and by what will occur in the immediate future. To put it bluntly, everything that exists now in the world emerges from the past and is a potential for whatever will come to exist in the future.

These twin principles of relationality and process give a new centrality and importance to the concept of *mediation* and the related notion of the *intermediary*. The *medium* is, on one level, fundamentally inseparable from what it mediates. Just as an art work – whether a painting, a sculpture or a movie – is a particular form in a more general medium, so all the things in the universe can be conceived as particular forms in a given milieu (interestingly, what the French call the *milieu* and the Germans the *mittel* relates to the English 'middle'). Things are always-already in the midst of other things and this means fundamentally *mediated* by other things. This, to repeat, applies both to space and to time: there is nothing without a constitutive environment (the environment, as we argued in the previous chapter, enters into the nature of each thing) and there is nothing which is a pure and simple *immediate* 'now'. Immediacy, pure and simple, is the suppression of mediation, mixed and complex.

Serres at the Interface

In this chapter we take Michel Serres as our guide to the mixtures and complexities of mediation and to the relevance of intermediaries to a psychology without foundations. Serres was born in Agen, France in 1930. Like Whitehead, he is celebrated, amongst other things, for his work on the foundations of mathematics, and has a keen interest in the natural sciences and their histories. Like Whitehead, Serres is informed by developments in the natural sciences and mathematics and argues for a move beyond an unbreachable nature/culture divide. In the quotation with which we started this chapter, for example, Serres likens the divide between the 'hard' and the 'human' sciences to the famous Northwest Passage. In his five-volume *Hermes* (1992) series, he invokes the Greek messenger god as a means of meditating upon the complications of mediation and the need for constant translations between different knowledge domains. A similar role is played by the figure of the angel (1995) in later work. *The parasite* (1980/1982) also deals with the pivotal role of questions of mediation, interception and interruption to numerous issues that cut across the physical, the biological, the psychological and the social domains. This last work is particularly relevant to us, since Serres proposes an alternative and paradoxical notion of *foundation* based on *flow* (homeorhesis rather than homeostasis), and upon the notion of the constitutive role of the *excluded third* (see Brown, 2004). In the previous chapter we saw how Whitehead rethinks the concept of atomicity, replacing the idea of atom-as-irreducible-substance with that of atomic actual occasion. For, Serres, as we will show, it is the *parasitical relation* that functions as the 'atomic form of our relations' (1980/1982, p. 8), and the principle for the production of change in those relations.

We are particularly interested in Serres, then, because of his rigorous and yet deeply poetic writing about the often unrecognised, vague and fuzzy spaces *in between* forms of reality, knowledge and practice, and for his concern with the role of things like error, imperfection, noise, accidents, opacity, interceptions and interruptions in the context of systems which 'work because they do not work' (1980/1982, p. 13). These are the mediating spaces, activities and processes that are neglected precisely because they lack the clarity and distinctness we have come to expect from positive knowledge. These are the spaces between the 'grooves' carved out by disciplinary specialisms, for example. Such special-ist grooves, as Whitehead was so well aware, prevent straying beyond estab-lished boundaries, and hence the spaces between the super-highways of knowledge remain neglected, as if they were unimportant. To switch metaphors, they exist in the dusty and dark corners that are the preferred territory of mythology and religion. They are populated by creatures that appear to disap-pear: angels that we think we catch a glimpse of out of the corners of our eyes; parasites that blend into the background but that irritate us and leave us unset-tled; winged gods that transform turtles into lyres and that appear and disap-pear as guides and go-betweens, leading mortals to death and the dead into heaven or hell. Serres has the courage to affirm the singular importance of these vague and disturbing spaces of transformation, mixture and confusion.

Where most thinkers perceive – if they attend to these spaces at all – disturbing *noise* to be avoided, Serres sees the remarkable constructive and destructive activities of mediators and intermediaries. In fact, for Serres these spaces are ultimately not only destructive but also constitutive of the nice, clean, orderly and predictable systems that we prefer to make the exclusive objects of our forms of knowledge. Perfect equilibrium, perfect homeostasis, and a perfect closed system are, for Serres, signs of death. Life begins and continues with *dis*-equilibrium, with homeo*rhesis*, and with the partially controlled openings between things. We cannot understand that clarity or those forms unless we grasp them in relation to the noise that they conceal, transform, pretend to understand, but ultimately depend upon:

> Maybe there is or never was a system … The only instances of systems are black boxes. When we do not understand, when we defer our knowledge to a later date, when the thing is too complex for the means at hand, when we put everything in a temporary black box, we prejudge the existence of a system. When we finally open the box, we see that it works like a space of transformation. The only systems, instances and substances come from our lack of knowledge. The system is nonknowledge. The other side of nonknowledge. One side of nonknowledge is chaos; the other system. Knowledge forms a bridge between the two banks. Knowledge as such is a space of transformation. (Serres, 1980/1982, p. 73)

Serres, in short, knows that the *interface* – the bridge between the two banks – is where the action is, but that such 'spaces between' are far from under our control. He thus provides invaluable conceptual tools for working up what William James called an 'ambulatory' (as distinct from a saltatory) approach that might better deal with the issues of multiplicity, complexity and difference that dominate contemporary life and knowledge practices.

This stance inevitably involves a rethinking of foundations, of rationality and of ethics. In the first place, it involves a reversal of the conventional relationship envisaged between terms like stability, permanence and essence and terms like flux, process and chaos. As we discussed in Chapter 2, it has long been conventionally assumed that true reality is permanent and stable and that flux and process are secondary distortions or degradations. This involves a certain negative ethical stance towards issues of disequilibrium, imperfection, error, noise, accident, change and so on, and a certain association of rationality with access to permanence and stability. Serres, by contrast, is clear that we must reverse this conventional relationship. From his work in information theory he is familiar with von Foerster's (1960) 'order from noise' principle and with Atlan's (1981) development of it into a theory of complexity-from-noise (see Brown, 2002b). 'In the beginning', as it were, we find not the serene stability of Platonic forms but the turbulence, noise and multiplicity of the untamed vortex. Order and stability emerge like Venus from out of a sea of noise. We thus do not begin with stability and order and, if we are unfortunate, add chaos and multiplicity to this. The opposite is the case: any temporary forms of stability that we find have emerged from out of a more tumultuous background. Notions of noise, multiplicity and process suddenly take on a new aspect. They cease to be dangerous and potentially irritating obstacles that must be removed in the name of rationality before we can gain access to stable fundamentals. From this perspective, 'old-school rationalism' appears to be 'more morality than research, more a social strategy than an intellectual one' (Serres, 1980/1982, p. 13). Disorder, opacity, noise and so on must no longer be considered as 'affronts to the rational'.

With respect to everyday human social existence, this shift in perspective also constitutes an abrupt challenge to the commonplace wisdom that open and transparent communication is a good thing, or that direct and undistorted access to one's 'true feelings' or 'real nature' is possible and desirable. From this perspective, differences in opinion, vested interests and disparities in knowledge, for example, may all be moderated by the creation of routes and channels where communication may flow freely between speakers. Removing the pre-existing barriers to the free flow of talk may then be seen as an unalloyed good. This view reaches its finest expression in Habermas' (1988) communicational utopia built around 'ideal speech situations'. Here bridges will be thrown across the great divisions within the social order – experts will talk to laypersons, government with citizenry. A modern, expanded agora will be founded upon a communicative rationality predicated upon the exclusion of obstacles such as the 'noise' of emotional bias and the opacity of dissembling and strategising. Axel Honneth has responded to criticisms of this Habermasian tradition by elaborating a psychosocial theory of the forms of mutual recognition that, when adequately understood, promise to open up 'the possibility of an undistorted relation to oneself' (Honneth, 1995, p. 1). Habermas' rational communicational utopia purged of the fluxes, instabilities and opacities of noise is thus seen to be dependent upon the interlocutors in turn having cultivated a relation to their own selves that is 'undistorted'. Self-confidence, self-respect and self-esteem must be intact and free from experiences of abuse, the denial of rights and insult.

Even critical responses to such utopias of purification tend to revert to very similar gestures of system-cleansing via noise-exclusion. In *Good to talk?*, for example, Deborah Cameron advocates resistance to what she presents as a performative 'culture of communication'. She locates the importance of the idea of open communication with the growth of 'enterprise culture'. This arises when a particular version of a business model, where flexibility and a calculative rationality serve as basic axioms, is seen as the basis of all forms of organisation. Enterprise culture identifies 'communication' as both a means towards efficient functioning and a target which should be subject to continuous improvement. Both aspects require the mobilisation of expert knowledges regarding effective communication such that the regulation of communicative acts becomes 'an important tool in the creation of a strong corporate culture' (Cameron, 2000, p. 16).

For Cameron, this colonisation of communication by enterprise culture means that the drive for open and transparent speech becomes yoked to the demand for increased performativity. Cameron's counter-demand, however, is that communication as a topic be 'liberated' from the expert knowledges and practices in which it is currently enmired. This may be done, she claims, through pedagogic practices which recover a notion of conversation as art, as storytelling endowed with 'ludic qualities' (p. 182). In this respect, her solution is similar to Lyotard's (1979/1984) turn towards 'petit' narratives as a way out of performativity. But what if the problem ran much deeper? Both Cameron and Lyotard assume that there is a richer, more positive version of communication and of identity to be rescued from its takeover within modern enterprise cultures. Here, presumably, communication is supportive rather than corrosive of social relations and personal wellbeing, if and when the distortions and noise of corporate performativity are removed. But what if this assumption were itself the problem? Michel Serres, we suggest, offers a very different understanding of the idea of 'free and open communication' and of 'undistorted relations' in general. For him, such positions are only achieved by silencing of alternatives and removing information, so that what is transmitted is only what is already known in advance. In its place, he substitutes a framework where the vagaries of what occurs between speakers, as messages become diffused, subject to interference, scrambled and translated, becomes the source of the rich texture of social relations ...

... THERE IS A KNOCK AT THE DOOR ...

Paul: Not again! There's always someone disturbing my peace! [he shouts downstairs] Steve! Would you mind getting the door please, I'm in the middle of a sentence here.

[The noise of stomping feet and creaking hinges can be heard downstairs, along with some muttering and some barely audible greetings.]

Steve: Hey – Paul. It's Beryl. Beryl Curt.

Paul: [With head in hands] She can't come in now, Steve – we'll never get this manuscript finished if she gets involved. Tell her it's not a good time. ... if we let her in now we'll have her whole entourage visiting, and that'll be curtains for ...

... [Beryl steps into the room, smiling broadly, holding a bottle of wine and wearing a full-length hamster-skin coat.]

Beryl: Hi guys! Long time no see.

[Steve enters the room behind Beryl, looking anxious.]

Steve: Hey Beryl ... look, it's really great to see you and all, but ... is there any chance you could pop back at the end of the month when we've got this work done, we ...

Beryl: I won't keep you – it's just that I heard on the grapevine that you were working on something ... hmmm, looks interesting ...

[She leans over Paul's shoulder, looks at the computer screen and begins reading the draft chapter on Michel Serres.]

Paul: [in a voice laden with unsubtle sarcasm] Be my guest Beryl.

Beryl: ... you know, of course, that you can't discuss Serres without first introducing René Girard and his theory of mimetic desire and scapegoating ...

[Steve looks at Paul and rolls his eyes in an expression of barely contained exasperation.]

Steve: Look Beryl, you know as well as we do that there are a thousand ways of presenting the work of a thinker as complex as Serres ... Let us do it OUR way... But, then again, I suppose you have a point ...

Beryl: Of course I have a point, particularly as this is supposed to be a book about psychology! Don't go banging on about the obscurities of information theory and La Fontaine's rats, get straight to the point about psychology and mediation: our very *desires* are mediated by others. Without models to emulate and heroes to copy, most of us wouldn't even know what we *want*, let alone how to get it. How can we 'get in touch with the real us' and with what we really want to do and really want to be, if these very desires are sparked in us by others?

[Beryl starts singing a Spice Girls song in an operatic voice: 'I'll tell you what I want, what I really, really want', but the song begins to mutate horribly, first into something approximating a line from Anarchy in the UK ('I know what I want, and I know how to get it, I want to destroy ... ') and then into something vaguely resembling a P.J. Harvey track ('All I want to do, and all I want to grow up to be, is all caught up with you, look what you're doing to me').]

Paul: Look, Beryl – with the greatest of respect, we were actually going to write about mimetic desire, but only after we'd introduced the idea of the *parasite*. Mimetic desire is, in a sense, desire that is parasited or parasitized, or however you should say it. Your horrible singing has made me think of the Sex Pistols and the Spice Girls in this light. For all the differences between them, both inspired millions of young followers who copied, not just their ways of looking and acting (this is something that social learning theorists have long been aware of), but also, to a large extent, their very aims, wishes and desires. Just look at…

Beryl: … Sorry for so rudely interrupting again [Beryl laughs], but are you guys really any different? Whose desires are you parasiting? When you write in your nice, detached, univocal prose you make out that you are simply 'presenting' the work of people like Whitehead and Serres, but what is really going on? Are you acting as neutral mediators and innocent 'go-betweens' here, or are you parasiting something? What is your role as intermediaries? Why not get it straight from the horse's mouth? Why not just tell your readers to read Whitehead and Serres in the 'original'? Are you feeding off scraps from their table, by any chance? Why else do you lodge yourself between your readers and these writers? And what about desire? Do you desire what Serres desires? Is it that you wish you could *be* Michel Serres, just as my little niece wanted to be Ginger Spice? And if so, do you do so in order that others may desire (to be) you as much as you desire (to be) him? Do you want others to eat the scraps off your table just as you feed off the great Michel? Come on … come clean! Arghhhh …

[Steve sneaks up behind Beryl and places a large sack over her head. Paul and he manage to wrestle Beryl to the ground and, amidst great struggle, gradually immobilise and bind her. They mutter in secretive tones something about sacrifice being for the common good as they drag their prisoner towards a dark cupboard.]

The noisy multitude that had so suddenly interrupted, returns to calm unity.

Parasite Logic and the Law of the Excluded Middle

We stated that the twin principles of relationality and process give a new centrality and importance to *intermediaries* and to the concept of *mediation*. We also stated that these mediating relations and processes are neglected precisely because they lack the clarity and distinctness we have come to expect from positive knowledge. Classical logic, for example, is founded upon the axiom of the excluded middle which holds that there is no third term which is simultaneously A and non-A. This axiom presupposes an axiom of identity (where A is A), and an axiom of noncontradiction (where A is not non-A). Classical logic is thus built upon the accord of the exclusion of any fuzzy territory between A and non-A. The muddle of the middle, as it were, is excluded from rational procedure. We now know, however, that neither logic nor the universe it presupposes, are eternal, static and unchanging things. We had assumed both to be watertight 'systems', but that assumption was based upon nonknowledge, upon 'black boxing', and upon the exclusion of all that did not fit the scheme. Especially since the definitive formation of quantum mechanics in the 1930s, a series of new logics have been proposed that go beyond classical logic (Nicolescu, 2002). Most of these, however, are concerned to resolve the new paradoxes introduced by quantum theory into the physical sciences. What is distinctive about Michel Serres' notion of *parasite logic* is that in his book *The parasite*, Serres attempts to progressively construct 'the field of human or social sciences. Not the sciences themselves, but their field and its conditions' (p. 130). In fact, in a good deal of his work, Serres deals with psychosocial questions of direct relevance to our project, and, as we shall see, he tends to draw his insights from a theoretically informed engagement with literature.

What Serres offers, however, is not a technical logic or proto-logic such as that provided by George Spencer-Brown (1969/1994). Rather, it could be said that he provides a naïve logic in the sense that he is concerned with a logic of the fresh creativity of new birth. Serres is not afraid to risk naïveté because, for him, 'the only new is naïveté' (1980/1982, p. 123). The strength of science in general has been in the realm of analysis, reduction and subtraction. Psychology, for its sins, has been no exception, and this despite the complexity and creativity of its subject matter. This has led to a preference for the preformed and the ever-repeated: a preference for the universal that is discovered via experiments that can be perfectly replicated. Serres associates this tendency with a thanatogenic philosophy 'that seeks to transform the world into a pillar of salt or a plain bestrewn with corpses' (1980/1982, p. 122). We know, by contrast, very little about *production, composition* and *combination*. And yet these are the issues that are relevant once we recognise that our key terms must be relationality and process in the key of creativity.

What, or who, is the parasite?

Serres distinguishes three different but related meanings of parasite, referring to biological, social and physical systems respectively. The technical, biological definition of a parasite is a heterotroph[1] that derives its food from other organisms (called 'hosts') when they are still alive. The word is also used in a human context to denote a guest who exploits their host, taking food and shelter and giving only talk, praise and flattery in return, for instance. In French, an obscure third meaning of *parasite* is the *noise* that interferes with a transmitted signal: static. Successful transmission of a message depends upon the exclusion of this parasite. None of these meanings should be given priority, as if, say, the biological were the real parasite and the others just metaphors. One could just as well point out that the 'intuition of the parasitologist makes him import a common relation of social manners to the habits of little animals, a relation so clear and distinct that we recognize it as being the simplest' (p. 7). In pointing to this dark spot in the French language where an abusive guest, a broken message and a host-dependent heterotroph are brought together,

Serres points to an instrinsic and nonarbitrary association: each has the same function within its system. Specifically, Serres tries to demonstrate that the parasitical relation (a relation of taking without giving) is no less than the 'atomic form of our relations' (p. 8) and, importantly, the principle for the production of change in those relations. If, as we have suggested, things are definable in terms of their relevance to other things and as the way other things are relevant to them, then, as we shall see, the notion of a parasitical relation goes a long way towards illuminating a basic feature of such relevance. We must ask, in other words, in what concrete and specific ways a parasite is relevant to its host and what ways a host is relevant to a parasite. A parasite, in whatever sense of the word, is literally a liminal figure, a figure on the side: para-site. Serres develops the thesis that any system (whether physical, organic, psychic or social) is based upon a relation to a third party – the parasite – which is thus an essential aspect of any system (Brown, 2004).

The parasite is the atomic form of relationality in the sense that we are in fact never dealing simply with a situation of a simple and unmediated 'relation' between two 'stations'. As Serres notes, 'as soon as we are two, we are already three or four. We learned that a long time ago' (1980/1982, p. 57). The relation is already a third term between station one and station two, for instance. If the exchange of messages between two stations by way of such a relation (or channel) were perfect and optimum then, precisely, there would be no relation. We would be dealing with a situation of immediacy, i.e. an absence of mediation. If the relation (and hence mediation) exists, if it is 'there', then by definition it has failed to some extent:

> The channel carries the flow, but it cannot disappear as a channel, and it breaks the flow, more or less. But perfect, successful, optimum communication no longer includes any mediation. And the canal disappears into immediacy. There would be no spaces of transformation anywhere. There are channels, and thus there must be noise. No canal without noise. The real is not rational. The best relation would be no relation. By definition it does not exist; if it exists, it is not observable. (1980/1982, p. 79)

There is always logically a third space between us, a third space in the process of opening up. To this notion of the parasite as mediation, Serres adds the notion of the *intermediary*. There is mediation involved wherever someone or something has a relation to someone or something else. That mediation, by definition, is never transparent, since transparency is immediacy. There is hence always a mediator or 'go-between'. But for Serres there is also always an intermediary: a third who may have no relation to the two stations but who only relates to their relation. To parasite in this sense is to branch onto an existing channel and hence to intercept or interrupt that existing relation. It is to relate to a relation. This parasite aims for what Serres calls the 'good position' – the position of complete dependence on a relation and the position in which no others depend upon or parasite them: to take without giving. We can thus envisage a primitive diagram in which two stations are connected by a relation (mediation) and in which that relation in turn is grasped as a station by a third who interrupts it (an intermediary), benefiting from whatever had been flowing along that relation. Serres finds these abstract relations in concrete form everywhere: in the activities of biological parasites; in the emergence of consciousness from brain states; in the development of institutions such as law and politics; and in the mundane activities of everyday human social existence. Consider the following example from the life of Jean Jacques Rousseau:

> Here follows the horrible tragedy, the history of the nut tree on the terrace. My uncle had it planted to have shade ... But my cousin and I wanted to plant as well, without dividing the glory with anyone else. A cutting of willow did the trick, and it was planted eight or ten steps from the august nut tree. But there was no water to water the cutting. We weren't allowed to run around enough to get some ourselves. Hence the industrious invention of the subterranean aqueduct, made of boxes and planks, which led to the willow, detouring the water destined for the nut tree ... The nut tree's basin, now with a hole, communicates with the hollow of the willow, at a low level. ... Suddenly, tragedy. Heavens! My uncle! Struck by the sight of the division of the nut tree's water between two basins, the uncle took a pick and shattered the aqueduct. There is always someone to surprise the parasite who has branched onto the channel. (Serres, 1980/1982, p. 111)

In this example we have the basic diagram of an existing relation between two stations (a channel carrying water between the uncle and the nut tree), and of the interception of that channel by a third, who branches a new channel onto the existing relation. The willow tree parasites its 'host', the nut tree, just as the boys parasite their 'host', the uncle. This 'good position', however, does not last for long before it in turn is interrupted or intercepted by the uncle, who destroys the new channel. As soon as we are two, we are already three or four.

A simple fable from La Fontaine allows Serres to develop some of the complexities of this thesis: relations branch upon relations which branch upon relations in a veritable parasitical cascade. The town rat invites his cousin the country rat to dine with him in the tax farmer's house. That is, in the city. In an ordinary sense of the word, the town rat is thus the host of the country rat, but in another sense, both rats parasite their host the tax farmer. The two cousins feast on the leftovers on the carpet in the farmer's dining room, whilst the farmer sleeps upstairs. In this sense the rats branch onto and siphon off some of what flows along an existing relation the tax farmer has with those he taxes (the tax farmer is thus in turn a parasite to another host). Suddenly their feast is interrupted by a noise outside the door. The two cousins flee, and their channel is destroyed. This is only temporary, of course, since they await the abating of the noise. The farmer returns to his slumbers, and the town rat urges his cousin to return to the feast. But the poor thing cannot bear it: 'Let's go to the country where we eat only soup, but quietly and without interruption' (Serres, 1980/1982, p. 3).

The fable can be diagrammed in the following way:

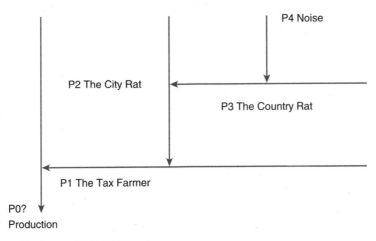

Figure 1 After Serres, 1980/1982, p. 4

Recall that the feast takes place in the house of a tax farmer. He produces nothing. The fine food he has on offer comes from elsewhere and is rendered to him as levy. Hence we must imagine a position (P0) where the foods are produced. All that follows will be a form of parasitism. The tax farmer parasites the producer – he then occupies P1. The town rat then parasites the farmer, seizing the position P2. The invitation to the country cousins makes space for a third parasitic position P3. So we have a kind of chain of parasites, which forms a clear sequence where each position in turn successfully parasitises the former, and temporarily assumes the good position. We might imagine such a chain stretching on without end. But it does end. With the knock at the door, or with an uncle brandishing a pickaxe. A noise from outside causes the chain to fall apart, and that noise comes from the parasite 'upstream' that had become aware that it had lost its good position. But the chain falls apart only temporarily. The town rat returns, the parasites come back. The lesson? You will never be rid of the parasite, send him away and he returns in numbers. The parasite is like nature itself: excluded with a pitchfork, it ever returns.

Note, though, the nature of the chain formed by the parasites in the fable. Every position is a parasitic one where 'the parasite parasitises the parasites' (p. 55). This is not so much a chain as a cascade, where the produce flows down through the chain of parasites. But this chain, this cascade, is not entirely random. Each link has a kind of specificity. Indeed, it is Serres' central claim that the singular attribute of the parasite 'is its specificity' (p. 230). The tax farmer is a farmer, like those whom he taxes. The town rat is small enough to eat undetected in his house. The country rat is his cousin. There is a chain of tiny specificities that makes the cascade of parasitism possible.

And this chain is itself not entirely random. It has its own direction. Each link is formed by a one-way relationship of taking without giving. Production is carried off, it is dragged down. The parasite takes without giving. It makes an unequal exchange which moves the chain away from any form of equilibrium. If we imagine production as the initial system, every act of parasitism (or parasitism squared, cubed, multiplied endlessly) drags the productive system away from its equilibrium point. It takes a further act of interruption – the noise at the door – to break the parasitic chain and restore the initial state. But the parasites always come back. The game they play is to always come last, to be in the last position in the parasitic chain. And thus to stand, open-mouthed, ready to absorb all of what flows down the chain. The last in line collects all: the good position.

Foundation by exclusion and paradoxical ambivalence

Serres' concept of the parasite conspicuously violates the axiom of the excluded middle in at least two distinguishable ways. First, the parasite is simultaneously inside the system and outside of the system. It both *is* the system and is *not* the system. Consider, for example, the diagrammatic representation of the story of the rats: 'is it something added to a system, like a cancer of interceptions, flights, losses, holes, trapdoors … or if it is quite simply the system itself' (p. 12). If a signal is to be transmitted, then noise must be excluded, which means that this exclusion of noise is essential to the system in the sense that it is constitutive of it. The noise, we might say, is included-as-excluded, much as the figure of *homo sacer* is held on the boundary of the social system in the work of Georgio Agamben (1998). We can thus talk of the parasite-as-noise (or static) as the *constitutive outside* of the system, and of the system as operating according to a principle of *foundation by exclusion* (Stenner, 2002, 2007a). This points to an intimate relationship between beginnings and *exclusions* and between identities and *expulsions*. The axiom of the excluded middle is thus informative but in a thoroughly paradoxical way. It is precisely through the expulsion of the noisy muddle of the middle that unity and identity are created and maintained. A clear implication of this is the essential relativity of what counts as 'noise' and what counts as 'signal'. What is a noisy interruption to the rats is an important signal of expulsion for the tax farmer. To give another example, the city rat appears largely immune to what the country rat experiences as an unbearable amount of noise and interruption. But no doubt the noises of the countryside would alarm the city rat in turn. What counts as signal and what as noise is, in short, a function of the position of the observer. Serres illustrates this with an example of the burden placed on a host at a dinner party who hears the unmistakable sound of a phone in the room next door:

> At the feast everyone is talking. At the door of the room there is a ringing noise, the telephone. Communication cuts conversation, the noise interrupting the messages. As soon as I start to talk with this new interlocutor, the sounds of the banquet become noise for the new 'us'. The system has shifted. If I approach the table, the noise slowly becomes conversation. In the system, noise and message exchange roles according to the position of the

observer and the action of the actor, but they are transformed into one another ... They make order or disorder. (Serres, 1980/1982, p. 68)

The hostess is distracted by the phone. It is noise, invading the pleasant repartee of the dinner table. Maybe she tries to ignore it. But it keeps on ringing. Like a taunt. Answer me! Answer me! The noise grows in strength as a signal as the host fails to repress its intervention (thus, as Serres describes, 'the repressed returns to parasite what I'm talking about. Such a force is in the third position that I repress', p. 78). The hostess gives in and crosses to the other room. At the threshold, at the point of commitment, the noise becomes fully signal and a new telephone conversation is begun. And now it is the delightful conversation of the dinner table which becomes noise which the hostess must repress in order to concentrate on the conversation with her new interlocutor. Everything happens at the threshold, Serres surmises. It is this boundary between two systems that is made permeable by the noise–signal interruption. This point becomes Serres' central concern – 'I have found a spot where, give or take one vibration, moving a hair's breadth in either direction causes the noises to become messages and the messages noises' (p. 67). Thinking what goes on at this boundary, the most intense point of relation between the two systems or stations, is the extended task of the entire text. Serres shows us, in this example, not just the relativity of the signal–noise couple, but also why it is that we tend to flee from the uncomfortable position in the midst of two systems, and hence why it is that we are motivated to exclude this mediate territory.

The second way in which Serres' notion of the parasite conspicuously violates the axiom of the excluded middle concerns the *value* accorded to the parasite. We have seen that 'old school' rationality conserves an ethical stance against the parasite. We do good to the extent that we kill the parasite, exclude it and keep it out. In that way we maintain the unity, the cleanliness and the purity (in short, the holiness) of 'our' system. But, inflect it a little, and this form of morality begins to look a little ethically suspect. Cleansing takes on connotations of ethnic cleansing and the task of eliminating the parasites comes to resemble the activities of a death camp. The one who thinks of themself as a rightful host becomes hostile and inhospitable. Complexity is reduced to the simplicity of a 'final solution'. The earth is cleansed of its manifold species. This ambivalence is fundamental. Who, after all, is the parasite? The tax farmer host who interrupts the feast of the rats is – for all the angry noise he makes about the parasitical rats – no less a parasite than they. The system continues to the extent that it excludes the parasites, but the system is itself the parasite of a broader system.

We must therefore be careful before assuming that a crude and simple negative value applies to the parasite. If that were the case, we would have to cleanse ourselves. Noise is not simply a threat to order: it is the basis from which order might emerge. It is simultaneously destructive and productive: it 'interrupts at first glance, consolidates when you look again' (Serres, 1982: 14).

Serres thus warns us against taking the side of the country rat who scurries away from the pressures of the city, in search of a simple life of truth, authenticity and belonging. It is, in fact, the country rat who *breaks* the system:

> He could live on simple and easy chains, but he is horrified by the complex. He does not understand that chance, risk, anxiety, and even disorder can consolidate a system. He trusts only simple, rough, causal relations; he believes that disorder always destroys order. He is a rationalist, the kind we just spoke of. How many of these rough political rats are there around us? How many of them break things they do not understand? How many of these rats simplify? How many of them have built such homogeneous, cruel systems upon the horror of disorder and noise? (p. 14)

The Parasite as Catalyst of Complexity

The parasite, looked at in one way, is the very principle of novelty: it invents something new: 'Since he does not eat like everyone else, he builds a new logic. He crosses the exchange, makes it into a diagonal' (p. 35). Or again:

> Theorem: noise gives rise to a new system, an order that is more complex than the simple chain. The parasite interrupts at first glance, consolidates when you look again ... are we in the pathology of systems or in their emergence and evolution. (p. 14)

For Serres, parasite logic underlies the very emergence of more complex grades of existence from out of a background of more simple grades. Let us put this first in a very abstract way. Parasite logic is the principle of system formation in the sense that a system, to exist, must find a way of converting the 'primal' noise of its inheritance into a temporary form of order. In this sense, systems literally exist 'on the side', as it were, of noise (this being a literal meaning of para-site). The process of system formation can thus be construed as the activity of parasiting noise. A system thus reduces the complexity of its environment, transforming (or 'digesting') its noise into what passes as 'signal' (as 'energy' or 'food' or 'meaning') for the system (cf. Stenner, 2006, for an application of these principles to a theory of emotion).

In systematising noise, emergent systems become fertile ground to be parasitised in turn by new systems. A new system (which is always the old system in new circumstances) can take advantage of the structured complexity produced by its host, and can thus afford a higher level of complexity. In other words, the production of order achieved by the parasited system can be taken for granted as an environmental given by the new parasite, and transcended. A new logic of exchange can be invented, that, having formed a diagonal, proceeds to run parallel to the old logic that it presupposes. But, at the same time, environments are never stable and can never be entirely taken for granted. An unstable environment always threatens to reduce a system once more to noise. Noise always threatens to perturbate, interrupt, and irritate the operations of a system. There is thus always a delicate balancing act at play, since no change would occur without such noise. Too much noise and the system would dissolve back into chaos: too little and it would become static, frozen, and maladapted. Our chance, says Serres, 'is on the crest', and on the threshold or the 'fringed, capricious curve where the simple beach of sand meets the noisy rolling in of the waves':

> Noise destroys and horrifies. But order and flat repetition are in the vicinity of death. Noise nourishes a new order. Organization, life, and intelligent thought live between order and noise, between disorder and perfect harmony. If there were only order, if we only heard perfect harmonies, our stupidity would soon fall down toward a dreamless sleep; if we were always surrounded by the shivaree, we would lose our breath and our consistency, we would spread out among all the dancing atoms of the universe. We are; we live; we think on the fringe, in the probable fed by the unexpected, in the legal nourished with information. There are two ways to die, two ways to sleep, two ways to be stupid – a head-first dive into chaos or stabilized installation in order and chitin. (1980/1982, p. 127)

Serres thus suggests an evolutionary principle that takes the form of a parasitical cascade. This would resemble the sequence of integrated interlocking entities described by François Jacob (1976), and it would also remain consistent with von Foerster's (1960) principle of order from noise as well as Atlan's (1981, p. 185) refinement of this as *complexity from noise*:

> Consider any level of an interlocking system. Locally ... it operates like a series of chemical reactions at a certain temperature. Let us forget for the moment their precise equations and the unique elements at work here. Let us consider only the energy conditions at this one level. It mobilizes information and produces background noise. The next level in the interlocking series receives, manipulates, and generally integrates the information-background noise couple that was given off at the preceding level. How does this take place? Several recent studies allow us to elucidate the answer to this question ... Indeed, if one writes the equation expressing the quantity of information exchanged between two stations through a given channel and the equation which provides this quantity for the whole unit (including the two stations and the channel), a change of sign occurs for a certain function entering into the computation. In other words, this function, called ambiguity and resulting from noise, changes when the observer changes his point of observation. Its value depends on whether he is submerged in the first level or whether he examines the entire unit from the next level. In a certain sense, the next level functions as a rectifier, in particular, as a rectifier of noise. What was once an obstacle to all messages is reversed and added to the information. This discovery is all the more important since it is valid for all levels. It is a law of the series which runs through the system of integration. (Serres, 1992, p. 77)

The parasitical cascade could thus be schematically visualised as follows (Stenner, 2006):

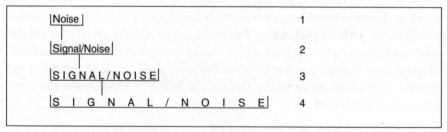

Figure 2   The parasitical cascade

Each system level in this four-level cascade would depend for its existence upon those situated 'upstream' from it. Level three, for instance, takes the entirety of the signal/noise couple of level two as its signal. Since there is no signal without noise, level three can function only by way of its own distinction between signal and noise. This signal/noise couple taken as a whole can then in turn become signal for a higher emergent level (level four), and so on. Despite these strict relations of dependence, each system level operates as if independently to the extent that it can take its host for granted. However, if noise levels exceed the tolerance capacity of a system in the cascade, it will collapse and return to the level of its host.

If a rubicon is crossed between a large-scale inorganic aggregate (say, for argument's sake, level one) and a single living cell (call it 'level two'), for instance, then we must attend to the possibility that a new logic has been built. If a threshold is crossed between life that must depend for the most part upon innately packaged information (level two) and life that can routinely *learn* from its experiences (level three), then, once again, we must suspect that an exchange has been crossed by the 'diagonal' action of parasitism. Further, biological systems that have evolved as *conscious* beings are organic creatures that both parasite and are parasited by a highly complex and novel principle of activity. And, as we reach the most complex grades of being we find that the speaking ape has a conscious existence that can never return to the state of innocence it left prior to its parasitism by language (although Serres also claims that nature may have its own forms of 'writing' – see Brown, 2003).

At each stage we have a 'jump' in complexity and at each jump in complexity, nothing less than a new medium comes into being. The medium that is a living organism is capable of activity that could not occur in the non-living medium of, say, a rock, or a beam of light. It might hear or see, for instance, and it might breathe. But mediation is always also between distinct forms of media, between the 'physical' and 'biological', for instance. In the case of organisms which can see, 'physical' light is the medium of vision (vision 'parasites' light); vibrations in the air mediate hearing; oxygen mediates breathing (breathing 'parasites' oxygen). But seeing and breathing are not light and oxygen, they are distinct processes that are particular to living beings. Note that in each case, for the biological message to pass through, the physical mediator must disappear. We do not see light as such and we rarely notice the air we breathe, unless that air is particularly polluted (and hence transforms from an invisible mediator to a noisy, inhospitable medium). In that case the physical mediator shows up, as it were, and interrupts the biological process, and in so doing transforms from medium to message. There can be no doubt that, at this level of existence, we are all creatures of biochemistry. And as creatures of biochemistry we presuppose the mediation of a hospitable physical universe, itself the product of long evolution.

Likewise, we rarely notice our lungs, unless we are unfortunate enough to be in poor health. To say that we notice the mediation of our lungs suggests that we have become *conscious* of them. In this case we are dealing with mediation not between physical and biological levels, but between a biological level and a psychological level that could be called consciousness. Consciousness too is made possible via biological mediation, itself mediated physically. But the same principle of the disappearance of the mediator holds true, as does the principle that interruption is the becoming-message of the mediator. We rarely notice, for example, the raging neural activity that doubtless makes our consciousness possible, nor the broader torrent of biological activity that sustains that neural activity in our brains. These mediators must disappear to allow the work of mediation to take place. Our conscious experience, however, is not just made possible by mediation but is itself a form of mediation at a different level of existence (which is to say that consciousness is itself a novel *medium*). As such, it too must disappear. Hence, typically it is not consciousness itself that shows up to us, but rather 'through it' and thanks to it we can imagine that we are in direct communion with the things in the world. We adopt the 'natural attitude' and take our perceptual experiences as if they were encounters with unmediated reality. However, when we get so nervous and emotional that we hear our hearts beating in our ears, these usually invisible biological mediators suddenly show up and dominate the conscious experience they were previously silently mediating. But they can only show up to consciousness in the medium that has been invented by consciousness. That is to say, our heartbeat comes to us, when it comes, as a conscious *experience* of that heartbeat. Further, when we faint or fit or pass out or take mind-altering drugs and then recover our former consciousness, we find ourselves in the rare position of having an experience of experience. We encounter the medium itself that is, on one level, ourself. It is not surprising that, despite a certain amount of suffering, such experiences are often highly valued and long remembered. There can be no doubt that, at this level of existence, we are all creatures of consciousness. And as creatures of consciousness we presuppose the mediation of those creatures of biochemistry which presuppose the mediation of a hospitable physical universe.

To give a final example, we rarely notice the language that mediates our communication with each other. When we share a language, and can communicate freely, the language itself seems magically to disappear, and we appear to understand each other as if we could experience one another's minds – as if we were 'open souls' one to another. But when we are learning a foreign language, or dealing with unfamiliar concepts or experiences, suddenly the language itself starts to obtrude and interrupt. When we can't quite find the words we need to express what we are trying to say, we suddenly have an experience with language itself. We become self-conscious and that consciousness starts to get in the way of our communication – to interrupt it. Suddenly your thoughts, feelings and intentions become opaque obstacles blocking the path of shared experience and expression, as do my own. Once again, the medium darkens and becomes the message. There can be no doubt that, at this level of existence, we are all creatures of communication. And as creatures of communication we presuppose the mediation of those creatures of consciousness which presuppose the mediation of those creatures of biochemistry which presuppose the mediation of a hospitable physical universe.

We are, in sum, simultaneously creatures of biochemistry, creatures of consciousness and creatures of communication (Stenner, 2007b). And yet, although each is dependent on the other (as a parasite depends on its host), each of these forms of mediation remains, in some important senses, radically inaccessible to the others. As we will discuss in greater depth in the following chapter on Luhmann, only communication can communicate, and it can only communicate with and as communication. The principle of connectivity which informs communication is communication. As will become clearer in the chapter on Artaud, no matter how hard we try to put our feelings into words, to the extent that we succeed we have succeeded only in converting an experience into a communicable expression. Only once we have changed media can we achieve systemic connectivity. In the same way, only consciousness is conscious, and it can only be conscious of what is conscious. The principle of connectivity which informs consciousness is consciousness. One thought or image or feeling can only flow from another. Consciousness is thus its own medium, and that medium is radically distinct from the biochemical medium of organic neural processes. These processes, to complete the triad, can only process what they process. The chemical process that releases a neurotransmitter at a neural synapse gives rise to an electrical impulse that in turn triggers a chemical process. This biochemical process of connectivity cannot 'connect up' with something like an 'idea', a 'conscious feeling' or a poem. We are thus dealing with the paradox of forms of dependence that lead to strict independence. To bring this discussion back to the work of Serres, this paradoxical parallelism should lead us to suspect the liminal activity of the parasite which paralyses one moment, and catalyses the next (Brown, 2004).

Another fable, by way of illustration. A poor man is starving with an empty belly. He approaches the kitchen door of a restaurant. The smells of the fine food inside waft over him and he finds that his hunger is somewhat sated. An angry kitchenhand comes out and demands that the poor man pay for having taken his fill, for the services rendered. An argument ensues. A third man arrives and offers to settle the matter:

> Give me a coin, he said. The wretch did so, frowning. He put the coin down on the sidewalk and with the heel of his shoe made it ring a bit. This noise, he said, giving his decision, is pay enough for the aroma of the tasty dishes. (Serres, 1980/1982, pp. 34–35)

Serres explains the fable in the following way. We have two orders, two systems. One where coins are exchanged for food, and another where sounds are exchanged for smells. No exchange was thought possible between these two systems. No communication was considered possible. The two systems are, in effect, completely *indiscernible* by one another. The action of the parasite – the third man – is to open up a channel where a new kind of exchange is possible, where coins are transformed into sounds which are exchanged with food transformed into smell. Communication becomes possible. This is something new, this is a transformation or a becoming of each system, or rather the two stations which now stand in relation to one another, by virtue of parasitism. In informational terms, we have a new form of complexity.

Collecting the Collective

> What living together is. What is the collective? This question fascinates us now. (Serres, 1980/1982, p. 224)

In this final section we will touch upon the ways in which Serres tackles the problem of the collectivity: of living together socially. Given that, for Serres, this grade of existence must count among the most abstract and complex, it is important to note that his first move is to insist that, despite our social sciences and our social practices, we *do not know* what the collective is. 'We do not know what "we" means nor what constitutes it. We do not know what happens between us and what passes between us' (p. 124). '[w]e understand nothing of the collective nor of the set' (p. 123). For sure, he states, the collective is not a 'pre-established harmony' or something that was 'always already there', and neither is it the product of rational deliberation and invention. The collective, in short, is a black box to us, and it is full of untranslatable noise.

In drawing attention to the abstract, diffuse, complex and difficult-to-grasp nature of social relations, it could be argued that Serres' thinking is in line with a tradition of French social theory that dates back at least to Emile Durkheim (e.g. 1912/2001) and his notion of a 'collective representation'. For Durkheim, a key problem of collective existence is how something as abstract and ineffable as a collective might come to 'recognise' itself as such, and thus treat itself as a recognisable unity distinct from its broader social and natural environment. The phrase 'collective' obviously requires some finessing here. By definition, a chaotic multiplicity is precisely not 'collected' into a collectivity. We thus suggest distinguishing two ideal typical modes of human *multiplicity* (cf. also Stenner, 2002; Middleton & Brown, 2005): a *gathered multiplicity* forms a kind of unity, a coherent, concerted collective; a *dispersed multiplicity* lacks form and unity and appears chaotic and incoherent. Of course, in any actual state of affairs we will always be dealing with a condition somewhere between integration and disintegration, and we will always be dealing with a *process* whereby a current state of integration is undergoing relative disintegration, and vice versa, and where new modes of integration are at play. For Durkheim, it is a key function of religion to bind the collective through the provision of collective representations that are provided by deities, totemic images, and so forth, and through ritualistic practices (we should not forget that the word religion – which derives from the Latin *ligare* – means to bind or tie together). Totemism, for example, is 'the most primitive and simple form of religion known to us today' (Durkheim, 1912/2001, p. 13). Totemism involves a system of gatherings known as clan groups in which each collective or clan is defined by, and named after a class of objects, usually an animal species: the wolf, the bear, the kangaroo; but sometimes also a species of plant or even, but less commonly, a type of inorganic object. The totem, an eagle for instance, is considered literally to be the ancestor of the clan, and at initiation clan members will, for example, have their ears pierced and decorated with eagle plumes. The totemic collective thus recognises itself in, and defines itself in terms of, a particular totemic animal, plant, or other object that functions as an origin myth, a principle of identification, and as a guide to the future. Much as something diffuse like 'love' might be objectified into a red rose passed from lover to loved, so through the totem the otherwise diffuse and ungraspable communal bond is objectified into a visible and tangible form. The collective acquires an 'objective' reality: a collective representation that allows it to recognise itself and to distinguish itself from its environment.

In the terminology of Serres, the totemic object would be called a *quasi-object*. Serres develops the concept of the quasi-object in various of his books, such as *The parasite* (1980/1982), *Rome* (1991) and *Genesis* (1998). This notion enables us to take very seriously the role that objects play in the gathering of human collectives. Arguably, this role has been obscured by the over-extension of certain 'top-down' social constructionist arguments. We are very used to arguments which quite correctly critique the idea of a naïve 'objectivism' which maintains the possibility of a direct and unmediated relation to objects. Human relationships to objects are always indirect or mediated, and always reflect and embody the concerns of socially organised actors. In other words, we are very used to the argument that objects are defined and constructed by the concerns of collectives. Accepting this, Serres adds another side to the story. Just as collectives construct objects, so objects are centrally implicated in the 'construction' of collectives (see Middleton and Brown, 2005 for practical examples). Serres thus describes the quasi-object as: 'the primary condition that brings about the birth of an elementary form of society' (1991, p. 106). In this sense, the collective is not generated by something like a social contract, or an abstract concept or a general will. Rather the collective relations are made concrete in and by objects. The quasi-object is hence a *marker* of collective relationships that would otherwise remain ineffable, abstract and gaseous. It 'collects' the collective. The quasi-object makes a network of relations more stable and thus allows them to endure in time (in Whiteheadian terminology we might say that it enables the spatial and temporal grouping of comparable occasions). Like the grain of sand around which a pearl takes form, the quasi-object crystallises the dynamics of the collective:

> The only assignable difference between animal societies and our own resides ... in the emergence of the object. Our relationships, social bonds, would be airy as clouds were there only contracts between subjects. In fact, the object, specific to the Hominidae, stabilizes our relationships, it slows down the time of our revolutions. (1998, p. 87)

The most simple example of a quasi-object is the French children's game called 'the ferret' or 'furet' which English children also play in the form of 'pass the ring', or 'pass the button' or 'hunt the slipper'. The button or slipper or ring is passed around the group of players until the music stops, or somebody shouts stop, or some other break occurs. The one who is caught with the button is 'it' – or sometimes 'dead' – and they have to pay a forfeit. In short, the one who is 'it' is marked with the sign of the ferret or the button. They are pointed out as an individual in the midst of a collective.

In this sense, the quasi-object *points out* a subject. This is why Serres calls it a 'quasi'-object. It is not simply an object, since, it is defined 'subjectively'. But conversely, the quasi-object is not simply a subject. It could be called a 'quasi-subject' 'since it marks or designates a subject who, without it, would not be a subject' (1980/1982, p. 225). By contrast, the players who are not 'it', who are not caught with the 'furet', are anonymous. They are part of an unindividuated, or uncut collective. So a sense of the collective is generated anonymously by the simple relationship of the passing of the button. The collective is made up of those who are not 'it' – those who pass the button. This passing of the quasi-object can be thought of as a stitching or weaving movement which binds the players into a collectivity. As Serres puts it:

> This quasi-object, when being passed, makes the collective, if it stops, it makes the individual ... the moving furet weaves the 'we', the collective; if it stops, it marks the 'I'. (1980/1982, p. 225).

For Serres, the human collective is unable to form unless this quasi-object circulates within it. Think of the team's ball, the peace pipe, the common cup passed around at the shared feast, or the small change circulating at the market. The circulation of the quasi-object transforms the dispersed multiplicity into a gathered collective. Serres asks us to think about a quasi-object as a kind of centre around which the collective circulates like planets orbiting around a sun. This is difficult to grasp because we are used to thinking of objects as passive servants which gravitate around active subjects. On the contrary, quasi-objects are the centre of attention around which people gravitate. In a ball game like football or rugby, for example, the whole game moves around

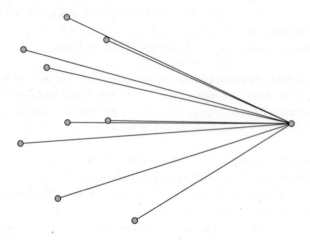

Figure 3   The many-to-one relationship of *concrescence*

the ball, and the players are merely relays or stations. The subject of the quasi-object is always multiple to the extent that all of the players are concentrating their attention and efforts onto this object, the 'ball'. Just as a cloud of vapour can condense into a single droplet of water, so the diffuse attention of a dispersed multiplicity gathers into the many-to-one relationship of *concrescence* represented above.

As with 'pass the button', the one with the ball is marked or designated. To be designated the 'I' or to become 'it' by receiving the ball is to be placed in a powerfully ambiguous situation. One can become the villain of the piece who loses the ball, trampled underfoot by the opposing team – literally sub-ject or 'thrown beneath', or one can become the hero who does something extraordinary – perhaps even scores a goal or a try. But more likely the 'hot potato' is quickly passed on, weaving the collective as it threads its way through the teams which move around it. Certainly, to hog the ball is a sporting offence.

This way of thinking suggests that it would be a mistake to imagine the 'we' or the 'collective' as a simple sum of 'I's'. The 'we' is less a collection of 'I's' gathered together than a *fluctuation* generated by the passing backwards and forwards of the 'I' – or rather, the 'we' of the relationship is 'embodied' in a quasi-object which can be passed from person or 'I' to person. The one who holds the quasi-object, despite being only one part of the collective, holds the whole thing: the essence of the relations which make up the group is in their hands (1991: 106). The we is thus 'woven' by the movements of the quasi-object as it is passed: 'Can one's own "I" be given?' asks Serres. 'There are objects to do so, quasi-objects, quasi-subjects' (1980/1982, p. 227).

For Serres, each social function has its own quasi-objects. Martial relations of warfare centre around weapons and stakes; money and goods circulate in the economy; relics and sacred objects constitute the circulations of religion, and so forth (see Brown, 2002b). We can thus begin to get a sense of the manner in which collectives might emerge and consolidate, but yet lack any understanding of their own emergence. Serres' denial of knowledge of the social that we stressed at the beginning of this section is important, particularly since there are many who would give the impression of having a clear understanding of the collective: 'The politician pretends to understand, as do the scientist and the theoretician. The religious man pretends to understand, as do the soldier, the inspector, and the militant. Each social function is a known and pinpointed variety of black ignorance intelligently disguised as white expertise' (1980/1982, p. 123). We must not be deceived, then, by those who claim to convert real noise into a harmony that is merely theatrical. Social functions, such as law, science, art and politics are, for Serres, forms that emerge to manage – and ultimately to disguise – the chaos of noisy complexity. Such social functions, in short, are parasites that eat and live off the specific type of ignorance and noise that they have made their own. Medicine lives parasitically off the noise of disease. Law off conflict, science off ignorance. Social functions are thus ways of closing black boxes, and of converting their noise into something that passes for understanding:

> Every social function from the judge to the professor and from the artist to the president, every function that is classified or classifiable in some theory of classes or functions, every function, I say, eats and lives on the aforementioned ignorance. It appears as soon as the black box must be closed. And this operation is paid for rather dearly, so that the holder of the key lives well off it. The one who holds the key does not necessarily have knowledge as well; he can also guard a lock and forbid it to be opened. Each social function is the guardian of a door of the ark, and a dangerous door, so it would seem. (1980/1982, p. 123)

A key motif for understanding the emergence and evolution of human collectives is thus the reduction of complexity or the containment of noise. This means that, once again, behind the foundation of a unified collective – of anything that might be described as a social *system* – there lurks an expulsion and exclusion which is not incidental but constitutive of the system.

As Beryl Curt correctly suggested before her untimely demise, the work of René Girard (1987, 1988, 1989) is important in this context. Girard draws attention to the large number of human collectives that form themselves around the figure of a scapegoat or sacrificial victim. For Girard, the 'scapegoat mechanism' is a recurrent means by which human collectives have managed the threat and the reality of internal chaos, conflict and disunity (we could call this 'noise' for short). Through nominating and excluding or sacrificing a scapegoat, a new unity is supplied to the collective. The scapegoat mechanism can thus also be viewed as a means of 'collecting the collective' or of transforming a dispersed multiplicity into one that is gathered. Although this may sound abstract, for Girard it is a brutal reality that occurs time and time again and that may be construed as a model for the very emergence of human culture.

Girard invokes two distinguishable arguments in his explanation of these processes, one distinctly 'psychological' and the other 'social'. He invokes his theory of mimetic desire to explain why collectives always risk dispersal into rivalrous conflict, and he invokes the scapegoat mechanism as a solution to this problem of disintegration. Given a 'mimetic' basis to human desire (i.e. that desire is mediated by a model rather than being essential to a desiring subject or inherent to a desirable object), human collectives are prone to intense rivalries as the 'acquisitive mimesis' of shared desire escalates into 'conflictual mimesis'. That is, to the extent that we fashion our desires on those of another who will stand as model, we take on 'their' object of desire (although their desire is also mimetic in nature, and may even be modelled on ours). To the extent that we are successful in satisfying our desire, this model is thus prone to appear as a rival, and hence rivalries become endemic. The social and material context is of course important here. Human collectives are more likely to enter a state of disarray and internal tension in situations of natural disaster or social crisis. But even without such events, Girard suggests that the noise of conflictual mimesis is likely to occur.

If Girard's notion of mimetic desire were considered a specific instance of parasitism (in which the desire of another is 'taken' for oneself), then one could approach the same problem of accounting for rivalry through Serres' conception of generalised parasitism:

> History hides the fact that man is the universal parasite, that everything and everyone around him is a hospitable space. Plants and animals are always his hosts; man is always necessarily their guest. Always taking, never giving. He bends the logic of exchange and of giving in his favour when he is dealing with nature as a whole. When he is dealing with his kind, he continues to do so; he wants to be the parasite of man as well. And his kind want to be so too. Hence rivalry. (1980/1982, p. 24)

Parasites will inevitably become rivals since mimetic relations of parasitism abound. We parasitise nature and, by extension, when dealing with our fellow humans seek to parasitise them also. Which serves in turn as the model for others. But if we follow the next stage of Girard's argument, then this likely war of all against all becomes the war of all against one. The collective will turn towards the scapegoat who must be expelled, murdered. But who will be nominated? Who will be 'it'? The scapegoat is likely to be either an outsider unlucky enough to be in the wrong place at the wrong time, or else a marginally placed insider. They will be broadly innocent, but will be blamed by the collective for the ills that are befalling them. This notion of blame and innocence is of decisive importance, and relates to the idea that we are profoundly ignorant about the processes by which collectives are collected. For Girard, scapegoating only occurs because those who engage in it truly *believe* that the victim is to blame and come truly to believe that the death or exclusion of this victim has indeed solved the problem of disintegration. This belief is not just an individual matter, but a collective belief, and it is not just any old belief but something that, because of its profound importance to the collective, is considered *sacred*. Sacrifice is thus at the origin of the sacred, and the sacred at the origin of the collective. A dark space of nonknowledge is thus a decisive actor in the operations of the collective. The gesture of sacrifice will be repeated ritually as a sacred core of collective activity.

Girard draws attention to the unifying effect of scapegoating: it actually works to newly unify the collective. First, it supplies a point of shared focus for the group – everyone focuses on the same victim. Second, everyone agrees that the scapegoat is to blame. Third, everyone participates in the violence or expulsion that follows. What was previously a group in disarray becomes a coherent collective with a shared focus, a shared desire and a shared course of action. The excluded victim in such a case is literally what the community has in common. In providing a shared object of in-group communication, the quasi-object of the scapegoated victim's body forms the foundation of the community. The muddle and chaos of dispersal is transformed into clarity as if by magic. Girard thus shows us how order arises out of disorder through the exclusion of a third party, and he gives us another reason to be troubled about the question concerning foundations.

... THERE IS ANOTHER KNOCK AT THE DOOR ...

Note

1. A heterotroph is a living system that obtains ready-made food molecules from other organisms. An autotroph (e.g. a plant), by contrast, manufactures its own food via photosynthesis.

FOUR

Luhmann and Communication

HR8.01ma&km/es.01.00-06.39\£7.46/brunel:

1. ((*fortissimo*))
   ↑AAAAAEEAAAAAAAAHHEEAAAAAAAAAAAAAAIIAA (.)
2. AHHHH (.)AYEEAAAAAAAAAAIAAAAAT↑IIIAAAAAAA (.)
3. AAAAAAIAAAAAA=
4. =AAIAAAAAIAAAAAAAAa↓ohh..

(Ashmore, MacMillan & Brown, 2004, p. 349)

Discursive psychologists work with finely detailed transcriptions of audio-tape recordings. A standardised set of transcription conventions, derived from the work of Gail Jefferson is normally used (http://www-staff.lboro.ac.uk/~sscal/notation.htm). Following is one example of a few seconds of talk transcribed in this way:

Extract 2 (DE-JF:C1:S1:9–10)

1 → M: 'cos ↑you think I'm the wor:st ↓person on this
2 ↑plan[↓et. (.) At the mo]ment.= ((plaintively))
3 J: [↑No ↓I do:n't,]
4 J: =That's not fai:r, no- (.) I ↓don't,
5 M: °That's what you've been telling me.°
6 → J: Hheh heh.

(cited in Edwards, 2007: p. 4)

The extract features Mary (M) and Jeff (J), a couple in their first session of relationship counselling with a trained counsellor (who does not speak in this extract). In these six lines only a few words are spoken, along with some laughter (Jeff at line 6). The symbols are meant to capture, as far as possible, the intonation and other features of naturally occurring talk. The aim is for the transcript to represent the sounds captured on the original audio tape as far as possible. The tape, in turn, is treated as a more or less faithful capturing of what was potentially hearable at the time the recording was made. In this way the tape is a sort of 'time machine' capable of transporting the listener back to the original event, and the transcript is the next best thing, a device for recreating the past in the absence of the tape itself (see Ashmore, MacMillan & Brown, 2004).

What can we read in these six lines? What would we be able to hear if we could listen to the tape ourselves? Here is how the author (and transcriber) describes it:

> Mary's turn at lines 1 and 2 deploys the ECF 'the worst person on this planet' in an ironic characterization of Jeff's opinion of her. The irony is signalled initially by the relativizing, counterfactual quotative '↑you think', with its individualizing, contrastive emphasis on '↑you'. But irony is also conveyed by the ECF's sheer implausibility as factual description; there are presumably worse people on the planet than Mary, even in Jeff's eyes. The softener 'at the moment' (line 2) comes just after she starts to hear Jeff's overlapping denial (line 3). The irony of Mary's ECF is hearable in how she vocalizes that assessment: it is mostly delivered at the top of her normal pitch range, and is plaintively delivered – I will return to the details of that vocal delivery in the second part of this chapter. The irony is picked up in Jeff's denials (lines 3–4) and laughter (line 6). Note some significant details here: Jeff's denial is not outright (e.g., 'I never said that'), but attends precisely to Mary's ECF as excessive ('that's not fair'). Further, his laughter (line 6) is minimal and constrained, sounding more like an appreciation of Mary's heavy irony, rather than ridiculing her distress; he is offering a bit of laughter with, rather than at her. (Edwards, 2007: p. 4)

Edwards uses a series of technical terms – ECF (extreme case formulation), counterfactual quotatative, softener – to point out key features of the exchange. Mary appears to be accusing her partner of bad feeling on his part through an ironic statement. As with all work inspired by Conversation Analysis (see Atkinson & Heritage, 1984; Sacks, 1992; Antaki, Biazzi, Nissen & Wagner, 2008), Edwards insists that the interpretation of each turn in the conversation be based upon its apparent 'design' (i.e. its rhetorical structure, based on local cultural conventions) and how the participants themselves appear to orient to what the other(s) have just said. Thus the claim that what Mary does at line 2 is 'ironic' is based on noting the way she addresses Jeff ('↑you think') and the 'sheer implausibility' of the strong way she describes the contents of Jeff's thoughts ('the worst person on this planet'). It is also based on Jeff's response, which deals with the way the accusation is made rather than the accusation itself.

This kind of micro-analysis has numerous qualities which distinguish it from the experimental tradition in social psychology. It emphasises that there is little need, at an empirical level, for imputing psychic or cognitive states as an underpinning for the conversation. Once adequately transcribed, naturally occurring talk – or rather talk-in-interaction – already contains the keys to its own intelligibility. We can perfectly well interpret what is going on here by attending to the subtle and creative aspect of how Mary and Jeff verbally interact with one another. What is more, by emphasising this creativity exhibited through the use of irony, extreme case formulations, softeners, etc., Edwards is making an implicit case that ordinary language users exhibit a degree of sophistication in their interactional competencies that vastly exceeds that which social psychologists would typically recognise. For example, an attributional approach might be tempted to see Mary's turn at line 1 as evidence of a bias in cognitive processes, that she really does imagine Jeff to have categorised her so negatively. Such approaches often use content analysis techniques to pull out interesting features from data, irrespective of the immediate conversational sequence in which they occur.

However, there are two moments in Edwards' analysis where this reliance on sticking to the details of the interaction threatens to break down. On line 2, Edwards includes the analytic gloss '((*plaintively*))' on Mary's turn. This is based on Edwards' interpretation of Mary's tone of voice as it is captured on the tape. The second moment is with regard to line 6, which contains the transcribed sounds 'Hheh heh'. Edwards refers to these as indicating 'some laughter'. In both cases we are obliged to trust in the analyst that this is really what is contained on the tape. In response to this perceived problem, Edwards offers a 'speech pressure waveform' and 'pitch trace' graph produced through computer analysis of the signals contained on the original recording transcribed as line 2. This is done, he claims, to 'show at least part of the basis on which such interpretative impressions are founded, and on which Jeff's hearing, as well as mine, must be based' (2007, p. 8). But rather than clarifying matters, this seems to add an additional level of complication. We now have to trust not just in the representational equivalence of the transcription and the tape, but also in the waveform to the tape, and all three of these mediators with the overall claim that Edwards makes and with the original events to which they are supposed to refer. Edwards wants to transport us as directly as possible to what Mary said as Jeff would have heard it at the time. But, rather in the fashion of the parasitic chain we described in the last chapter, we now seem to have to go by way of many more points of call to reach that destination. And the longer the journey takes the greater rather than the lesser our dependence grows on the analyst as our indispensable guide and authority.

Ashmore, MacMillan and Brown (2004) refer to the general problematic we have been describing as that of 'tape fetishism'. This is the notion that at some point in their argument the analyst will be forced to claim that the tape is a straightforward representational record of an actually occurring event – that the tape "is what it is": an aural record of, and practically-adequate substitute for, some event' (p. 354). To do so is not to deny that the claims made by the analyst who speaks on behalf of the tape are mediated, since of course *they are* by the use of transcription conventions, waveforms and whatever else. Rather, it is to claim that these mediators are not really relevant, they are simply supports or neutral assistants. All the mediators do is to facilitate transport back to the counsellor's office where Mary and Jeff once were, such that we can hear their words as they themselves would have heard and spoken them.

But tape fetishism requires the continuous intervention of the analyst in order to sustain its peculiar magic. We need Edwards to reappear at crucial moments to tell us that 'Hheh heh' marks laughter or what the amplitude variations on the speech pressure waveform mean. Ashmore et al. (2004) call this 'professional hearing'. This occurs when naturally occurring data is 'seized upon by a formal body of expertise able to construct a set of distinctive yet credible claims about the "correct" way that this record should be understood' (p. 353). Professional hearing instructs listeners on how to hear the tape, the implications and inferences they should draw. However, despite the treatment of the tape as an 'evidential resource for a complex series of analytic moves' of an 'elaborative and interpretative nature', professional hearing is nevertheless 'dependent on maintaining the status of the record as itself clearly unmediated' (p. 353). It does this by holding to the assumption that at the bottom of this chain of mediations the original scene is itself not mediated. In other words, once we have completed our journey, we can arrive back at the scene in the counsellor's office. It may take many listens, many interpretations, much collective analysis involving the use of transcription conventions and sound-analysing software, but after weeks and months of analysis we can finally hear these few seconds of talk in pure, unmediated glory.

The kind of approach taken in discursive psychology is a 'radical empiricism' of sorts. That is to say, discursive psychologists eschew theoretical speculation in favour of demonstrating the supposedly clear evidential basis on which their particular claims are made. Refreshing as this is in contrast to the tendency towards highly speculative readings of data and the overall dominance of the hypothetico-deductive method in the discipline, the hostility towards theory is ultimately counter-productive. It ends up making the clear decipherment of small slices of talk-in-interaction the only meaningful ambition for social psychology, where these slices are treated as pure givens, self-contained blocks of sociality.

Taken together, tape fetishism and professional hearing amount to what William James (1910/2003) would call a 'saltatory' understanding of relations. The aim is for the analyst to jump from the tape to the original event as directly as possible, making use of mediators merely to prepare as well as possible for their landing. By contrast, 'radical empiricism' means for James taking the 'ambulatory' relations between mediators seriously. The point is not to get from A to B, from tape to world, directly, but rather to understand the variety of ways in which the identity of 'A' and 'B', 'tape' and 'world', emerge from these relations, from the process of mediation itself, from which, for James, there is no exit. If identity is a moment in a process, rather than being that which underpins and makes sense of the process, empiricism cannot then be a matter of simply 'seeing better' or 'seeing more' (as it appears to be for the tape fetishist/professional hearer). It will be necessary to deduce aspects of the process on the basis of these moments, to engage with the ambulatory movements of mediation as a matrix of potentials.

The overall aim of this chapter is to provide the broad outline of an account of communication compatible with our critical notion of reflexive self-grounding and consistent with our process-centred cosmology of assembled and coordinated 'events', 'occasions' or 'operations'. In the case of Mary and Jeff we would need to examine the specific conditions under which the very particular events occurred, and we would need to begin by affirming the mediated becoming of such talk-in-action.

Communication as Mediation

Communication is amongst the most unavoidable of all mediators. Whenever concepts of the 'social' and the 'cultural' are invoked, communication is at play. Linguistic communication, as we discussed briefly in Chapter 3, mediates our relation to the world in profound ways. Only rarely, however, do we recognise our relationship to the language we use. That is to say, we experience and communicate *through* or *by way of* language, but it is only rarely that we have an experience *of* language. This reflects our general notion of the disappearance of the mediator: an effective mediator renders itself invisible. We only tend to have experiences of language qua language when there is some problem with the smooth functioning of mediation. When we learn a new language, for example, at first only the brute sounds show up to our frustrated consciousness, and we do not feel at home with ourselves uttering strange vowels. The mediator itself then obtrudes into consciousness as a figure standing out from its ground. But the fact is that significant aspects of our social and personal existence are unconsciously shaped and conditioned by the forms of mediation we employ.

Many have argued that communication is the primary medium in which human beings live out their existence. Language, as Martin Heidegger (1990) put it, is the house of our Being. It is no exaggeration to say that it was insights such as this that provoked the massive transformation in thinking about human psychosocial existence that took place in the twentieth century. Significant portions of each of the human or social sciences – but most notably sociology, anthropology and social psychology – have recently gone through a phase variously known as a 'discursive' or 'textual' or 'postmodern' or 'poststructuralist' or 'social constructionist' turn. Communication, as some of these labels suggest, is pivotal to this turn. The discursive turn in psychology is well expressed in the following quotation from Rom Harré:

> The fundamental human reality is a conversation ... to which ... individuals may make contributions. All that is personal in our mental and emotional lives is individually appropriated from the conversation going on around us ... The structure of our thinking and feeling will

reflect ... the form and content of that conversation ... not only are the acts ... individuals perform and the interpretations we create ... prefigured in collective actions and social representations, but also that the very structure of our minds (and perhaps the fact that we have minds at all) is drawn from those social representations. (1983/4, p. 20)

It is important to realise that this turn was itself influenced by the gradual diffusion of some rather core ideas characteristic of twentieth-century philosophy, particularly the three strands of existential hermeneutics (especially Heidegger's [1982; 1990] insistence on the discursively mediated worldly dwelling of human existence [Stenner & Eccleston, 1994], and the subsequent work of Gadamer and Ricoeur), post-structuralism (e.g. Foucault [1977], Derrida [1978a] and Lyotard [1979/1984]: Lyotard's book on the postmodern condition of knowledge, for instance, talks of the dwindling plausibility of the 'grand-narratives' and other taken-for-granted monuments of would-be-truth) and pragmatically oriented ordinary language philosophy (including Austin [1962] and Ryle [1975], but marked especially by Wittgenstein's 'turn' from the *Tractatus logico-philosophicus* [1921/1981] to the *Philosophical investigations* [1958] which put ordinary language at centre stage in contrast to a celebration of scientific language as the bitter medicine for muddled thinking).

Each of these strands defines itself against the idea of a timeless and universal metaphysics supposing a context-free and neutral observer position. As a result of this refusal of metaphysics, each strand, in its own way, deconstructs 'truth' as the possibility of an ultimate access to 'reality' and replaces it with the idea of a multiplicity of polyvalent versions, perspectives, language games, meanings, narratives, discourses, etc., each firmly located in its worldly nexus of space and time. Each strand then makes linguistic communication its central concern and uses this focus to 'dethrone' previously held metaphysical ambitions to truth and to replace them with concern for the local vicissitudes of communicatively mediated activity. These strands, both separately and in combination, have in turn given rise to various influential movements in social and psychological theory and practice (cf. Curt, 1994, and Stainton Rogers, Stenner, Gleeson & Stainton Rogers, 1995 for summaries). These movements have championed language-centred qualitative methodologies and proposed radical shifts in ontology and epistemology compatible with the turn to text. These developments, we suggest, directly reflect the twin concerns of twentieth-century philosophy: the dethroning of metaphysics, and the enthroning of language as the source of meaning (the rise of language-centred practice).

Our concern here is not to celebrate this discursive turn in a complacent way. On the contrary, despite support from most of what was interesting in twentieth-century philosophy, this discursive turn has itself run up against serious problems that provoke a rethinking of the entire settlement. The core recurrent problems include accusations of the neglect of all that is not discourse (the 'extra-discursive', including embodiment and material objects); inattention to nonlinguistic communicational forms; the impossibility of an adequate specification of context; neglect of the connection between inter-personal (social) and institutional (societal) communication; the premature settlement of the relationship between subjective experience and language-use; and a poorly developed conceptualisation of questions of process. An account of communication compatible with our critical notion of reflexive self-grounding and consistent with our process-centred ontology contributes to a rethinking of communication that directly addresses these weaknesses, albeit at the cost of challenging some cherished (but we think flawed) foundations.

The core foundational weakness which supports an avoidance of all of these problems is the assumption that, ultimately, discourse is both the source of meaning and the site at which meaning is at stake. This conceptual starting point reproduces on a vast scale the gesture of the bifurcation of nature into a realm of meaningless and objective causality and a human socio-cultural realm of meaning. In so doing, it has direct implications for how the psychic is conceived in relation to the social, and hence how psy-chology is conceived in relation to sociology. This in turn has implications for how psychology's relation to the biological and physical is negotiated. Namely, it encourages the tendency to reduce the psychic to discourse. Indeed, the term 'discourse' is often used in a massively over-extended way, as if it covered everything from unconscious biological processes to institu-tional power dynamics.

Our point is not to deny that communication is indeed perhaps the most conspicuous and important site for the organisation of meaning, but to insist that what we now think of as discourse is – evolutionarily speaking – in fact something of a late arrival on the scene of meaning. As a late arrival, of course, communicative processes simultaneously partake in, reap the benefits of, and transform the nature of other modes such as affect, imagery and thinking. Our affective experiences, our sensory perceptions, and our conceptual thought processes are in many ways radically altered through our 'entry into language'. They are selectively sharpened here, dulled to nonentity there, for instance. However, none of these processes was primarily communicative or linguistic, and each retains something of their distinct experiential qualities. These other modes of experience, and the worlds in which they unfold, are presupposed by communication.

It is one thing, then, to affirm the singular relevance of communication to the psychic as a profound shaping force, but it is quite another to exclude any-thing but the discursive and hence to reduce the psychic to patterns of dis-course. It is instructive to note that this tension has been with us since at least the 1920s when the great Soviet socio-psychologists, such as Vygotsky, Bhaktin and Volosinov contributed to the formulation of a psychology com-patible with Marxism. Their starting point was that communicational dynam-ics are the source of mental processes. For Vygotsky (1934/1987), for instance, mental processes are mediated by language. Since language is inherently social, then so are mental processes (but see González Rey, 2007, for a discussion of Vygotsky's notion of 'sense' as a specifically subjective form of process). Socially structured communicative activity hence becomes the fundamental issue, since psychological activity can only be understood with reference to it: what is 'in the mind' has its primary reality 'in communication'. For Volosinov this becomes a matter of affirming that 'the human psyche and consciousness reflect the dialectics of history to a much greater degree than the dialectics of nature' (1987, p. 83).

From our perspective, this kind of argument represents a laudable and perfectly justifiable effort to begin from the full complexity of complex communicative activity, and to move from there to examine the shaping influence of communication on each of the other experiential modes of psychological process. To the extent that our thinking is linguistically mediated, for instance, it is clear that communication has a profound transformative effect on our thought processes. Vygotsky's observations about the social origins of 'inner speech' thus make a decisive contribution. A large and growing literature likewise testifies to the fact that this principle can be extended to perceptual 'images', memories, emotional experiences, and so forth, none of which remains untouched by the influences of communication or by the lie of the land of power and status relations. But such results flow precisely from an attempt to work back from expressive communication through to other psychic modes. This speaks of one's departure point and not of the essential nature of the issues at play. It is to argue that the 'dialectics of nature' have, in effect, *become inextricably enrolled within* the dialectics of history. But to put it this way is not to deny the dialectics of nature but to presuppose them. To study communication in isolation is to study a chimera. It is to miss the point that it could never exist nor have come into existence in isolation. The distinction between the psychic and the social thus cannot be solved simply by privileging the social term.

The key concept for this chapter is communication. We use the word communication as opposed to the more familiar notion of discourse for three reasons. The first reason is to better enable a distinction (but not a sharp one) to be drawn between communication and the other modes of psychological process that constitute 'the psychic'. Such a distinction permits a re-consideration of their relations. The second is that it enables us to draw attention to the broader *process* of communication that is often obscured by the textual turn in psychology. As a process, communication can be considered thoroughly *social*. Although the centrality of language should not be downplayed here, it should be noted that this process exceeds the linguistic (discursive psychologists tend to restrict themselves unnecessarily in this respect). The third reason is that this enables us to connect up with a long tradition of scholarship on communication processes that has been largely ignored in recent psychology, critical and otherwise.

In addressing communication we wish to step away a little from the commonly evoked Saussurian weaponry of binaries such as *langue/parole*, diachronic/synchronic, signifier/signified, and so on. We wish to do this, however, without returning to a conception of language as a nomenclature or a mirror-like expression of thoughts. We will therefore replace dualism with a concern for triads. The introduction of a third term brings a dynamism that dualities lack. A German sociologist, the late Niklas Luhmann, will be our guide and mediator in the remainder of this chapter. In various works of his, Luhmann (1982; 1995; 1998a; 2000a) offers a radical account of communication as a synthesis of three selections: utterance, information and understanding.

Luhmann on Communication

Luhmann defines communication as 'the synthesis of three selections, as the unity of information, utterance, and understanding' (1995, p. 147). Hence communication 'occurs whenever the utterance of an information is understood' (Luhmann, 2000a, p. 40). The concepts of 'information', 'utterance' (actually the German term used is *Mitteilung* which also conveys the sense of a report or notification, which may be verbal or not) and 'understanding' are not to be interpreted as primarily psychological issues but as components that, taken together, constitute a communicative *event* or 'operation' as a unity. The first point to be grasped, then, is that a given, actual communicative event is a synthesis or unification of (at least) these three components.

This unification provides a 'meaning' which can be accepted, rejected or otherwise modified by further communicative events or operations. That is, the unity provides a connective basis upon which further communicative operations can unfold. The second point to be grasped is that these synthesised unities of the event are assembled or grouped together into a temporally unfurling chain of linked events or operations. Communication in the full sense can thus be thought of as this unfolding process. A communicative event arises out of the meaning created by an immediately preceding communicative event and, in providing new meaning, supplies the connective basis that enables a further communicative event in the immediate future to be realised.

Communication in this sense is a distinct process unfolding in real-time (or, as Wittgenstein said, *im Laufe der Zeit* – in the course of time). It does so by way of recursive connections between the events of its operations. This recursivity is crucial: every communicative operation recalls a previous operation and anticipates a future one. The synthesis of the three selections therefore supplies a basic communicative unit which is ripe with connective possibilities. This is the basic unity of a communicative event. The process of communication emerges through the binding of a number of such unities into a temporal chain through reciprocal conditioning. Communication is an emergent reality. As an emergent reality it can be considered as an independent formation.

It presupposes beings capable of operating in the medium of meaning, but, as an independent formation, it cannot be reduced to such beings. Communication has its own manner of being-in-the-world.

In unpacking Luhmann's rather abstract definition and theory, it may be helpful to consider the following example involving data collected during a recent morning:

1. Paul: ↑Good mor [↓ning! (raises right hand slightly whilst smiling) [8.47am]
2. Steve: Good morning (.). (nods and raises eyebrows) [8.47:1.3 secs]
3. Paul: [How are ↑You↓ today?] (eyebrows raised towards the middle) [8.47: 3 secs]
4. Steve: Not so ba:d, (.)thanks (audible exhalation). And you? (looks Paul in the eye) [8.47: 5 secs]
5. Paul: Mustn't grumble. (audible exhalation) [8.47: 7 secs]
   (Paul passes a £10 note to Steve, who folds it and places it in his trouser pocket)
6. Steve: (looks upwards and moves eyes upwards) Sod's law! [8.47: 10 secs]
7. Paul: This is no good at ↑all↓ [8.47: 12 secs]

The clock times indicated in square brackets above illustrate that this process unfolded in the real world relatively slowly. Perceptions and thoughts, for example, can take place far more quickly, as can neural processing. This means that both Steve and Paul could have been following long trains of thought or taking in a good deal of perceptual information in between their utterances. It is important to recognise that the above transcription, no matter how detailed, remains merely a partial trace of what actually transpired during those 12 seconds at 8.47 am. It is also important to recognise that much transpired during those 12 seconds we wouldn't necessarily wish to call 'communication'. The wind blew and trees grew. Neurones fired in brains and blood coursed through veins. The planet turned. Senses perceived. The transcription record displays merely a sequence of sign transformations in the medium of written English, some of which translate spoken utterances into a conventional format, and some of which code for additional information (nonverbal material, speaker identifiers and clock time). Naturally, any distinction between what is communication and what is not must be made via the medium of language. This paradox need not prevent us from drawing a distinction, however, so long as we are aware that any distinction produces an unmarked space that must remain obscure if we are to indicate the marked side of our distinction (Spencer Brown, 1969).

Through the transcription, an observer can reconstruct a sense of the communication that is represented as having transpired. For both Steve and Paul, however, these events unfolded in a perceptible world: Paul *saw* Steve at 8.47 and Steve *heard* Paul's voice before turning to look at him. The communication is thus far from being self-sufficient. It presupposes a *perceptible world* and what Whitehead calls *sense-awareness* (1920/2004, p. 3). It also presupposes what Volosinov called an 'extraverbal pragmatic situation' (1987, p. 98). Steve and Paul met on a Saturday morning near the clocktower in Brighton. The communication remains tightly coupled with its extraverbal circumstances.

Ethnomethodologists, conversation analysts and discursive psychologists typically use the concept of *indexicality* or the 'occasioned' nature of talk to mark the context-dependent nature of the meaning of an utterance. Potter (1996, p. 43), for instance, states that 'to say an utterance is "occasioned" is to say that it is fitted to a sequence of talk, which is part of a broader social setting'. Clearly, however, more is at stake here than merely the verbal circumstances of a 'sequence of talk' or even the 'broader social setting'. Both of these can and do, of course, provide information that is relevant to communication, but neither approaches the more far-reaching conclusion that 'verbal communication is always already established in the world of perception' (Luhmann, 2000a, p. 16) or that 'the verbal form is never the whole phraseology of the proposition; this phraseology also includes the general circumstances of its production' (Whitehead, 1920/2004, p. 9).

We will dwell a little on this issue, since it is central to many current debates about linguistic relativism. Indeed, at times it seems as though conversation and discourse analytical approaches were deliberately trying to remove the possibility of considering a world outside of language. Consider the following quotation from Speer:

> Utterances are 'doubly contextual' (Drew and Heritage, 2005): they are *context shaped* in the sense that they 'cannot be adequately understood except by reference to the context in which they participate' (1992b:18), and they are also '*context renewing*' in that 'every current utterance will itself form the immediate context for some next action in a sequence'. It follows that the interactional context is not exogenously (i.e. from outside) predetermined, but is 'continually being developed with each successive action' (1992b:19). The process of analysis does not require us to look *beyond* the talk to establish the context and understand what the talk is orienting to. Instead, participants' talk constructs and orients toward the relevant context, and does so on a turn-by-turn basis. (Speer, 2005, p. 101)

The 'doubly contextual' nature of communication seems clear enough. Our earlier discussion of the recursive connections mirrors Drew and Heritage's concept, yet their sense of the 'doubly contextual' is limited to one of the three selections that are actually synthesised in any communicative event. That is to say, the notion of an utterance being 'context shaped' relates to the process of unification effected in all aspects of a communicative event – of all there is in the world at this moment, a partial and graded selection is actualised in a given utterance. The context is grasped in the synthesising operation of utterance, one might say. The notion of an utterance being 'context renewing' likewise relates to the recursive connections between such events. This means that the proximal determinant of the next communicative event is what is supplied by the previous one to which it must in some manner conform. This can indeed be grasped as a kind of endogenous determination – such self-foundationing production is exactly what is meant by autopoiesis, as will be discussed later. Our disagreement is rather with the resulting *a priori* exclusion of extraverbal considerations. It is one thing to say that such considerations are external to the system (which is true), it is another thing to say that the system functions in isolation from them.

Although, as we will go on to show, the relation to the extraverbal can never be avoided, some aspects of the interaction appear less dependent upon extraverbal circumstance than others. The greeting ritual, for instance, is highly familiar to English speakers. Utterances 1 to 5 are highly conventional to the point of being ritualistic. This form of communication has a high degree of redundancy since it is designed precisely to be repeatable on an indefinite number of different occasions of greeting. Of course, it remains tightly linked to the extraverbal pragmatic situation of a greeting scene in which two familiars involved in an encounter first perceive one another, but its redundant nature makes it easily understood in isolation from other circumstantial particularities. The form, however, is nevertheless flexible enough to permit idiosyncratic expression. Paul's concerned frown at 3, for example, was predicated upon his knowledge that he and Steve had drunk rather too much the previous evening, and Steve's audible exhalation expressed his hungover state. These idiosyncratic details are, as it were, embedded in the ritual like a soft snail in its hard shell. In this example, the communication at issue presumes a prior recent history shared by the interlocutors. This history can be presupposed and hence does not require *utterance* in order to nevertheless feature as *information* which can be *understood*. It is part of what Volosinov calls the 'assumed' of discourse (1987, p. 99).

The passing of the £10 note, to give a rather different example, constitutes a form of communication so compact and conventionalised that no accompanying verbal discourse was required. Money simplifies highly complex economic communications in the form of a medium that can be used and reused indefinitely, precluding the need for complex bartering arrangements or other debates concerning relative value (Luhmann, 1999). The medium, we might say, assumes this complex economic communication into the conventionalised form of money. Here we need only know that Paul borrowed ten pounds from Steve the night before. Both could presuppose this information, and also presuppose the nature and meaning of money.

The penultimate utterance of this little interchange is worth dwelling on since it is so tied to its extraverbal circumstances that without them it cannot be understood. Whilst 'good morning', thanks to its redundancy, appears almost self-explanatory, 'Sod's law!' cries out for interpretation: what does Steve mean? The point we wish to make is that no amount of attention to this utterance, or to the utterances that accompany it, will furnish this interpretation. No subtle exegesis of the semantics and morphology of the phrase will clarify the situation. The reason is simple. The meaning is not contained 'within' the utterance, nor within the sequence of utterances, nor in a vaguely defined 'broader social setting', but in the conjoining of the interlocutors as co-participants in a commonly evaluated situation. This will require unpacking.

It so happened that it started raining at 47 minutes and 8 seconds past 8.00 on that Saturday morning. Paul and Steve couldn't avoid perceiving the rain (and they could jointly assume this aspect of a shared perceptible world). Both of them knew that they had a plan to go to the beach (they could assume this aspect of knowledge-shared-between-them). And both of them knew that this plan would now have to be called into question (they could assume a negative value judgement about the state of affairs this information reveals). Steve's 'Sod's law' thus articulated a shared negative judgement about this situation which presupposed their shared perceptions (the rain) and shared knowledge (their plans). We have thus distinguished, adapting Volosinov, three aspects of the assumed: shared perception, shared knowledge and shared evaluation. None of this information needed to be uttered in order to be understood, and hence it could be communicated in an impressively minimalist and even obtuse manner.

The utterance can thus be thought of as what Volosinov called a 'resolution of the situation'. Clearly this utterance does not somehow 'mirror' the extraverbal situation (which is not mentioned at all) and hence we must avoid this longstanding way of thinking about the relationship between 'words and things'. Rather, the utterance grasps and transforms that situation into what is uttered as a shared evaluation. This kind of utterance is possible because Steve and Paul, having a history and being co-present in the same circumstances, can take for granted a shared perceptual, epistemic and evaluative reality. Steve did not need to say that it had started raining, that he and Paul planned to go to the beach, and that the rain would make this less desirable, since all of this, given the circumstances, could be presupposed. All of this, we might say, was assumed into the evaluative form of 'Sod's law'. As put by Volosinov (1987, p. 100):

> The utterance depends on their [the interlocutors'] real, material appurtenance to one and the same segment of being and gives this material commonness ideological expression and further ideological development.

Whitehead (1920/2004, p. 6) makes the same point when he distinguishes demonstrative and descriptive phrases in propositions, and Wittgenstein deals with it when he grapples with the problem of 'ostensive definition' and the peculiar status of the demonstrative 'this' (1958, p. 38). The point can be further clarified by examining the final utterance of our transcribed exchange. This final utterance requires that we understand what detachable segment or factor of the world the 'this' in 'this is no good at all' refers to. The word 'this' is typically used in demonstrative rather than descriptive phrases since it is used to demonstrate some factor in the world. Hence Wittgenstein suggests that 'the word "this" has been called the only *genuine* name'. The reason for this is that familiar nouns such as 'rain' and 'clocktower' can always be uttered in the absence of what it is that they name, whilst 'the demonstrative "this" can never be without a bearer. It might be said: "so long as there is a *this*, the word 'this' has meaning too'" (ibid.).

Wittgenstein and Whitehead were far from being naïve realists. Even in the presence of its 'bearer', the word 'this' will remain indeterminate unless it can be given a shared meaningful place within an unfolding communicative encounter. This is why, in the absence of clarity, we can give numerous plausible interpretations of what the 'this' might indicate. Perhaps Paul is referring to the whole spoiled situation in which he and Steve now find themselves, and *that situation* is the bearer of the 'this'? Or perhaps he is referring to his hangover, and the underpaid transcriber just happened to miss the nonverbal gesture of a head-clutch? In this case the 'this' would be his invisible but partially communicated pain. Or perhaps, unbeknownst to all, a seagull had just defecated onto Paul's shoulder? As Wittgenstein (1958, p. 28) observed, the word remains meaningless except in so far as its 'place is already prepared' within the presupposed circumstances of the interlocutors, and these circumstances include the commonly available perceptual background.

This problem is not just that of the bemused discourse analyst. Steve may also fail to understand what Paul meant. In this case, Steve would be placed in the predicament that Wittgenstein called not 'knowing how to go on'. The lack of meaning constitutes an obstacle to the connectivity necessary for communication. Since every communicative operation recalls a previous operation and anticipates a future one, any lack of understanding threatens to rupture the flow of communication since it leaves the interlocutor with no basis upon which to proceed or 'go on' with a further utterance that anticipates a further utterance via its recollection of what came before. This is the reason for our previous comment that the notion of 'understanding', like 'utterance' and 'information', are not primarily psychological issues but components that, taken together, constitute a communicative event as a unity. Wittgenstein (1958, p. 154) communicates this neatly to his imagined interlocutor when he says:

> Try not to think of understanding as a 'mental process' at all – For that is the expression which confuses you. But ask yourself: in what sort of case, in what kind of circumstances, do we say, 'Now I know how to go on,'... In the sense in which there are processes (including mental processes) which are characteristic of understanding, understanding is not a mental process.

Unlike the discourse analyst, however, Steve has the reflexive option of real-time metacommunication (communication about communication). That is, he can directly or indirectly ask Paul what it is that he means. As a matter of fact, Paul had been muttering to himself whilst trying unsuccessfully to get his umbrella to open. In response to Steve's query, Paul displayed this nonfunctioning umbrella-opening mechanism, making it clear that 'this is no good at all' was about the broken umbrella and was something of an inconsequential change of topic prompted by these unpredictable but nevertheless apparent circumstances.

Without this clarification the demonstrative phrase 'this is no good at all' failed to demonstrate, since the background of sense-awareness which it presupposed (i.e. the demonstration of the broken umbrella) was absent. Once the utterance is understood, new connective possibilities open up, and the process of communication can continue. Of course, communication can, and usually does, also proceed on the basis of misunderstandings, so long as these are misunderstood as such, or simply ignored.

In sum, we can assert with Volosinov that the 'distinguishing characteristic of behavioural utterances consists precisely in the fact that they make myriad connections with the extraverbal context of life and, once severed from that context, lose almost all their import – a person ignorant of the immediate pragmatic context will not understand these utterances' (1987, p. 101). Without knowledge of the faulty umbrella, we lack the 'password' that would enable us to understand the meaning of Paul's utterance, and without the rain we lack the password that makes sense of Steve's. In the discussion above we have tried to show that this dependency upon the unsaid varies greatly depending upon form, context and medium of communication. When we are dealing with a face-to-face situation of two people standing by a clocktower, then both interlocutors can largely take for granted a shared recognition of even the most fleeting of perceptual events and changes of circumstance. The communication process is, we might say, highly sensitive to its unspoken perceptual background, and modifies itself accordingly.

This sensitivity is directly proportional to the incomprehensibility of much of such discourse to an observer who does not share that circumstantial purview. However, if the domain of 'the assumed' is to extend further in space or in time, or to encompass more interlocutors, then its circumstantial sensitivity must be reduced and more durable forms of the assumed must be provided. The conventionalisation of communication is thus a hardening of communication designed to maximise the likelihood of achieving the meaningful synthesis of a communicational event.

One example we provided was that of the exchange of money, which involves a medium that permits a vast extension beyond the immediate pragmatic context of its use as a compact economic communication, but there are many other examples. As Harvey Sacks (1992) was well aware, for instance, speakers on the telephone must make adjustments to their communication in order to accommodate the lack of a shared perceptual purview. The medium of writing likewise massively transforms the relationship between the said and the unsaid, and hence brings about dramatic changes to the communication process. This situation reaches its illogical conclusion in the burdensome contortions of legal discourse or 'legalese' (Luhmann, 2004). The paradox of confusion in the name of clarity results from the fact that clarity at-a-distance requires painstaking attention to the unsaid details that can precisely no longer be presupposed and taken for granted.

The Importance of the Third Selection

We hope that the above makes it clear why it would be problematic to imagine that having access to a transcription gives the analyst access to the phenomenon of communication. Rather, it makes available to an observer a record of a sequence of utterances (like 'Good morning!') and some additional information (like the amount of time an utterance took to utter). Luhmann's third term of understanding, if it is considered at all by an analyst of such a transcript, must be inferred from these two sources. We can infer, for instance, that Steve understood Paul's question ('How are you today?'), since he replied with a plausible answer (he knew how to 'go on'). Such an inference, however, involves the *understanding* of the analyst-as-observer, who thereby uses the transcript as an utterance that may or may not provide a connective point in a new process of communication (perhaps publishing the analysis so that it might be read by others in further chains of communication). This is less an 'analysis' of the discourse than a continuation of the communication by other means: a discursive hijacking, as it were. In this way, the supposedly neutral observer must unwittingly become a participant.

The problem here outlined – i.e. the unavoidability of the 'third term' of understanding – would therefore not be solved by, for instance, having the transcriber include a note about Paul fiddling with his umbrella or about the rain. Such notes merely already presuppose that the transcriber has *understood* what the utterance means, and hence can communicate this to the reader by supplying a selective slice of extraverbal activity that serves as the 'bearer' of the otherwise ambiguous 'this'. The transcript, and also the analysis, always remain as *parts* of a communicative process that can never 'escape' itself through reference to an object outside itself (in this case the chunk of communication being analysed), since it must bring such objects into itself if it is to 'go on' at all. Such is the paradox at the heart of the relation between words and things or the said and the unsaid: communication needs things to talk about, but it can only ever use them in and as communication. Communication is always already established in a world of perception which forever escapes it. In a sense, that is why we need communication.

Luhmann's 'third selection' of understanding must therefore be given its decisive place in the process of communication since 'communication is only realized if and to the extent that understanding comes about' (1995, p. 147). This means that, in a very important sense, communication is always and only made possible 'from behind'. The utterance or *Mitteilung* taken alone is merely a suggestion that may or may not be taken up into communication. It is, in Luhmann's terms, 'nothing more than a selection proposal' (p. 139). Hence although the *Mitteilung* may well come first in the temporal course of events, it can belong to the unity of communication only after its connective possibilities have been realised through an understanding that makes a new utterance possible. If, for whatever reason, understanding fails, then communication breaks down. The lost soul desperately shouting for help in the midst of a vast, dark forest fails to achieve what she most desires: communication.

This unpleasant image of a person lost in a forest enables us to focus in on a further crucial point that has so far been left implicit: that understanding relates precisely to the difference between utterance and information. So far we have distinguished utterance and information only implicitly. We have recognised, for instance, that utterances convey some information. Paul and Steve exchange information about their current state of wellbeing, for instance. We have also recognised that utterances can convey information without mentioning it: we have explored the nature of demonstrative phrases, and we have indicated how communication can work on the basis of knowledge and values that are assumed. Considerably more information is available to the understander than that which is uttered, and understanding takes this into account.

Understanding: the Difference Between Utterance and Information

We must now focus more sharply on this difference between utterance and information that is 'built into all communication' (Luhmann, 1995, p. 151). The person lost in the forest shouts at the top of their voice: 'Help! Can anybody hear me?! Help!' Their utterance is not yet communication, since nobody is there to understand it (although this raises the thorny question of whether the understanding of one's own utterance constitutes communication, which we will not pursue here). The squirrels and birds hear the noise of the cries, but hearing and understanding are not the same thing. These creatures flee from the noise. This means that they are *informed* by it. It is information in Bateson's sense since it is a difference that makes a difference to them (otherwise they would not flee). But they do not respond to the cry as an *utterance*. That is to say, their rapid flight is surely a response but it is not a reply. For the squirrel and the woodpecker there is no difference between utterance and information. The difference between utterance and information that we humans take for granted makes no difference to them. Utterance and reply belong to the form of life that is communication, and this means that both utterances presuppose the possibility of being *understood*. It takes a particular kind of being to reply to an utterance. That being must grasp the difference between utterance and information, and must manage that difference. So what is that difference?

As a form in the medium of meaning, an utterance is there to be understood. It is wasted on those who, for whatever reason, cannot understand its meaning or, more primordially, cannot grasp that meaning is at issue. The cry as an utterance was uttered in the desperate hope that it might be heard by one who might understand. In this case, it is an understatement to say that this person intended to communicate. Unlike information more generally, an utterance is specifically designed for communication. This means that the possibility of it being understood, or at least attended to in the hope of understanding, is already built into the form of the utterance. This is most obvious when an utterance is formed using language, since a language is a highly specialised and highly coded medium for communication. If somebody says 'hey you!' it is hard not to understand that they may be trying to attract one's attention. It should be recognised, however, that the distress signal of a cry for help need not be primarily linguistic. Indeed, such signals exist at the very borderline of utterance and information. The person lost in the forest first of all wants to attract someone's attention. A high-pitched whistle might be enough to alert a passer-by that a human being is in a distressing predicament. But the distress signal must be distinct from other noises that might lead a passer-by to attribute the information to local wildlife or some other source. This is why repetitive, high-pitched signals are recommended. In principle, this is no different to the clearing of a throat prior to a speech.

An utterance is an utterance to the extent that it is *understood* to be distinct from mere information. Intentionality forms the basis of that distinction, since what is uttered is selected from a repertoire of possibilities for the purposes of being understood. But this does not mean that actual intention of utterance is necessary for communication to occur. All that is required is that some event be taken as such. Many furious arguments, for example, hang on the meaning attributed to a frown here or a scowl there. The scowler might doggedly insist that the scowl was either involuntary or no scowl at all, but this does not prevent its recipient from insisting that it was deliberate and deeply meaningful. For the scowler, the alleged scowl ought to be taken merely as information, whilst for its recipient it was a *Mitteilung* (here the reader can hopefully understand the inadequacy of translating *Mitteilung* into utterance), to be replied to as such.

It should be noted that this distinction corresponds directly with what the communication expert would distinguish as nonverbal behaviour and nonverbal communication. MacKay (1972, p. 5) is worth quoting on this:

All would agree … that a measly face can be *informative* to a qualified onlooker. But is it useful to speak of the sufferer himself [*sic*] (who may be unaware of it) as *communicating* this information? Is there no distinction to be made between the passive manifestation of a symptom and the deliberate (even if instinctive) production of words or non-verbal behaviour (including perhaps pointing to the spots) *calculated* to inform the observer? Again, shifts of gaze or posture may play a subtle part in coordinating the behaviour of two persons (Argyle, 1969); but may it not be useful to have different terms for those acts that are expressive of the originator's purpose and *perceived* or *interpreted* as such, and those that are not?

Not all nonverbal activity is correctly grasped as communication, though all of it can be used as information. Slow movements can be interpreted as a sign of boredom without inferring that the slow mover intended to communicate this.

In this case the slow movements serve as information, much as the red sky at night might inform shepherds of a pleasant day to follow. None but the most superstitious of shepherds is likely to take the sky as having intended to communicate this meaning to her. On the other hand, a skilled communicator might precisely wish to communicate their boredom through the medium of their slow movements. Of course there is a grey area between the information and utterance, and this grey area is exploited regularly by skilled communicators who rarely mean exactly what they say or say exactly what they mean. The bored individual does not risk an *explicit* communication of boredom, and thus leaves open the possibility of denying it should the issue be raised verbally. What matters is that those who 'understand' can – correctly or not – distinguish utterance from information and manage that difference. That is to say, this is not merely a distinction that an external observer might usefully draw (a communication expert, for instance). Rather, it is a distinction that any communicator must draw, or must have drawn, if they are to communicate. Communicative understanding is understanding the difference between information and utterance: 'The inclusion of this difference is what makes communication communication, a special case of information processing per se' (Luhmann, 1995, p. 143).

One implication of the tailoring of utterances for understanding is that the communicators must constantly anticipate and manage the ways in which utterances will be understood, and constantly check and manage the ways in which they appear to have been understood. Utterance implies understanding which implies information which implies utterance, and so on. We not only routinely anticipate that we will be understood, but we also routinely anticipate the ways in which these understandings may deviate from what we hope to communicate (we like to think of these as misunderstandings, but our interlocutor often has a different perspective). Likewise, we routinely anticipate the anticipations of our interlocutor, and use these expectations to steer the selection of our own utterances and our understanding of those of our interlocutor. Sometimes we even take the trouble to communicate all of this, but, understandably enough, this tends to clog up the communication somewhat. Sometimes – particularly in ritualistic situations – we simply accept that an utterance may be a hollow form with no expectation of truth or depth. 'Good morning', for example, need have no reference to any qualities of the morning, just as 'How are you today?' need not be spoken or received as a heartfelt enquiry. Some may choose to deliberately misunderstand this situation, of course, no doubt explaining the evolution of the 'mustn't grumble' response.

Such observations point to a further crucial aspect of Luhmann's theory: 'communication is possible *only as a self-referential process*' (1995: 144). Luhmann calls *basal self-reference* (as distinct from forms of reflexive communication-about-communication discussed above) the fact that the process of communication is composed of elements that 'refer to themselves by including their connection with other elements of the same process' (p. 144).

This is arguably a more rigorous theoretical construct than the related notion of *implicature* as used by linguists (Forrester, 1996, p. 89–90):

> When one communicative action follows another, it tests whether the preceding communication was understood. However surprising the connecting communication may turn out to be, it is also used to indicate and to observe how it rests on an understanding of the preceding communication. The test can turn out negative, and then it often provides an occasion for reflexive communication about communication. ... This implies time. Only in the process of connecting can one tell whether one has been understood; but one can use one's own experience to set up communication in such a way that one can expect to be understood. In every instance every individual communication is recursively secured in possibilities of understanding and the control of understanding as the connective context for further communication; otherwise it would never take place. It is an element only as an element of a process, however minimal or ephemeral that process may be. (Luhmann, 1995, p. 144)

In sum, each communicative operation is a synthesis of information, utterance and understanding, and none of these components alone constitutes communication. Together, however, they constitute a negatable meaning that can, in referring back to past communication, provide a connective node that can, in turn, give rise to more communication. This is the basic self-referential unity of a communicative event that gives rise to the higher-order unity of an unfolding procession of comparable component unities. This basal self-reference, in other words, endows communication with a high probability of forming into a process that continues over time through the binding of a number of communicative operations into an unfolding and reciprocally conditioned temporal chain. Luhmann thus supplies us with a way of grasping communication as an *emergent reality*. The reality of communication is created in communication, by communication, for communication, but it is real nonetheless. That is to say, as an emergent reality communication has its own manner of being-in-the-world, a manner organised through the synthesis of utterance, information and understanding.

The self-referentiality of communication means that, despite always being 'about' something beyond itself, communication is destined nevertheless to refer only to itself: to communications past and future. More specifically, communication can only connect up with further communication or, to put it another way, anything that connects up with communication is also communication. The 'brute reality' of the naïve realist has no place in the communication process itself, other than as something communicated. Talk about really real reality is just that: talk about really real reality. An action, such as the kicking of a stone, can enter the process either as communicated information or as a *Mitteilung* (provided that someone attributes to it a communicative purpose, and hence takes it as communication). At the risk of labouring the point, this is not a comment about the ontological status of stones but about what we have called the *reality of communication* (Luhmann, 2000b). Communication can thus be seen as a process with its own unity or, in other words, as a system with its own distinct and irreducible mode of operation.

Communication recursively recalls and anticipates further communications, and solely within the network of self-created communications can it produce communications as the operative elements of its own system. In so doing, communication generates a distinct autopoietic system in the strict (not just 'metaphorical') sense of the term. (Luhmann, 2000a, p. 9)

Autopoiesis, as we discussed in Chapter 2, means 'self-production' and names the way in which self-referential systems reproduce themselves from out of their own elements. Living cells, for instance, are autopoietic systems in that they are to some extent *self-creating* or self-foundationing. The elements that organic systems process, however, are the biochemical elements that they themselves produce in interaction with their environment. Luhmann makes the controversial move of applying autopoeitic theory to social systems. Communication is so central to Luhmann's theory because, for Luhmann, only communication can play the role of element-producing basal process in social systems (cf. Clam, 2000). Social systems are hence communication systems.

Some Implications for Contemporary 'Psychosocial' Thinking

If Luhmann is correct that communication forms a complex system then it is important to address it as such, and not, for example, to attempt to reduce it to its components. In fact it seems to us that there are, broadly speaking, two typical ways of neglecting the principle of non-summativity with respect to communication. Practitioners of qualitative research in psychology have, we will suggest, fallen prey to both of them. It is necessary to briefly dwell on these in order to maximise the chances of avoiding their pitfalls in the future. Together these reproduce the typical binary distinction between object and subject. Indeed, one might say that the subject/object distinction, as an epistemological theme (i.e. as mapped onto the difference between a knower and a known), is itself an expression of the more general need – on the part of knowers – to reduce the complexity of complex systems to something more intellectually and communicatively manageable (and hence connectable). The dependence of psychology on the knower/known dualism is thus an expression of its ability to evade the complexity of its subject matter (Stenner, 1998). To the extent that Klein can be read in complexity theory terms, this is directly comparable to the psychoanalytical notion of splitting.

Reduction to the object side of the distinction is achieved through a focus on utterance (or text) in isolation from the other two selections (understanding and information). Attention in this case is directed solely towards the analysis of a given utterance or text (as is typical in discursive psychology), or a given sequence of utterances or texts (as in conversation analysis). This is a tempting reduction, since one can fix such an utterance into a material form (a transcript, for instance) with an objective (publicly shareable) reality. This might provide the scientist who is anxious in the face of ephemeral complexity with the comfort of the present-at-hand. It creates the illusion that one *has* the thing (e.g. the 'discourse') at one's disposal and hence something like 'analysis' is possible. However, such reductions quickly run into scientifically paralysing paradoxes since they evade the unity of the phenomenon they actually seek (i.e. communication). They dissect the songbird to find the song. Naturally, when presented with such criticism, analysts devoted to this form of reduction (unless they discover new resources for managing complexity) will find themselves either driven further and further into the minutiae of their 'data', or driven outwards into the territory of structuralism where language *tout court* is presented as a vast facticity of fluctuating differences. Dwelling amidst increasingly specialised concerns, which do indeed yield novel findings, they find that their powers to communicate outside of their own community dwindle at the same rate that their resources for dismissing outsiders increase (e.g. for not using elaborate enough transcription conventions). This increases the likelihood of the formation of isolated communities.

Reduction to the subject side of the distinction is achieved through an equally unjustifiable, but equally understandable, prioritisation of understanding. If 'meaning' cannot be found in the material marks that compose a text or in the structure of a language, then where can one hope to find it but in the mind of an individual – either that of the speaker or that of the listener? Subjectivity takes centre stage, and with it the need to address the paradox of 'inter-subjectivity' and the 'sharing' of meaning (the word communication, let us not forget, denotes sharing or distributing). In this context one finds that the labyrinthine resources of phenomenology are drawn upon, and intentionality becomes a decisive concept. However, the thoughts, feelings and intentions of a given individual may well be a necessary condition of communication, but they are not the complex beast itself. To paraphrase Wittgenstein, explaining communication via subjectivity is like getting at the true artichoke by divesting it of its leaves.

Efforts to combine these two forms of reduction in some neo-Hegelian synthesis do not help matters, since adding one reduction to another does not permit access to the excluded systemic synthesis which unified those selections in the first place. Despite much rhetoric about overcoming the type of subject (information processing system)/object (environmental information) distinction that grips experimental psychology, contemporary qualitative psychology is dominated by a different manifestation of the very same dualism. We wish to suggest that, in this sense, phenomenological approaches collude with discourse analytical approaches in evading the complexity that properly belongs to their subject matter.

These two forms of complexity reduction (to utterance and to understanding) are, in an unexpected way, the product of a residual acceptance of the now defunct *transmission model* of communication that such approaches were actually set up to challenge. According to this deeply ingrained model, communication is about transmitting a message along a channel from a sender to a receiver. This model brings with it a good deal of metaphorical baggage. We are led to think of the message as a 'thing' that is passed from a sender to a receiver much like a gift might be. The sender loses it and the receiver gains it, but what passes between them is basically the same thing. As Luhmann states: 'The metaphor of transmission locates what is essential about communication in the act of transmission, in the utterance' (1995, p. 139). Those discourse analysts that concern themselves entirely with transcribed utterances thus tacitly inherit this bias towards the act of transmission. They become fascinated with the rhetorical skills evidenced in the utterance and they neglect the insight that the utterance is in fact 'nothing more than a selection proposal, a suggestion' (Luhmann, 1995, p. 139). As a result they tend to neglect the vast gaps in understanding that routinely occur in everyday discourse and that cast a grave doubt over the idea that the 'same object' has been passed from sender to recipient. What is communicated is never 'housed' within the utterance.

The urge to interpret the phenomenology at play in discourse is also governed by these residual transmission metaphorics. Here, interpreters take all too literally the idea that something is passed between the otherwise isolated subjectivities of the interlocutors. It is as if communication were a magical process in which the subjective meaning of one individual were transmitted, via language, into the subjective world of another, and vice versa. Discourse is misconstrued as a vehicle which somehow carries psychic meaning between people. The whole notion of intersubjectivity which informs such approaches is an oxymoron. Nothing is passed from ego to alter in communication.

Qualitative developments in psychology have in these ways also fallen behind the work of linguists, who have long taken the temporal (process oriented) and systemic aspects of communication seriously (Hopper, 1992) and have even begun tackling issues such as syntax in terms of unfolding temporal processes (Auer, 2005).

We hope we have conveyed the meaning behind Niklas Luhmann's insistence that communication is an 'independent type of formation in the medium of meaning' (2000a, p. 9). The unity of communication cannot be explained on a purely psychological basis since its unity exceeds and, as it were, incorporates the psychic. This is not to deny the necessity of the psychic, however, since neither utterance, information nor understanding is possible without other modes of psychological process such as affective experience, sensory perception, memory, conceptual thought and reflexive consciousness. Communication thus certainly presupposes a sophisticated psychic system, even as it transforms it. When we address somebody, for instance, we assume that they will perceive this, and that they will take the strange noises we emit as something meaningful that was intended as communication, i.e. as an utterance to be understood and replied to with a reciprocal utterance that has similar qualities. Likewise, our powers of perception are to no small extent devoted to the concerns of communication. If someone says 'look at that tree', we must hear them, and we might look, or refuse to look. Either way, our consciousness is, as it were, 'captured' by the communication, and transformed by it. Communication thus occupies vast swathes of our conscious attention. But this by no means implies that such psychological processes are the foundation of communication any more than a devoted secretary is the foundation of an executive boss. The boss might depend upon the personal assistant, but is distinct from, and not reducible to them.

To develop this analogy further, one might think of communication as a parasite of psychological processes. Communication takes from consciousness. For example, communication uses perceptual resources, but uses them for its own ends, which are radically distinct from those of perceptual consciousness. Just as personal assistants always run the risk of being taken for granted, so communication can usually afford to entirely presuppose the sophisticated psychic systems it requires for its existence. But in some ways the relationship is symbiotic, doubtless as an unanticipated byproduct. For example, communication takes perceptual resources, but lends in return the possibility of an order – a linguistically mediated order – to conscious and indeed unconscious, processes. When considering the 'autopoiesis' of 'mind' and 'language' it is thus important to recognise their mutual co-creation, i.e. the extent to which mind and language have created each other. As we will touch upon in Chapter 7, articulated memories, are a gift enabled by language from oneself in the past to oneself in the present. Our mentality, particularly in its higher forms, can usefully be thought of in these terms as a gift of sorts from language to humankind (Whitehead, 1938/1966, p. 41). In the following chapter, however, we will see that sometimes that gift can be *giftige* or poisonous.

As the synthesis of three selections, communication has a unity that exceeds the psychic, which remains a part of the environment of communication. Reciprocally, communication, once it exists, comes to be presupposed as the environment of psychic processes. This means that the psychic can by no means be taken as the foundation of communication and ought not to be assigned a foundational role in conceptualising social systems. One cannot understand communication by attending to the minds of those communicating. On the contrary, social systems of communication provide their own foundation and in so doing, acquire their own psychology: a psychology without foundations.

FIVE

Artaud and Embodiment

On the outside grows the furside, on the inside, grows the skinside. So the furside is the outside and the skinside is the inside. Oneside likes the skinside inside and the furside on the outside. Others like the skinside outside and the furside on the inside. If you turn the skinside inside thinking you will side with that side then the softside furside's inside which some argue is the wrong side. If you turn the furside outside as you say it grows on that side then your outside's next to skinside which becomforts not the right side. For the skinside is the cold side and your outside's not your warm side And the two cold sides coming side-by-side are not the right sides, one 'side' decides. If you decide to side with that 'side', turn the outside furside inside. Then the hard side, cold side, skinside's, beyond all question, inside outside. (Herbert George Ponting, *The Sleeping Bag*, from *Scott of the Antartic* (1948))

A strange short film appeared on the BBC website in late November 2007. The words 'The hinderer' flashed onto the screen in stark black and white. A scene follows which is dominated by a badly focused model sloping landscape. A small red wooden ball with eyes crudely attached moves up the slope. It appears to falter. A pink cube, again resplendent with eyes, bursts into frame from the left, at the top of the slope. It descends, making contact with the ball, and both move down the slope, before the cube retreats to the top, leaving the ball at the bottom. More words flash up: 'the helper'. The scene cuts back, apparently to the point where we left. The ball repeats its previous movements up the slope, but this time from bottom right a yellow triangle, again with eyes, shoots towards the ball and both move to the top. The triangle then exits, leaving the ball to make a curious bouncing motion. Final words: 'the choice'. A new scene appears. A baby pictured in profile, stares towards something out of shot. A pair of hands holding what seems to be a tray appears. On the tray are the cube and the triangle, which now look oddly flattened when shot from a different angle. The baby looks at the objects and then bangs her hand near the yellow triangle.

This was not, tragically, historical footage of an entry from some half-forgotten Central European short film festival. It purported to be a record of a developmental psychology experiment conducted at Yale University. The research question addressed in the study was whether babies (6- and 10-month-old-infants) could make 'social evaluations'. The researchers – Hamlin, Wynn and Bloom (2007) – hypothesised that this could be imputed on the basis of a 'preference' shown towards those who help rather than those who hinder others. If babies could be shown to prefer 'helpers' over 'hinderers' purely on the basis of observing their behaviour then this would imply that the capacity to make social evaluations is 'universal' and unlearned; i.e. innate or 'wired in'. The logic of the experimental procedure runs as follows: the shapes are anthropomorphised, they are meant to serve as analogues of human behaviour. 'The hinderer' is preventing the red ball from climbing 'a hill'. Contrastingly, 'the helper' provides assistance to the red ball. Having viewed both scenes, the baby is then presented with the two shapes on a tray. If the baby 'chooses' one this is taken to be a display of preference. Displaying preference for 'the helper' is seen as evidence for a social judgement. The baby orients towards the shape that appears to help others. In order to do this, the baby is presumed to have implicit knowledge of social relationships. This was indeed what the researchers claimed to have found: more babies (26 out of a sample of 28) expressed a preference for 'the helper', therefore they demonstrated the ability to make social judgements, ergo they are endowed with innate sociality.

What to make of this study? The experimenters took care to limit the role of a range of well known potential 'artefacts' (i.e. effects which arise from the nature of the procedures). Care was taken to counterbalance the choice of shape (the pink cube and the yellow triangle swap roles in different trials), the direction (sometimes the red ball/baby was helped up the slope, sometimes down) and the order of presentation (whether the helper or the hinderer was seen first). We must take the experimenters at their word as having demonstrated a robust effect. However precisely what it is that they have shown is open to question.

The researchers assume that a display of preference for the helper exhibits the ability to make social judgements. But would this not also be the case were a preference for the hinderer to be shown? In what sense is 'helping' social and 'hindering' not? Presumably hindering is understood to be 'anti-social' in the very particular ideological sense that it frustrates individual intentions, and that imposing oneself on the 'freedom' and 'choices' of another is corrosive of social life. This libertarian individualism is a very narrow view of social life. It would be very surprising indeed to find that such a historically and culturally specific world view were innate. It is more likely that babies have acquired such a belief on the basis of their limited experience, perhaps in the course of their interactions with the researchers. In which case, the research team are to be congratulated for their discovery of the means to rapidly ideologically condition such young minds. What, though, if it were true that babies could make social judgements? Presumably there are several kinds of things they might be judging. They could, as the researchers claim, be making a judgement about the 'behaviour' of the shapes. But equally they could be making a judgement about the behaviour of the experimenters. They may be choosing the helper because they believe that is what the experimenters want them to do. In other words they are trying to help the experimenters by not merely choosing but also emulating the helper. But would such behaviour be a genuine demonstration of the ability to make social judgements? Surely a judgement reflects the ability to apply evaluative criteria to a given case. Who is to say that the red ball actually deserves to be helped? With its irritating bouncing behaviour and its frankly lazy inability to climb a small slope on its own, the babies might conclude that the hinderer is more worthy of their preference. Perhaps the choice of helper here might not be a preference but an accusation: 'that one gave too much help, it should have left the red ball alone'. Or, pushed further, would not the best display of innateness of sociality be in a refusal on the part of the baby to participate in the experiment altogether? For are we not, in fact, at our most social when we are exercising our ability to refuse and protest and to demand different kinds of social arrangements? Maybe the best demonstration of innate sociality would be for the babies to knock over the tray, to throw away both helper and hinderer and the whole damn corrupt social order that they both represent.

The Hamlin et al. experiment is an open text, ripe for endless interpretative speculation. We will stop our own here with the conclusion that what this experiment tells us is very little about babies per se and a great deal about the way psychologists mobilise implicit assumptions about the nature of the social and seek to naturalise them through experimental procedures. In a way we are picking the wrong fight here. Given the range of things that psychologists have tried to claim as innate – including aggression, sexual violence, the capacity to manipulate, 'schizophrenia' – our natural sympathies lie closer to the Hamlin team than they do with their opponents. It seems somehow ethically preferable, for example, to believe in Rousseau's vision of natural goodness rather than Hobbes' notion of primal, wolfish self-interest. It might even be possible to imagine ways of reading the experiment which would render it as evidence of a Spinozist account of human development where we associate with others to manage our own inherent vulnerability (about which we will have more to say in the next chapter). But the problem remains one of seeking to ground social order in apparently natural order without having interrogated the idea of 'order' itself as it applies in both domains.

As we will present him in this chapter, Antonin Artaud – actor, writer, theatre practitioner, poet and mental health patient – remains one of the most trenchant critics of 'assumed order' in twentieth-century thought. Through his varied, complex and at times downright bizarre works, Artaud takes aim not merely at social order but at the very idea of there being any necessary order at all in the natural world. Artaud's mantra 'the sky will fall on heads' is meant to express what he came to call 'cosmic strictness' or the idea of the implacability of forces of nature and their capacity to overcome human consciousness and society. We must build our lives around this always possible apocalypse, for only on this basis can we truly begin to think. As Anaïs Nin wrote in her diary in 1933:

> Artaud sat in the Coupole café pouring out poetry, talking of magic: – I am Heliogabalus, the mad Roman emperor, because he becomes everything he writes about. In the taxi, he pushed back his hair from a ravaged face. The beauty of the summer day did not touch him. He stood up in the taxi and, stretching his arms, he pointed to the crowded streets: – The revolution will come soon. All this will be destroyed. The world must be destroyed. (Barber, 2006: 7)

The details of Artaud's extraordinary life are well documented (see Esslin, 1976; Barber, 2004), as are the debates around the problematic status of his writing (see Scheer, 2002; 2004). We will avoid prolonged engagement with those questions here (see Brown, 2005; 2007 instead), and confine ourselves to reading Artaud as illustrating a variety of creative practical responses to the problem of social interaction and order. In the last chapter, we saw that Luhmann's response was to put communication on a different footing, based on the recursive connections between utterance, information and understanding. This somewhat rational response has an equally relevant flip side that no one deals with better than Artaud, who found himself malformed with respect to the normative forms of life created in part by these recursive connections. Artaud thus makes a very different response – he demands that we place the body, the fleshy envelope of organs and fluids, at the centre of social order. We will describe how Artaud's response evolved by considering a series of works, more or less chronologically.

Suspended Thought

In 1923, Artaud submitted a selection of his poetry to *Nouvelle Revue Française* for consideration for publication. The editor, Jacques Rivière, sent Artaud a polite letter of rejection, but 'found them sufficiently interesting to want to make the acquaintance of the author' (Artaud, 1968a, p. 27). Thereafter a partly written conversation developed between the two. This revolved around Artaud's confessed inability to translate his thoughts into creative expression. As he puts it:

> I suffer from a fearful mental disease. My thought abandons me at every stage. From the mere fact of thought itself to the external fact of its materialisation in words. Words, the forms of phrases, inner direction of thought, the mind's simplest reactions, I am in constant pursuit of my intellectual being. Thus, when *I am able to grasp a form*, however imperfect, I hold on to it, afraid to lose all thought. As I know I do not do myself justice, I suffer from it, but I accept it in fear of complete death. (ibid., p. 27)

The reason for the relative failure of his poetry, Artaud suggests, is that he suffers from a unique condition where thought eludes him at the very moment when it becomes materialised in words. The difficulty is not with his thought itself, nor necessarily with the 'forms' themselves, but rather with the process of rendering thought material. He latches onto inelegant and insufficient poetic forms out of fear of not being able to write at all. Artaud writes under the influence of 'a sickness affecting the soul in its most profound reality, poisoning its expression. Spiritual poison. Genuine paralysis. Sickness robbing us of speech and memory and uprooting thought' (1968a, p. 41). In subsequent responses Rivière notes the contradiction between the elegance with which Artaud expresses himself in these letters, with his 'extra-ordinarily precise self-analysis' (p. 34), and the relative failure of the poetry. He eventually proposes to instead publish their correspondence. Blanchot argues that whilst Rivière's sensibilities are worthy in noting the contrast, he fails to notice the significance of Artaud's cries to be defeated by poetry:

> Common sense immediately poses the question why, if he has nothing to say, does he not in fact say nothing? We may reply that one can content oneself with saying nothing when nothing is merely almost nothing; here, however, we are apparently confronted with such a radical nullity that, in the exorbitance it represents, the danger of which it is the approach, the tension it provokes, it demands, as if it were the price to be freed from it, the formulation of an initial word which would banish all the words which say something. (Blanchot, 1959/2004, p. 112)

Although Artaud professes that he has 'nothing to say', that he suffers from a 'powerlessness', an 'unpower' that interrupts his work, Rivière is wrong to assume this 'nothingness' is a crisis suffered by thought. Rather it is a 'radical nullity' that is itself 'thinking', or rather an image of thought as withdrawn from speech. What Artaud experiences as a 'void' is the 'tension' or the 'danger' which arises as speech confronts the absent traces of the thinking which serves as its conditions, and which correspondingly must be effaced in the act of speech.

What Artaud describes here is an elegant psychological paradox. We may treat thought as the foundation of language, as what is straightforwardly expressed in the words we employ in utterances. And yet we do not really experience language as such in this way. To speak is to distance oneself from one's thoughts, to become immersed in communication, in the mediator. It is as though we were forced to expel thought in order to be able to speak. Conversely, the maintenance of a separation between thought and utterance requires that we impute some difference in form – whatever thinking is, it must somehow be different from language. But when we start to explore this difference we inevitably do so from within language itself, we create a discourse *about* thinking rather than engage directly *with* thinking. In the last chapter we described several responses to this difficulty. Discursive psychology, drawing on the later Wittgenstein, chooses to avoid the problem by insisting that the majority of what is psychologically meaningful and certainly all that is amenable to empirical inspection is already contained in utterances (or rather talk-in-interaction) as a kind of 'public mentation' (see Edwards, 1997). An alternative response is to the follow the psychoanalytic tradition in treating thought as always-already seized upon by language such that only its traces or symbolic residue can be detected within utterances (as in Lacan's famous dictum that 'the unconscious is structured like a language').

It is fitting that Artaud should provide an alternative to psychoanalysis, given that in 1937 Lacan was the psychiatrist who first diagnosed Artaud as 'incurably insane', thereby consigning him to nine years in the French secure mental health system. Rather than create a conceptual model of thought and language, Artaud instead seeks to dramatise the experience of the 'banishing' of thought by language. He attempts to intensify rather than domesticate this sense of thinking being stolen or spirited away in the lived act of speaking or writing:

> There is, therefore, one single thing which destroys my ideas. Something which does not stop me being what I might, but if I may express it thus, leaves me in a state of suspense. Something furtive which robs me of the words *I have found* (Artaud, 1968a, p. 31).

Blanchot hails Artaud's poetry as an attempt to think the 'impossibility of thinking'. That is, to confront thought as it absents itself from the formal, rational organisation of expression (of which poetry is emblematic). It is this absence that Foucault (1989a) would later famously refer to as 'the thought from outside' in his well known essay on Blanchot. It becomes important for Blanchot to distinguish the character of this struggle from 'madness' per se:

> We must not make the mistake of reading as analysts of a psychological state the precise, unflinching and detailed descriptions of this which Artaud offers us. Descriptions they are, but of a struggle. This struggle is in part imposed on him. The 'void' is an 'active void'. The 'I cannot think, I cannot manage to think' is an appeal to a deeper thought, a constant pressure, a forgetting which, unable to bear being forgotten, none the less demands a more complete forgetting. Thinking now becomes the step back which is always to be taken. (Blanchot, 1959/2004, p. 114)

Artaud's struggle is to evacuate language in such a way that it is adequate to the task of going after 'the void'. This would not be a language which says nothing, but one which says the nothing: a language capable of expressing the nullity that oppresses him. Blanchot uses the language of forgetfulness to describe the trace-like character of thought as both perpetually absenting itself from expression, and yet making that absence felt within whatever is expressed. To go after the void is then to turn expression back on itself so there is nothing left but the traces of absenting thought (a 'complete forgetting').

Surrealist Thought

In one of his most pithy statements, Artaud succinctly declares his opposition to what we might call a 'psychological' view of literature and the arts: 'All writing is pigshit. People who leave the obscure to try to define whatever it is that goes on in their heads, are pigs' (Artaud, 1965b, p. 38). Beneath the apparent irony of these written words is a serious objection to the idea that the text is a material document of the thoughts, intentions and emotions of the author. To treat the text in this way is to subscribe to a certain form of humanism that Artaud finds untenable:

> If man in Shakespeare's plays is sometimes concerned with what is above him, it is always finally to determine the result of that concern within many, that is, psychology. Psychology persists in bringing the unknown down to a level with the known, that is to say with the everyday and pedestrian. And psychology has caused this abasement and fearful loss of energy which appears to me to have really reached its limit. And it seems to me both theatre and ourselves want nothing more to do with psychology. (Artaud, 1974, p. 58)

Samuel Weber (2000) notes that there are some infelicities with this translation, but nevertheless offers the following gloss. Shakespeare's plays are often taken to contain themes dealing with extreme human experiences (i.e. passion, revenge, jealousy, fate). Yet, for Artaud, these themes are always bent backwards into somewhat cod psychological speculation about character and motivation. This he sees as a disease that has taken hold of theatre in general, reducing it to the status of a 'digestive' recreation where the bourgeoisie can see their own pathetic concerns reflected back. But it is not simply that a particular kind of psychology is reflected in the theatrical obsession with the correct staging of 'masterpieces'. It is the central role accorded to 'humanity' itself that is problematic: 'what is at the heart of "psychology", as Artaud here uses the term, is the underlying *humanism* it conceals, an anthropomorphism that places not just individuals, but through them the very idea of "Man" himself at the centre of things' (Weber, 2000, p. 14).

Writing is 'pigshit' when it reduces the movement of thought (aka 'the obscure', 'the unknown') to the empty abstraction of humanism, i.e. the self-contained, self-possessive model of the person whose mind is dominated by the faux-drama of petit bourgeois morality and intimacy. Artaud demands that this writing be rejected in order to allow living, vibrant arts to be created: 'let us do away with this foolish adherence to texts, to written poetry. Written poetry is valid once and then ought to be torn up. Let dead poets make way for the living' (Artaud, 1974, p. 59). In this sense, what is required is a non-anthropocentric theatre and a non-psychological literature. We will turn to the theatre in a moment, but with regard to literature Derrida's essay 'La parole soufflée' neatly identifies an immediate difficulty. Derrida refers to a double movement of 'furtiveness' in Artaud's description of consciousness and language. Thought is initially stolen or 'spirited away' by speech. But having been materialised it then becomes subject to a second form of theft once it is passed on and rendered as an object for critique, commodification, or simply as no longer belonging to the speaker. On the basis of this double movement of 'theft', Derrida reads the Artaudian consciousness as fragmented by this undecidability about 'who speaks':

> I am in relation to myself within the ether of speech which is always spirited away [*soufflé*] from me, and which steals from me the very thing that it puts me in relation to. Consciousness of speech, that is to say, consciousness in general is not knowing who speaks at the moment when, and in the place where, I proffer my speech. (Derrida, 1978a, p. 176)

The speaking subject is riven with a fissure. To be conscious of one's own speech is to not know with any certainty 'who speaks'. Speech is dominated by the figure of theft, or, as Derrida will have it, rather the stealing of language from our mouths by 'the thief who has always already lost speech as property and initiative' (p. 178) is itself the exemplary scene of theft from which all other instances will borrow their determination. The question Derrida then asks is whether this fear ultimately leads to a kind of complicity with the metaphysics that Artaud denounces (i.e. of self-presence, of capturing thought itself, etc.). In seeing speech as the theft of thought, Artaud does appear at times to privilege a sovereign consciousness that is somehow entirely outside of language. Perhaps unsurprisingly Derrida argues that such complicity is a 'necessary dependency of all destructive discourses: they must inhabit the structures they demolish, and within them they must shelter an indestructible desire for full presence, for nondifference: simultaneously life and death' (p. 194).

In Artaud's work language is disorganised, twisted into unexpected shapes. Sometimes this falls into apparent disorder – for example, in Artaud's lecture performances which would descend into stylised screams and enactments of agony, plague and sickness (see Barber, 2004). But more usually Artaud punctuates his texts with peculiar phrases, non-standard use of grammar, invented words and expletives. At these moments it is as if a kind of space is hollowed out within language where unexpected or 'chance' singular moments occur. In an early essay, Foucault (1995) claimed this disruptive experimentation with language as evidence for a new form of communication between madness and literature. The basis of his claim is that one form in which madness has been classically understood is that of:

> subjecting an utterance, which appears to conform to the expected code, to another code whose key is contained within the same utterance so that this utterance becomes divided within itself. It says what it says, but it adds a silent surplus that quietly enunciates what it says and according to which code it says what it says. (Foucault, 1995, p. 294)

Such utterances would then necessarily take the form of singularities, since they would not entirely obey existing codes for the formation of discourse (despite broadly resembling such codes), but would rather contain within themselves the keys to the articulation of a second code which have the effect of not only transforming the utterance but also of rendering the utterance entirely unique. Foucault points to Artaud, Nerval and Roussel as having made this technique 'the place of literature'. But in so doing, this gesture – which, for Foucault, brings literature and madness into close proximity – means that literary criticism assumes a new importance, for it becomes essential to handling the singularity of texts and the distribution of codings, and that, perhaps even more importantly, it now becomes impossible to consider the authors of such work as endowed with an 'oeuvre' in the classical sense. Crudely put, if each text is singular, there can be no overarching code – the 'life-work' – under which these texts can be gathered. Their power resides instead in the 'empty form from where this work comes, in other words, the place where it never ceased to be absent, where it will never be found because it had never been located there to begin with' (Foucault, 1995, p. 296).

Foucault gave the term 'the absence of work' (more properly the 'absence of the Life-Work') to this emerging practice, of which he saw Artaud as one principal exemplar. Now this absence, or rather deliberate attempt at absenting the work from subordination to a given set of codings, certainly captures one other key aspect of Artaud's theorisation of language. Namely that language 'works', at its most efficacious, precisely when it appears to be 'not working', giving rise to a body of texts which gain their standing not through what they appear to affirm, but through the avoidances, side-steps, omissions and 'failures' that they perform. In this respect each text is to be judged in terms of the 'silent surplus' of meaning it hollows out in its carefully constructed apparent misfiring.

Vital Thought

So far we have seen how Artaud views consciousness as split asunder in its encounter with language. But consciousness is also split, perhaps more fundamentally, in another sense. It is estranged from the body. In Western philosophy, Descartes' division of mind from body sets the conditions for a peculiar kind of self-experience. Descartes founds his philosophical system on the notion of a subject made of pure thought, who can reflexively recognise itself as such (the infamous *cogito ergo sum*). To experience oneself as a 'thinking thing' is then to experience oneself as immaterial, as divorced from a dubious and untrustworthy body (in the next chapter we will show how Spinoza provides an intriguing alternative to this bizarre proposition). Artaud rejects entirely the naturalness of such a view. For him, thinking is a work of the body. Consciousness cannot be divorced from embodiment: 'I do not separate my thought from my life. With each of my tongue's vibrations I retrace all the paths of my thought through my flesh' (Artaud, 1968c, p. 165).

Considered as a 'total organism', the body, by virtue of its very existence, is that which apprehends the world and acts within it. The body *thinks* as it *acts*. Consciousness is rooted within the flesh. Why then should we imagine otherwise or experience ourselves as Cartesian beings? Because of the systematic rationalisation of consciousness that occurs at an institutional level throughout all Western societies, Artaud claims. He rails against the then modern education system as involved in the production of 'engineers, magistrates, doctors, who know nothing of the true mysteries of the body or the cosmic laws of existence'

(Artaud, 1968b, p. 179). These 'experts' know nothing of the body, save as a vehicle for an overly prescriptive and ultimately fleshless version of thinking. Thought is thereby locked into a 'narrow tank' or else 'lost in its own labyrinth' (ibid., p. 179). The Cartesian experience of the body is not a natural state for Artaud – it is a cultural-historical state of affairs whose time is finished.

Susan Sontag (1988) acutely observes that in the course of railing against what he saw as the dominant tendencies in Western culture, Artaud aligned himself with three 'frequently travelled imaginative routes' (p. xl) to find a more vital alternative. The first of these is the 'turn to the East' which took hold in the early twentieth century. This involves the wholesale 'othering' of the East in order to reflect on the West so brilliantly described by Edward Said (1978). Second, the rediscovery of suppressed 'heterodox spiritual or outright magical tradition' (p. xl) in the history of the West. And finally, an interest in so-called 'primitive people' whose civilisation had somehow been preserved in the face of Western colonialism.

Taking the first of these, whilst editor of *La révolution surréaliste*, Artaud alternated between writing vitriolic attacks addressed at Western authority fig-ures, such as the Pope (including the immortal lines 'we are thinking of a new war – war on you, Pope, dog' [Artaud, 1968d, p. 180] with affectionate pleas to the Dalai Lama and 'The Buddhist Schools' soliciting their help in the over-throw and ultimate salvation of Western civilization: 'you who know how one can turn in one's thinking, and how the mind can be saved from itself … come, tear down our houses … Come. Save us from these larvae. Design us new houses' (Artaud, 1988a, pp. 104–105). However, in the brief few months Artaud spent back in Paris following his release from the Rodez asylum before his death in 1947, Artaud had revised his views. He came to believe that all hope for 'Tibet' and for Buddhism was lost, that it had been subsumed by 'the West'. Now Buddhist monks were plotting against him, willing his death through bizarre collective sexual rituals (see Marowitz, 1977).

Artaud's engagement with the repressed 'magical' history of the West is illustrated by his history of the Roman emperor Heliogabalus, whose reign was notorious for its violence and sexual excess. Artaud writes with relish of this 'example of laxity, disorder and depravity' (2006, p. 114), savouring the details of ritualised mutilation and orgiastic frenzy. At first glance what Artaud describes are scenes of utter disorder, driven by an unhinged mystical fanati-cism. However, Artaud notes that 'I see Heliogabalus not as a madman but as a rebel. 1st Against the Roman polytheistic anarchy. 2nd Against the Roman monarchy that's been buggered through him' (Artaud, 2006, p. 121). What Heliogabalus does, Artaud claims, is dismantle the existing Roman order through deploying a set of mystic principles, primarily based around codes of gender (woman/man) and cosmology (sun/moon; light/dark). These principles are to a certain extent nominal – it doesn't really matter what they consist of, merely that they are applied as a 'superior idea of order' to the existing order 'like a slap on the face of the Latin world' (p. 115).

The story of Heliogabalus enables Artaud to imagine what the Surrealist Revolution might have become. That too was a 'revolution of the mind': 'Heliogabalus undertook a systematic and joyous demoralisation of the Latin mind and consciousness' (p. 115). Although mind and consciousness are the targets, they are attacked not through oratory or by superior rationality, but through the body itself. Heliogabalus is in effect restoring the unity of mind and body. This Artaud names as 'anarchy'. The anarchist is he or she who is able to crack open social order and expose it to the vital forces which it believes it has domesticated. From the time of Roman polytheism, Western religion imagines it is possible to use the name of its Gods as founding principles. Artaud argues that 'these names were names for forces, ways of being, modes of a great power of being that changed into principles, essences, substances, elements' (p. 60). Anarchistic vital thought treats principles as 'definite organisms', as agitated states of matter which demand expression in human thinking. Thought does not arise from within the mind, but rather is amplified or transduced through consciousness, having emerged directly from the living forces of matter and the body: 'every shot life fires at things is equivalent to a thought' (p. 64). When principles are abstracted and treated as distinct from a lived engagement with the world they become 'nothing', in the same way that when the body is treated merely as a functional machine for sheltering mind it too becomes a parody of living:

> Matter exists only through spirit, and the spirit only in matter …[I]t now seems to me easy to reply that there are no principles, but that there are things; and likewise that there are solid things, and rarity in these solids; and assemblages of unique matter that give an idea of perfection … Nothing exists only as a function, and all functions lead back to one; – and the liver than turns the skin yellow, the brain that syphilises itself, the bowel that extrudes ordure, the blazing look that takes the place of flames – they boil down for me, when I die, to my regret at living and my desire to be finished with it. (Artaud, 2006, p. 66)

Heliogabalus discovers the terrible truth of anarchist thought. In order to re-establish the physical basis of mind, to reconnect consciousness with the forces expressed in matter, it will be necessary to subject our common notions of living, of what our bodies are and what they can do, to strict experimentation. This is one sense of the term 'cruelty', which would be developed at length in Artaud's writing on theatre.

The last source explored by Artaud came about during an arduous trip to Mexico in 1936. In a piece entitled *What I came to Mexico to do*, Artaud (1988b) describes the country as possessing 'a cultural secret' bequeathed by the ancient Mexicans (p. 372). This secret is the means of accessing 'subtle forces' which are 'part of the vital realm of nature as men knew it in pagan times' (p. 373), a cultural inheritance entrusted to the few remaining indigenous tribes. Artaud journeyed to visit one such tribe, the Tarahumaras of Sierre Madre, with the express aim of participating in a peyote ritual, which he believed would enable him to share their experience of 'vital natural forces'.

After a considerable wait whilst his participation was negotiated, the experience proved to be a disappointment:

> After twenty-eight days of waiting, I had not yet come back into myself, or should I say, *gone out* into myself. Into myself, into this dislocated assemblage, this piece of damaged geology … this ill-assembled heap of organs which I was and which I had the impression of witnessing like a vast landscape of ice on the point of breaking up … For to have come this far, to find myself at last on the threshold of an encounter and of this place of which I expected so many revelations, and to feel so lost, so abandoned, so deposed. (Artaud, 1988c, pp. 382–383)

If Artaud was unable to properly experience the access to cosmic forces unlocked in the peyote ritual then this was, he considered, due to his constitutional inability to mobilise his body as fit to think the 'thoughts shot by life'. Consciousness and embodiment are as one in the anarchic vital thought that Artaud discovers in his turn to the East. Rationality and language then take on an entirely different status. They are no longer mediators, the material medium through which consciousness is expressed, but rather a material swarm around the 'ill-assembled heap of organs' which further enable it break up.

Cruel Thought

Artaud viewed *Lot and his daughters*, painted by Lucas van Leyden in 1521, hanging in the Louvre. The canvas contains a strikingly literal depiction of the culmination of the Biblical story of Lot, who escaped the destruction of Sodom and Gomorrah to drunkenly father a new nation with his daughters. His wife had already met a different fate (see Haaken, 1998, for a reading of the contemporary relevance of this story for psychology). Van Leyden frames the incestuous scene with fire and brimstone catapulted to earth from the exploding heavens, shattering buildings and sinking ships. It is an apocalyptic scene.

Artaud was greatly struck by the painting which seemed to him to affect the mind directly 'by a kind of striking visual harmony, intensely active in the whole work yet caught at a glance' (Artaud, 1974, p. 22). Although Artaud appreciated the work in the traditional sense, in terms of its composition, it is the uncanny way that the artist has manipulated formal techniques to make the painting 'affect the mind directly like a physical reagent' (p. 24) which fascinated him, making it akin to kind of nonrepresentational 'primitive' art. The painting was, he claimed, 'what theatre ought to be, if only it knew how to speak its own language' (p. 25). What language would this be?

In describing such a language, Artaud offers an analogy with the bubonic plague outbreak which struck Marseilles in 1720. As the plague spread through the city, social order broke down, 'society's barriers became fluid with the effects of the scourge' (1974, p. 7). This occurred in several stages (see Weber, 2000). First, normal communication is disrupted and civil services fail. This is high drama. Second, a new emergent form of communication occurs as 'victims disperse through the streets howling, their minds full of horrible visions' (Artaud, p. 14). Tragedy ensues. Third, bizarre and comic scenes occur in last- ditch efforts to halt the progress of the plague – 'strange men clothed in wax, with noses a mile long and glass eyes, mounted on kinds of Japanese sandals' (ibid., p. 14). Farce arrives. Finally, 'the remaining survivors go beserk' in a kind of 'frenzied pointlessness' (ibid., p. 14). Absurd acts of violence, 'erotic fever' and stylised reversion of values occur – 'Dandies deck themselves out and stroll among the charnel-houses' (ibid., p. 14). Here the desired language of theatre emerges 'At this point theatre establishes itself. Theatre, that is to say, the sense of gratuitous urgency with which they are driven to perform useless acts of no present advantage' (ibid., p. 14).

During the plague, the presence of death enables the emergence of an experience of 'an extreme force' where all the 'powers of nature are newly rediscovered the instant something fundamental is about to be accomplished' (Artaud, 1974, p. 17). This is the same 'anarchy' that Artaud pursued through his personal 'turn to the East'. In his most famous work *The theatre and its double*, Artaud expounds at length on how the theatre may be a privileged space in which a different route to anarchy is possible. Artaud proposes a practice where theatre becomes a spectacle. Its task will no longer be the slavish presentation of great works, but an experimental or 'alchemical' work of rendering the world as 'virtual reality'. What Artaud means by the term 'virtuality' is close to the sense given to it by Bergson (see Chapter 7). Virtual is a synonym for process and change. We typically see some aspect of the world in terms of its abstracted concrescence or 'actuality' – what it appears to be for us, at this given point, and what sorts of possibilities it offers for current and future action. Actuality is always the outcome of a concerned simplification. We are forced to reduce the world into manageable chunks in order to act upon it. Yet, for both Bergson and Artaud, what eludes simplification is still real. The forces and processes which are at work in any given 'body' or 'thing', albeit typically at the edge of the thresholds of our perception, are no less real than the apparently stable qualities that we perceive. Indeed they are the matrix out of which our particular concrete experiences are extracted. 'Virtuality' names this doubling of the world into process/change and thing/stability.

As virtual reality, theatre will allow something of change, of process and forces in their incomplete, raw state to emerge. The last stage of plague is, in effect, the condition of all the preceding stages. Here humanity exists in its most fluid and febrile state (much like the plague-stricken bodies themselves), from which, at any moment drama, tragedy or farce might develop:

The plague takes dormant images, latent disorder and suddenly carries them to the most extreme gestures. Theatre also takes gestures and develops them to the limit. Just like the plague, it reforges the links between what does and does not exist, between the virtual nature of the possible and the material nature of existence. (Artaud, 1974, p. 17)

In an infamous lecture given at the Sorbonne in 1933, Artaud attempted to literally perform the relationship between plague and theatre through a mixture of screams and violent exhortations. He subsequently distilled his notions of performance into a set of propositions mapping out the techniques on which the plague-theatre, now renamed 'The Theatre of Cruelty' would be based. The phrase 'cruelty' is subject to many interpretations (see Scheer, 2000). Artaud defined it in the following way:

I use the word cruelty in the sense of hungering after life, cosmic strictness, relentless necessity, in the Gnostic sense of a living vortex engulfing darkness, in the sense of the inescapably necessary pain without which life could not continue. (Artaud, 1974, p. 78)

Cruelty does not mean the deliberate harm of self or others. It is rather a studied attitude of accepting that social order is intrinsically adrift in a 'living vortex' of forces which may at any moment engulf humanity. To adopt cruelty as an attitude is to attempt to engage with these forces directly, to recognise the 'far more terrible, essential cruelty that objects can practise on us. We are not free and the sky can still fall on our heads' (p. 60). Recognising that there are forms of 'relentless necessity' beyond our human powers raises the perpetual question of how we are to respond, how we are to live, how we can engage with a 'cosmic strictness' that can at any moment dismantle the comforts of commonsense existence.

Critical to Artaud's shift toward formal theatrical production was his reflections on a Balinese performance he had seen at the Colonial Exhibition in 1931 (1974, pp. 38–55). In Balinese productions the precision of ritual gestures is critical, such as certain movements of the eyes or lips, which produce 'studiously calculated effects' (p. 39). Staging is used not in support of words, but as part of the symbolic coding of activities wherein a gesture, a visual symbol or a particular mask may be combined together, without differentiating 'word' from 'image', in order to form complex expressions:

In fact the strange thing about all these gestures, these angular, sudden, jerky postures, these syncopated inflections formed at the back of the throat, these musical phrases cut short, the sharded flights, rustling branches, hollow drum sounds, robot creaking, animated puppets dancing, is the feeling of a new bodily language no longer based on words but on signs. (Artaud, 1974, pp. 38–39)

The Balinese theatre showed Artaud that a radical distinction between discourse ('word language') and speech ('sign language') is possible. Taken in its widest sense, language is any system of codified elements, a broad grammar constituted by heterogeneous materials, whose fundamental operation is to order space through the assembling of intricate spatial forms. Language does not 'signify' anything, that is, it does not point outside of itself to worldly referents, since it is the things themselves that are being put into play to construct a complex lived space. And as part of that language – since there is no external 'God's eye' position from which to observe the proceedings – we apprehend what comes to pass through the affects which arise as we are ourselves put into play and moved about.

This conception of language holds that the linguistic need not be seen primarily as a medium for the constitution of meaning, but rather for the generation of *affects*. Artaud suggests that words themselves are physical beings with their own particular affective force. Words and the human voice itself literally 'strike us', and in so doing establish connections, an ordering between things in the world. Our apprehension of the world is always initiated by the 'shock' or 'tension' that language engenders within us. In seeing language as a physical gesture rather than the transmission of meaning, Artaud again harked back to what he saw as a pre- or non-modern conception of the word that was rooted in the anarchic and vital thought of primitive ritual. It is because language is able to literally push people around and generate intense emotions – 'sudden silences, fermata, heart stops, adrenalin calls, incendiary images surging into our suddenly awoken minds' (p. 17) – that it can bring about a confrontation with 'living powers' (p. 65).

In its First Manifesto, Artaud announced that The Theatre of Cruelty would engage the audience in a complete sensory assault:

> Every show will contain physical, objective elements perceptible to all. Shouts, groans, apparitions, surprise, dramatic moments of all kinds, the magic beauty of the costumes modelled on certain ritualistic patterns, brilliant lighting, vocal, incantational beauty, attractive harmonies, rare musical notes, object colours, the physical rhythm of moves whose build and fall will be wedded to the beat of moves familiar to all, the tangible appearance of new surprising objects, masks, puppets many feet high, abrupt lighting changes, the physical action of lighting stimulating heat and cold, and so on. (Artaud, 1974, p. 71)

New techniques in stage lighting would be coupled with a revolutionary approach to stage design. The audience would no longer be sat in the darkness before the stage, but would be placed in the centre, with the performance occurring around them, on all sides. Fantasy-like props and devices would be employed, coupled with innovative musical scores designed to highlight the rhythmic and ritualistic quality of the performance. The status of the script – the play itself – was to be entirely rethought, the words now becoming one element amongst many in the *mélange* of effects brought together. The script would no longer be the ultimate repository of meaning, becoming instead a set of sonic weapons or tools with which the actors could generate affects in both the audience and one another.

Mômo Thought

During his incarceration at the Rodez asylum between 1942 and 1946, his psychiatrist Gaston Ferdière asked Artaud to undertake a number of translations of Lewis Carroll's work, with therapeutic ends in mind. Artaud's translations rather predictably diverged considerably from the source material. Gilles Deleuze (1990a) observes of Artaud's translation of a 'fragment' of Lewis Carroll's poem 'Jabberwocky' that there is a real difference between the way language is handled. Carroll, Deleuze claims, prodigiously maintains a gap between expression and denotation in language – between what language does, in its transformation and movement, and that to which it ostensibly refers. Artaud, by contrast, collapses any such gap by treating language in purely physical terms, as that which directly strikes the body. For Deleuze, treating language in this way creates the impression of endless depth:

> Things and propositions have no longer any frontier between them, precisely because bodies have no surface. The primary aspect of the schizophrenic body is that it is a sort of body-sieve. Freud emphasised this aptitude of the schizophrenic to grasp the surface and the skin as if they were punctuated by an infinite number of little holes. The consequence of this is that the entire body is no longer anything but depth – it carries along and snaps up everything into this gaping depth which represents a fundamental involution. Everything is body and corporeal ... Every word is physical, and immediately affects the body. (Deleuze, 1990a, pp. 86–87)

If we leave to one side the rather problematic use of the term 'schizophrenic', Deleuze's claim is that Artaud envisages a 'language without articulation' (p. 89) consisting of 'breath-words' and 'howl-words' in which 'all literal, syllabic, and phonetic values have been replaced by values which are exclusively tonic and not written' (p. 89). This appears to be the inevitable conclusion of Artaud's experiments with language. If 'suspended thought' led Artaud to see language as the spiriting away of expression, and 'cruel thought' to the view of language as a toolkit for generating affects, then the gap between language and consciousness is collapsed. Words do not refer to anything outside of themselves, they are physical beings in themselves which are emitted and absorbed by the body as it engages with the world around it: 'everything is body and corporeal'.

We might then say that the central fact of psychology for Artaud is that we are bodies, bodies which think, feel and act and are engulfed by a cosmos whose powers greatly exceed our own (again, this is also the point of departure for a Spinozist psychology, as mapped out in the next chapter). Sontag (1988) makes much of Artaud's interest in Gnostic thought. Although it takes many forms, the basic tenets of Gnosticism are that the cosmos is driven by conflicting forces within physical matter itself, which take on the appearance of 'good' and 'evil'. Social order and law are merely human expressions of these fundamental conflicts. Apprehension of conflict creates a profound sense of anxiety, not least because these cosmic dramas will be played out within our own bodies. This sets up a paradox whereby we may use our embodied powers to transgress laws and boundaries, thus accomplishing a kind of freedom by overcoming the play of good and evil. But ultimately we are unable to escape the conflicts embedded in the very design of our own bodies; thus transgression may drive us into ever more complex anxieties about the corrupted nature of the flesh. It is not far-fetched to regard the contemporary psychological concern with problems related to embodiment – from body dysmorphic disorder and eating disorders through to self-harm – as reflecting a Gnostic current in contemporary culture.

Throughout his life Artaud maintained a scorn for what he considered to be the failings of human embodiment. From the moment of birth, one is forced to endure a botched and impoverished physical form, a set of 'conditioned reflexes' and organs which are 'badly correlated' with the directions in which thought needs to press. In a short note *On suicide*, Artaud imagines humanity as simply badly designed:

> Life was not an object or form for me, it had become a series of rationalisations. But these rationalisations never got off the ground only freewheeled, they were like possible 'diagrams' within me which my will-power could not light on. (Artaud, 1968e, pp. 158–159)

To live under such circumstances is to accept the fate of a 'walking automaton' which is 'kept alive in a void of denials and furious disavowals' (p. 158). The alternative, to commit suicide, is then not an act of despair or self-destruction, but rather the rejection of a flawed design and the submission of a new set of plans:

> If I kill myself, it won't be to destroy myself, but to re-build myself. For me, suicide would only be a means of violently reconquering myself, of brutally invading my being, of anticipating God's unpredictable approach. I would reintroduce my designs into nature through suicide. For the first time I would give things the shape of my will. (ibid., p. 157).

Derrida notes that Artaud's concerns with the body mirror those over language. What Artaud decries in each is formal organisation, such that movement is subordinated to function: 'Organization is articulation, the interlocking of functions or of member, the labor and play of their differentiation … Artaud is as fearful of the articulated body as he is of articulated language, as fearful of the member as of the word' (Derrida, 1978b, p. 186). If consciousness is made extensive with embodiment then it follows that Artaud's struggles against language – as seen in the screams of the public lectures and the Theatre of Cruelty – will become struggles against the body itself.

This becomes apparent in the art that Artaud produced in the last few years of his life. His drawings and portraits are savagely executed. They range from cartoonish scribbles illustrating his notebooks (see Artaud, 2008) and decorated 'spells' sent to real and imagined addressees, through to formal portraits of friends, often emphasising unnatural and disruptive elements, and complex coloured works dramatising key themes in his thought (see Rowell, 1996 for a selection).

The spells, for example, are complex mixtures of text and symbols. A spell addressed to Sonia Mossé in 1939 (see Rowell, 1996, pp. 46–47) has the following message scrawled in thick ink on both sides of exercise book paper: 'You will live as dead, you will never stop the process of dying and descending. I cast upon you a Force of Death. And this Spell will not be recalled. It will not be deferred. And it breaks all other witch's spells. And this spell will act instantly' (cited in Ho, 1997, p. 20). The text is defaced with a scattering of symbols, some of which have been scribbled over, and looping knots of yellow and red crayon, symbolising death. Finally the paper has been burned through with cigarettes so holes erupt into both sides of the text.

Artaud intended the spells and associated drawing as nonrepresentational: 'these drawings that have nothing to say and represent absolutely nothing' (Artaud, 2008, pp. 11–12). They were instead 'magical actions', physical exhortations 'felt in the body and by the body like a conglomeration (p. 20), designed to produce effects on the recipient. Through the spells Artaud extended himself out physically, and treated the spells as literally the embodiment of the other. His aim was usually to offer protection (the spell to Mossé is actually intended to defend her from evil), but sometimes to engage bodily in other more complex affects (as with a spell addressed to Hitler – see Deleuze & Guattari, 1988). Derrida and Thévenin (1998) pick up on the term *subjectile* which Artaud occasionally used when discussing art. One meaning of this term is the surface, the paper on which the drawing it done, its material support. But it also refers to the act itself, the *jetée* or movement by which the drawing is rapidly executed, a projectile thrown into the world. The movement is an expressive 'spurt', a movement of ideas. Yet since Artaud refuses to separate consciousness from embodiment it is also a 'spurt of blood' (echoing the title of a 1925 Artaud script). The subjectile is then potentially a surface on which consciousness reflects itself and a part of the body which has been expelled: 'neither object nor subject, neither screen nor projectile, the subjectile can *become* all that, stabilizing itself in a certain form or moving about in another' (Derrida and Thévenin, 1998, p. 77). Derrida plays at length on these alternating senses. As a surface, the question will be how to locate subjectivity in the work, since it will always be 'behind' or 'thrown under' the drawing (making it necessary for the surface itself to be burnt or scored in an effort to let subjectivity through). As a projectile, a spurt, the question will be instead how this thing which is expelled serves as a foundation, as a work, a basis on which to discuss art or the artist (making it necessary for Artaud to ruin or reclaim what is expelled, to re-envelop it within his body).

The reclaiming of what has been expelled becomes a major preoccupation in Artaud's later work. In *Heliogabalus*, the expulsion of bodily substances is associated with transgressing boundaries, but by the time of the 1946 text

Artaud the Mômo, the reclamation or enveloping of sperm, excrement and mucous has become a necessity: 'Desired, say I, but without juicing off white, lapped up, bone splinters (buttes of mucous the saliva) the saliva from her false teeth' (Artaud, 1995a, p. 119). If, following Derrida, we see subjectivity as constituted in the subjectile, in the play around that which is expelled and the proprietary relationship the person develops in relation to this act of expulsion (whether it be words or substances – the difference being moot for Artaud), then Artaud's anxieties become an entirely practical matter. Whoever takes possession of the subjectile effectively determines the subjectivity of she or he who has 'thrown it out' into the world:

> If I wake up every morning surrounded by this appalling odor of jism, it is not because I have been succubused by the spirits from beyond – but because the men of this world here pass the word around in their 'perisprit': rubbing their full balls, along the canal of their anus nicely caressed and nicely grasped, in order to pump out my life. 'It's that your sperm is very good, a cop from the Dôme said to me one day who set himself up as a connoisseur, and when one is "so good", "so good", by god one pays too much for fame'. (Artaud, 1995a, p. 149)

Although written in his uniquely obscene prose style, Artaud's concerns may be located within a tradition of 'biopolitical' readings of the relationship between embodiment, subjectivity and power. Beginning with Spinoza, passing through Lacan and Althusser, and culminating in Foucault (the subject of Chapter 8), this tradition emphasises that subjectivity is produced through a disciplining of the body by the institutional apparatuses of the state. Artaud's fantasy around the 'cop from the Dôme' is a visceral version of Althusser's (2001) famous example of 'appellation' involving the cop on the street who hails the subject: 'hey you!'. In both cases the subject is told who or what they are as they are addressed by the cop. Subjectivity receives its determination from outside the person, through the process of being recognised in an institutional encounter. The difference here is that for Althusser power is mediated by the semiotic, whereas for Artaud power is expressed directly in the way bodies envelop and connect with one another: 'I abject all signs. I create only machines of instant utility' (Artaud, cited in Barber, 1993, p. 151).

The self-description Artaud the Mômo, adopted by Artaud in 1946, literally means 'the fool' or 'village idiot' in Marseilles slang (Barber, 2004). It is significant because it is a self-assumed name, a self-created identity. During his Rodez years Artaud developed an elaborate fiction around a group of women, including his grandmothers, friends and former lovers, whom he collectively named 'daughter of the heart to be born'. The 'daughters' served for him as guardian angels, ready to free him from Rodez. They are also literally his creation, his offspring. Artaud then lays claim to his own lineage. As he famously expressed it in the poem *Here Lies* – 'Me, Antonin Artaud, I am my son, my father, my mother and me' (1995b, p. 193).

As a theme, self-creation and physical self-modification runs through Artaud's portraits and drawings. In a small essay written to accompany a display of his Rodez potraits (1995c), Artaud argues that the human face itself bears 'a kind of perpetual death on its face' (p. 277), from which it is the painter's task to save it. By this he means that the physical organisation of the face acts as a barrier to the expression of the vital forces which are obliged to pass by way of it. It is as though, throughout history, the face has breathed and spoken without yet starting to 'say what it is and what it knows' (p. 277). The human face is then a screen, emitting deathly signs denuded of all vitality. Artaud's own portraits seek to recover these vital forces by staging focused and concentrated attacks on the faces in various ways (see images in Rowell, 1996, pp. 98–132). His 1946 works concentrate on distorting a single feature – Roger Blin's nose appears as a giant fold of flesh (p. 103), Jacques Prevel's face is split in two with the right side sliding away, an image referencing a scene from Germaine Dulac's *The seashell and the clergyman*, a film based on a scenario by Artaud (p. 108), a dancing figure appears across Colette Thomas' pursed lips (p. 113). By 1947 this gives way to wholesale assaults – Paule Thévenin's entire head chained by tiny figures (p. 115), Henry Pichette's neck erupts with spikes and thorns (p. 124) and in a self-portrait completed four months before his death, faces appear to erupt everywhere from a blurry stem-like body and torturously erect fingers, all of which dissolve into scratched lines of graphite (p. 128).

We might call this experimentation with a remaking or reclamation of self centred on the body 'Mômo thought'. One of its central notions is 'organless living'. Since his 1920s' work, Artaud associated the general idea of 'function' with the term 'organ'. An organ is a point of articulation which sets up an automatic normative relation between two elements, whether it be the use of adjectives in grammar, the script in theatrical production or the liver in the human body. In all cases the organ forecloses on the possibility of the relation being rendered differently; it is a barrier set against the will:

> The time when man was a tree without organs or function, but possessed of will, and a tree of will which walks will return. It has been, and it will return. For the great lie has been to make man an organism, ingestion, assimilation, incubation, excretion, thus creating a whole order of hidden functions which are outside of the realm of deliberative will. (Artaud, 1988d, p. 515)

As with so much else in Artaud's work, the bizarre nature of this claim may blind us to what is important here. If consciousness and embodiment are co-extensive, if subjectivity is physically occasioned by the relations our body enters into with other bodies (including human-bodies, word-bodies, sound-bodies, institution-bodies), then we have to ask ourselves which sets of relations we are prepared to take as givens, as having already been decided and settled upon, and which are open to modification or recreation. An organ is in effect a materialisation of a prior judgement. It is against this central idea of 'assumed order', or judgement-in-advance, that Artaud railed throughout his entire life. There can be no possibility of change, of difference, revolution even, if we are prepared to simply cede some aspect of existence as a done deal, as outside of deliberation. And yet the giving up of the ontological security that comes with this rejection of assumed order exacts a terrible price: 'It is this contradiction between my inner facility and my exterior difficulty which creates the torments of which I am dying' (Artaud, 1988e, p. 93).

In Artaud's infamous banned radio performance, *To have done with the judgement of God*, the ends of Mômo thought are outlined. The piece closes with the much discussed scene of humanity placed on an autopsy table where the 'sickness' of God is removed. As Deleuze (1998a) makes clear, 'God' is here cipher for the ultimate guarantee of reason in and by itself, the projection of transcendent values which will secure perpetual judgement. It is the constant withdrawing, or rather deferment of the basis on which judgement is made that constitutes God's will. By having reason emanate from elsewhere, life is turned into a perpetual waiting for ultimate judgement by God, a deferment and debt without end which will make up the business of living. But Artaud demands a reversal of terms. Rather than accept life as that which is judged by God, life will be turned inside out as the process of putting God, putting reason itself on trial. And to the extent that such a trial will involve dragging the traces of reason from our own bodies themselves, it will become a forensic autopsy. Hence the significance of the following lines:

> Man is sick because he is badly constructed. We must decide to strip him in order to scratch out this animalcule which makes him itch to death, god, and with god his organs. For tie me down if you want to, but there is nothing more useless than an organ. When you have given him a body without organs, then you will have delivered him from all his automatisms and restored him to his true liberty. Then you will teach him again to dance inside out as in the delirium of the dance halls and that inside out will be his true side out. (Artaud, 1995d, p. 307)

To 'have done with judgement' it is necessary to have done with God, with the notion of a prior organisation that already determines the vitality of human life. Rooting out this organisation, wresting 'life' from the 'badly constructed' designs which force us to embody a prior judgement in our very embodiment, is essential to achieving 'true liberty'. As Deleuze puts it, 'judgement implies a veritable organization of the bodies through which it acts: organs are both judges and judged, and the judgement of God is nothing but the power to organize to infinity' (1998a, p. 130). The vitality of life ripped away from the apparent strictures of given designs, and treated as a site for the play of affects and intensities – 'a nonorganic vitality' as Deleuze puts it (p. 131). Living without judgement, beyond power, is the final object of 'cruelty', through the making over of life as 'theatre' ('the delirium of the dance halls'). It may well be that here, as elsewhere, this confrontation is yet another grandiose failure on Artaud's part – perhaps the attempt to live without judgement can only ever end in the 'mis-trial' of reason – but in Artaud's layered descriptions of experimentation, affect, doubling and the judging of judgement, what it means to see consciousness and the body as subject to self-creation is joyously stated:

> Who am I? Where do I come from? I am Antonin Artaud and if I say it as I know how to say it immediately you will see my present body fly into pieces and under ten thousand notorious aspects a new body will be assembled in which you will never again be able to forget me. (Artaud, 1995e, p. 323)

Psychological Theatre, Once More

We began this chapter by describing a film which on first viewing appeared to have certain Surrealist qualities. However, it rapidly became apparent that the film was no free play of images, no experiment with thought and emotion. It was dominated by an explicit notion of social order which it sought to affirm and naturalise. The Hamlin et al. (2007) study is then rather like the traditional notion of theatre, as Artaud describes it. It is structured in advance by a clear script, a set of assumptions about the normative which are dramatised for purely digestive reasons. Hamlin et al. help us to feel better about ourselves by reassuring us that whilst the world may often feel hostile and torn asunder by conflict we humans come already formed as pro-social beings oriented towards cooperation.

This sort of experiment is then not just theatrical; it belongs to a certain kind of theatre, the morality play. Hamlin et al. claim that what they are offering is evidence for the innate basis of a capacity that can serve as 'the foundation for a developing system of moral cognition' (2007, p. 558). In effect, they are arguing for an innate organ of moral ordering. They dramatise the origins of what they take to be moral thought in general. In so doing they seek to inflate their very narrow and particular version of morality and their highly local assumptions about social order into a universal model. This is not just flawed logic, it is also bad theatre. And it seems to us that if theatre wants nothing more to do with psychology, then equally psychology ought to have nothing more to do with this particular kind of theatre.

Developmental psychology of this sort envisages not a *body-without-organs*, but a set of *organs without a body* (see Deleuze & Guattari, 1988; Zizek, 2003). It wishes to align itself and celebrate a veritable judgement of God, a grand principle of order given in advance, whether that be an innate capacity for social evaluation or whatever else. A tradition of anti-developmental thought within the discipline has long detailed its objections to such thought and the impoverished view of both children and adults that it offers (see Stainton Rogers & Stainton Rogers, 1992; Morss, 1995; Bradley, 2005).

But perhaps there is another way. Just as Artaud saw a new kind of theatre emerging from an intensification and transformation of certain practices in the existing theatrical traditions, so too we might imagine a kind of 'script-less' performative version of the experimental theatre of developmental psychology. What if Hamlin et al. had not posited any hypotheses in advance? We can certainly read their data in all manner of different ways, see all kinds of possibilities in how their tiny participants reacted. And what if the participants and props in such experiments were permitted a more active role in defining the forms of normativity at play? Imagine the children tormented in Albert Bandura's 'Bobo doll' studies simply refusing to play along with the experiment ('I didn't want those toys anyway. They're rubbish. And so are you nappyhead'). John Bowlby's '44 teenage thieves' arriving at his home late at night to raise the issue of their delinquency. Jean Piaget's plaster mountains ground underfoot, the only sound being children laughing, laughing .....

SIX

Spinoza and Affect

In *Descartes' error*, the neurologist Antonio Damasio recounts an episode involving one of his patients:

Not too long ago, one of our patients with ventromedial prefrontal damage was visiting the laboratory on a cold winter day. Freezing rain had fallen, the roads were icy, and the driving had been hazardous. I had been concerned with the situation and I asked the patient, who had been driving himself about the ride ... His answer was prompt and dispassionate: it had been fine, no different from the usual, except that it had called for some attention to the proper procedures for driving on ice. The patient then went on to ... describe how he had seen cars and trucks skidding off the roadway ... a woman driving ahead of him who has entered a patch of ice, skidded and, and rather than gently pulling away from the tailspin, had panicked, hit the brakes and gone zooming into a ditch. One instant later, apparently unperturbed by this hair-raising scene, my patient crossed the ice patch and drove calmly and surely ahead ... The scene now changes to the following day. I was discussing with the same patient when his next visit to the laboratory should take place. I suggested two alternative dates, both in the coming month and just a few days apart from each other. The patient pulled out his appointment book and began consulting his calendar. The behaviour that ensued, which was witnessed by several investigators, was remarkable. For the better part of half-hour, the patient enumerated reasons for and against each of the two dates: previous engagements, proximity to other engagements, possible meteorological conditions, virtually anything that one could reasonably think about concerning a simple date. Just as calmly as he had driven over the ice, and recounted that episode, he was now walking us through a tiresome cost-benefit analysis, an endless and fruitless comparison of options and possible consequences. It took enormous discipline to listen to all this without pounding on the table and telling him to stop, but we finally did tell him, quietly, that he should come on the second of the alternative dates. His response equally calm and prompt. He simply said 'That's fine'. Back the appointment book went into his pocket, and he was off. (Damasio, 2006, pp.193–194)

It is the contrast between the assured, rapid responses the patient makes whilst driving and the laborious and ultimately pointless way he attempts to choose between the two appointment dates which fascinates Damasio. Both events involve decision-making processes (crossing the ice instead of braking, choosing one or other date). According to Damasio, the precise form of neural damage suffered by this patient compromised his ability to make decisions in a unique way. Rather than being unable to make decisions at all, the patient lacks the automatic ability to limit and circumscribe the process. He is unable to immediately recognise that labouring over the choice between the two dates is 'useless and indulgent' (p. 194). By contrast, he is able to calmly make decisions under terrifying conditions that would lead most people (including the unfortunate fellow driver) to respond in a panicked and irrational fashion. The moral of the story, for Damasio, is that the ability to make automatic rather than conscious decisions is usually highly beneficial, except under these very special circumstances.

Damasio tells the story to illustrate his 'somatic marker hypothesis'. A somatic marker is a pattern of feelings which intervene in cognitive processes associated with decision making. These feelings 'stamp' or 'mark' the possible outcomes of various courses of action, thereby according them a positive or negative valence. They allow for a sort of pre-selection or reduction of the number of options before they are subjected to conscious, rational processing. Damasio proposes that somatic markers depend upon basic 'innate regulatory dispositions, posed to ensure the survival of the organism' (p. 179). However, their content and association with mental representations is not in itself a biological given. This is acquired through experience throughout the lifespan (although childhood and adolescence is seen as a critical period), in the context of local cultural conventions and moral codes. This gives somatic markers the special quality of being parasitic on both biology and the social. Cromby (2004) demonstrates that this status accorded to somatic markers makes Damasio's work highly compatible with a constructionist form of psychology.

But let us return to the story for a moment. As befits a work of popular science, *Descartes' error* contains many such stories and anecdotes. These are not meant as primary evidence for Damasio's proposals, they are merely interesting illustrations. The story dramatises or stages the neuroscience. In this sense it has something in common with the kind of empirical practice we considered in the last chapter. In the same way that Hamlin et al.'s (2007) video frames and communicates their experiment in a way that distracts attention from the precise claims the work itself is making, so Damasio's stories may potentially blind us to the wider import of his research. Damasio seeks nothing less than a dethroning of rationality. He wants to treat emotions and feelings as the bio-social matrix out of which the experience of self is forged. Reason and social order are not a priori conditions, out of which our particular experiences are constituted, but rather effects or expressions arising from the evolution of biosociality: 'The immune system, the hypothalamus, the ventromedial frontal cortices, and the Bill of Rights have the same root cause' (p. 262).

In the last chapter we saw how Artaud ultimately sought to make judgement an embodied matter, where we must question assumed order even at the level of the organic itself. Whilst Damasio is certainly no Artaud, there is some relationship between Damasio's neurological refiguring of experience and Mômo thought. The question we will explore in this chapter is with the turn to emotions of which Damasio is one example, and the extent to which it can be grasped as a reflexive foundation for the psychological.

The Affective Turn

There is currently much talk of an 'affective turn' within the social sciences (e.g. Massumi, 2002; Sedgwick, 2003; Clough, 2007), and there has been a striking increase of interest in affect and the emotions across the full range of the social sciences. This turn to affect follows on from, and in some senses deepens, the 'textual turn' that, as we have discussed, characterised much activity in the social sciences and humanities in the last few decades of the twentieth century. A rethinking of 'the emotions' was a key ingredient of the textual turn. Arguments were repeatedly put forward for the symbolically mediated, discursively organised and socially constructed nature of emotional experiences and expressions that had, or so it was argued, previously been approached as natural mechanisms (Averill, 1980; Harré & Parrott, 1996).

For many, the affective turn involves drawing a clear distinction between affect and emotion (cf. Greco & Stenner, 2008, p. 10). For example, Barry Richards stressed the importance of this distinction at a recent conference. He suggested that 'affect' refers to deep and often unconscious organismic processes, whilst emotion is a more superficial and conscious affair. This kind of argument is part of a resurgence of interest in psychoanalytic thinking, within which the concept of affect has a long pedigree (Green, 1977; Redding, 1999; Matthis, 2000). On the basis of his drive theory (and its pleasure/displeasure polarity), Freud tended to define feelings and emotions as psychic expressions of an underlying physiologically grounded affective matrix. A re-engagement with psychoanalytical theory is thus one clear pathway into the affective turn (see also Hollway & Jefferson 2000; Rustin 2002; Froggett, 2002).

Another pathway stems from Deleuzian post-structuralism. Although Deleuze himself did not make a clear-cut distinction between affect and emotion, his followers have tended to. Thrift (2008), for instance, distinguishes his preferred concept of affect from what he refers to as the 'touchy feely' territory of 'emotion' (cf. Thien, 2005 for a critique). Likewise, McCormack contrasts the limitations of 'emotion' with the 'creative potential of affect'. Emotion is associated with the individual person and with a certain fixity within regimes of discursive meaning, whilst affect is associated with an 'unqualified intensity' that is 'never reducible to the personal quality of emotion' (2003, p. 500). Both cite the influence of Brian Massumi who defines affect as 'unqualified intensity' and as a 'nonconscious, never-to-be-conscious autonomic remainder' whilst stressing that affect and emotion follow 'different logics and pertain to different orders' (1996, p. 221). Those who equate affect with emotion are thus sharply criticised (1996, p. 237), since the latter concerns a 'subjective content' characterised by 'qualified intensity'. To give a final example, in Hardt and Negri's (2004) version of Deleuzian philosophy 'emotions ... are a form of mental phenomena, [whilst] affects refer equally to body and mind. In fact, affects, such as joy and sadness, reveal the present state of life in the entire organism, expressing a certain state of the body along with a certain mode of thinking' (p. 108).

There are some bigger issues in the background of these debates, and these issues relate directly to the bifurcated conception of nature that we described in Chapter 2. Both the textual turn and the affective turn constitute challenges to the notion of a rational and unitary conception of the human subject that has dominated the modern period (Henriques, Hollway, Urwin, Venn & Walkerdine, 1984). This is the self-contained 'cogito' that was split off from the rest of the mechanistic material world placed at its disposal. This cogito was closely related to the subject of the new alignments of law and politics that constituted the modern era of the 'sovereign' nation state (Stenner, 2004). According to Venn (1984), it was this conception of the subject that was implicitly taken up by modern psychology and thus 'naturalised'. There is more to this story, however. Depending upon which side of the bifurcated divide is concentrated on, the subject could either be presented as a part of nature, and hence as an object absolutely determined by material causal laws, or as a pre-given, completely free rational agent. Depending upon which factor is at play, different critiques appear necessary. Sometimes it appears necessary to challenge mechanistic determinism for its reductionism and for its neglect of the symbolic and its denial of agency (as has tended to occur with the textual turn), and sometimes it appears necessary to challenge the notion of a free and self-contained rational decision maker for its occultism and for its denial of structural forces, unconscious motives and irrational desires (as has tended to occur with the affective turn). It is no surprise, therefore, that psychology has been riven by debates concerning 'free will' and 'determinism' and, in particular, concerning the role of the affects and emotions in these matters.

We will deal in this chapter with the seventeenth-century philosophy of Spinoza because it is of direct relevance both to the psychodynamic and to the Deleuzian turns to affect. Spinoza, for example, has been dubbed 'the philosopher of psychoanalysis' (Neu, 1977, p. 148), and direct comparisons have long been made between Freud's psychology and Spinoza's philosophy (Rathbun, 1934; Hampshire, 1988). On the other hand, Deleuze characterises his own philosophy as 'Spinozist' and has dedicated two books to this topic (Deleuze, 1988a; 1992). Spinoza's thought thus constitutes a certain 'common ground' between these two strands of influence. Finding notions in common is important, given that relations between these two camps, where they exist, are typically hostile (see the rather rough treatment meted out to psychoanalysis – and to Melanie Klein in particular – in Deleuze and Guattari's *Anti-Oedipus* [1983], for instance).

Spinoza is also relevant to the bigger story concerning the modern conception of the subject and the articulation of a more viable alternative. Like Leibniz, Spinoza offered an immediate critical response and alternative to the Cartesian proposal of a strictly bifurcated nature. Already in the seventeenth century, much criticism was voiced of the Cartesian tendency to strip nature of creative force and power and to concentrate it all in the figure of a super-natural self-contained cogito (which in turn refers to a transcendent God). This critique was not just negative but also involved the articulation of a new form of naturalism: a completely different conception of a nature that fully includes the human subject and that does not rely upon occult entities in order to explain its emergence, its powers and its creativity. Affect is central to this Spinozist alternative.

As well as placing the affects at centre stage, Spinoza is relevant to our rethinking of the foundations of psychology because: a) he offers a unified conception of nature that problematises distinctions such as natural/unnatural, nature/technology and nature/society; b) through his distinction between *Natura Naturans* (nature involved in infinite active self-creation, or 'naturing' nature) and *Natura Naturata* (nature as finished product, or 'natured' nature), he constructs a vision of nature in which nature is a creative force that consti-tutes its own foundation. It is thus an early version of what we have called 'critically reflexive' or 'creative' foundationalism; and c) through his emphasis on the *felt relations of affecting and being affected*, notions of *value* and *ethics* are brought to the foreground as an irreducible aspect of nature in which the key ethical issue is the practical question of *becoming active*. Affects thus relate to *emergent orderings of the relational field made up in the encounter between mani-fold finite beings*.

In the remainder of this chapter we will offer an exegesis of Spinoza's account of the affects that we will then use to illustrate some of the limitations of Damasio's approach.

Spinoza's Critique of Descartes

Compared to Descartes who, for the most part, set up pure (and that means *disembodied*) thinking as the essence of the human being and envisioned the felt body as 'confusing' this purity, Spinoza effectively affirmed that we are never *not* embodied and that one cannot conceive knowledge without affect. We do not know 'the world' but rather the *way in which the world affects us*. 'We' – and that means our bodies – mediate our relation to the world. In the *Ethics* of 1677, Spinoza sought to explicitly challenge the Cartesian model of the body-as-machine animated by the will of an immaterial mind or soul. Recourse to such 'mystic' explanations was for Spinoza a sign of inadequate understanding of the actual workings of the human body and of its place in broader nature:

> Whence it follows that when men say that this or that action arises from the mind which has power over the body, they know not what they say, or confess with specious words that they are ignorant of the cause of said action, and have no wonderment at it. (E. III. prop. 2, note)[1]

The problem of mind–body interaction, as formulated by Descartes, involves the strict separation of the two elements of being, and the exclusion of the former from the concept of nature. This reflects Descartes' commitment to the idea of two radically different substances: *extension* (the physical field of objects positioned in a geometric space that can be the subject matter of the scientific enquiry of natural philosophy) and *thought* (that property which distinguishes conscious beings from objects). Thought, as displayed by the human subject qua 'thinking thing', is precisely that which is not object (not an extended substance). Likewise, extension is that which thought is essentially detached from, but can come to know 'clearly and distinctly', and thus render controllable, through mathematics for instance. This distinction also involves political and ethical questions of power and governance. For Descartes, the subject is active, the object is passive, hence our minds are (or *should* be) active, whilst our bodies are passive. Personal being is thenceforth identified with an active thinking mind, which must exercise its control over a passive body that it happens to own (but which by no means defines it). In short, all creative and self-generating properties are allocated to thought, leaving extension a realm of barren and dependent passivity. For Descartes, bodies are nothing but machines.

Now the same relation of domination and ownership applies to emotions or, more accurately, *passions* in Descartes' philosophy. Passions of the soul are depicted as entirely passive (they are passive perceptions of the active desires of the will), and thus the mind should strive to gain absolute dominion over them. The mind is authorised to exercise this absolute control over the body and emotions because, being active, it depends upon nothing but itself, whereas the body's 'activity' (strictly we should say 'movement') depends either, as with the passions, upon the mind, or upon some physical proximate cause (an encounter with another passive body).

Once body and soul are cleaved apart in this Cartesian fashion, however, the question arises as to precisely how it is that the mind may become connected to the body such that control may be exercised. That is to say, we are presented with two quite separate notions of causality. On the one hand, a familiar causality in which one might demonstrate the effect that one physical entity might have upon another physical entity (as when the cue ball strikes the black ball in a game of snooker). On the other hand, we have an unfamiliar form of 'master' causality in which a nonphysical thinking substance supposedly effects a demonstrable change in an extended substance. The first process takes place 'within' entities of a single substance (within modes of extension), whilst the second must take place 'across' entities belonging to supposedly different substances (from thought to extension). In other words, once thought is cast as a 'master cause' of extension, then the question arises as to how exactly that process of causation takes place. Spinoza attacks Descartes for his inability to adequately conceive of what establishes a bridge between and holds together the two supposedly separate substances:

> Truly I should like him [Descartes] to explain this union through its proximate cause. But he conceived the mind so distinct from the body that he could not assign a particular cause for this union, nor for the mind itself, but he had perforce to recur to the cause of the whole universe, that is, to God. (E. V. preface)

Descartes, then, is criticised by Spinoza because, through excluding thought from the concept of nature, he is only able to reformulate the subject through the transcendental power of God. Furthermore, the same relationship of control and ownership that obtains between the two substances of thought and extension obtains for Descartes between God and World. Just as the mind governs the body from a position of radical externality, so a transcendent God has in eminence this power of governance to oversee the world of nature that He created.

Spinoza's alternative: one substance, two attributes, many modes

Spinoza's alternative conceptualisation involves completely dispensing with the chain of eminent relations to posit an *immanentist* conception of a single substance that composes the universe, known as either God or Nature (E. IV. preface). Nature, for Spinoza, is thus fundamentally a *unity* and any natural principles must apply throughout nature. There are not two separate 'substances' – thought and extension – but a single substance. This rethinking of 'foundations' does not mean, however, that Spinoza simply fails to make the rather obvious distinction between 'thought' and 'extension' or between 'mind' and 'body' that had preoccupied Descartes, or that he simply does away with the ethical idea of a dimension from passivity to activity. On the contrary, the neo-Cartesian separation between extension and thought that Spinoza subsequently performs is then conceived as occurring between different *attributes* of the singular substance. Thought is one 'attribute' of the singular substance, whilst extension is another. Individual minds and bodies are considered in turn as finite 'modes' of these attributes, with mind being a mode of thought and body a mode of extension. If the human body, for example, is a mode of extension more generally, then this means that, first of all, a human body is part of and continuous with the broader universe (considered as extensive).

This concern for the body as continuous with the rest of nature fits well with Artaud's Mômo thought. Similarly, when Whitehead (1938/1966, p. 28) defines the human body as 'that region of the world which is the primary field of human expression' he is being rigorously Spinozist. A 'region' of extension is a definite 'mode' of extension capable of its own particular forms of modification as it encounters other modes. In a comparable way, a particular thought, feeling, memory or perception that might constitute a given person's mind at a given moment in time is a particular and finite 'mode' of the attribute of thought (or, as we expressed it in Chapter 3, a particular *form* in the *medium* of 'mind'). The difference between mind and body is thus clearly recognised by Spinoza – but, importantly, they are ultimately considered as *expressions* of a fundamental unity of composition:

> The mind and body are one and the same thing, which is conceived now under the attribute of thought, now under the attribute of extension. Whence it comes about that the order of the concatenation of things is one, or, nature is conceived now under this, now under that attribute, and consequently that the order of actions and passions of our body is simultaneous in nature with the order of actions and passions of our mind. (E. III. prop. 2, note)

Here the Cartesian hierarchy of relations (in which mind should govern body) is systematically dismantled and replaced with a system where 'the order and concatenation of things is one'. Personal being is thereby revealed as both mind and body, seen 'now under this' attribute and then 'now under that attribute'. Spinoza then goes on to make the assertion that the 'object of the idea constituting the human mind is the body, and furthermore the actually existing body' (E. II. prop. 13, proof). This position draws upon the fact that our personal experiences, perceptions, feelings and sensations depend entirely upon the physiological functioning of our personal bodies (we see with our eyes, for instance, and with a little help from our visual cortex). The proposition that the body is the object of the mind has two major effects. First, it means that although thought (as an attribute) is infinite, mind (as a mode of that attribute) is located firmly in duration by virtue of its constitution around the finite 'object of the body'. Mind thus approximates to a *particular* lived time and space. Second, Spinoza may further demonstrate that:

> The human mind has no knowledge of the human body, nor does it know it to exist, save through ideas of modifications by which the body is affected. (E. II. prop. 19)

This crucial proposition couples movements in ideas to modifications in the body (by way of 'ideas of modifications'), or, to put it more plainly, knowing (as a mode of thought) proceeds in parallel fashion to the body's physical engagements in unfolding scenes of encounters. As we will discuss later, this is the relational basis upon which Spinoza constructs an intimate relationship between affects and knowing (since an emotion [*affectus*], considered as a mode of thought, is the idea of a modification of the body). What is more, within the 'parallelism' adopted by the *Ethics*, activity and passivity cease to be uniquely identified with particular attributes, contra the Cartesian formulation. They become instead potential and actual properties of both attributes, since both attributes are 'expressions' of the underlying unity of these unfolding scenes of activity, encounter and transformation. A 'body' whose powers decrease as a function of an encounter is, when conceived under the attribute of thought, simultaneously a 'mind' with resultant diminished powers. The equal standing of each attribute in turn as *expressions* means in addition that they are no longer successively weaker parties in a relationship of control or ownership. Indeed, the very notion of a relationship between them is undermined by the assertion of their unity.

These moves may be characterised in several ways. They serve, initially, to remove the need to imagine some kind of 'holding power' or a mechanical point of connection between body and mind, there being no absolute difference in the substantial composition of the attributes. There is simply an ordering of things expressed in two registers. Beyond this, Spinoza may be read as performing an emancipatory act of awarding the body its full and proper standing in the definition of personal being that is not unlike that in critical psychological theory (e.g. Harré, 1991; Stam, 1997; Brown, 2001). But it is important to recognise that the 'levelling' of the attributes is ultimately warranted as the exercise of reason. What offends reason, for Spinoza, is the hitherto ignorance of the actual nature of the body displayed in conceiving of it as a simple vehicle for the mind. Such a conception fails to question what powers and capacities may be immanent to the body qua body:

> For no one has thus far determined the power of the body, that is, no one has yet been taught by experience what the body can do merely by the laws of nature, in so far as nature is considered merely as corporeal and what it cannot do, save when determined by the mind. For no one has acquired such accurate knowledge of the construction of the human body, as to be able to explain all its functions; nor need I omit to mention the many things observed in brutes, which far surpass human sagacity, and the many things which sleep-walkers do, which they would not dare to do when awake: this is sufficient to show that the body itself, merely from the laws of its own nature alone, can do many things, at which the mind marvels. (E. III. prop. 2, note)

Spinoza and Affect | **117**

Spinoza thus takes aim at the central Cartesian notion that acts of will depend on nothing but will itself (the proof of mind-as-active). Neither determination for action nor 'decisions of the mind' are, for Spinoza, equivalent to effects produced by the will of the 'thinking thing'. They are instead related to a wider series of determinations (of which 'appetites' and 'dispositions' are the most proximal) that have their place in the ongoing encounters between bodies and between ideas in which the human individual is perpetually engaged. Now inasmuch as the power of thought or action is taken to define the individual, these powers emerge from a process of sustained engagement with the world. Here Spinoza is entirely consistent with the notion of a single substance.

The Subject of Spinozism

Although many of his most illuminating illustrations draw upon human examples it is important to remember that, for Spinoza, the human being is but one of an infinity of existing *modes* or complications of the single substance. If this single substance with its infinite modes and attributes taken in its entirety is called Nature or God, then Nature/God is the only entity that has the 'absolute' freedom and independence that Descartes attributes to thought, as Nature/God alone is *causa sui* or cause-of-itself (being infinite, there is logically nothing outside God upon which God might depend). All other things have Nature/God as their formal cause because they are in, or of, Nature/God. However, since any given mode is necessarily finite (and hence dependent), it is also necessarily affected and variously determined, that is, subject to modification by its encounters with other finite modes. A given mode can never be absolutely free in the sense of *causa sui*; it is always subject to external determination.

Spinoza, then, makes a distinction between the formal cause (Nature/God) and the proximal cause of a modification (an encounter with another finite thing). The proximate cause of a finite thing is always another finite thing rather than an omnipotent intervention or a mysterious act of will. There is no room for transcendental explanations in Spinozism, whether these are called the 'will of God' or, in the present context, any of the grand explanandum of the social sciences – 'class', 'culture', 'history' or 'biology'. Spinoza evokes Nature/God as formal cause not as an end in itself, but rather in order to establish the immanence of a single substance and thence to proceed rapidly to more proximate causes (Deleuze, 1992). Each finite thing or mode is then understood as an unfolding of substance in a certain determinate manner. This manner is circumscribed by what Spinoza calls a thing's *essence*:

> From the given essence of a thing certain things necessarily follow, nor can things do anything else than that which follows necessarily from their determinate nature. Wherefore the power or endeavour of anything by which it does, or endeavours to do, anything, either alone or with others, that is, the power or endeavour by which it endeavours to persist in its own being, is nothing else than the given or actual essence of that given thing. (E. lii. prop. 7, proof)

An essence is, therefore, both the effort to maintain form and the potential that a thing has so to do. Spinoza defines essence as power in a double sense and terms this *conatus*: the endeavour to persist in being. In keeping with his system, *conatus* can be seen under both attributes:

> This endeavour, when it has reference to the mind alone, is called will (*voluntas*); but when it refers simultaneously to the mind and body, it is called appetite (*appetitus*), which therefore is nothing else than the essence of man, from the nature of which all things which help in his preservation necessarily follow; and therefore man is determined for acting in this way. Now between appetite and desire (*cupiditas*) there is no difference but this, that desire usually has reference to men in so far as they are conscious of their appetite; and therefore it may be defined as appetite with consciousness thereof. (E. III. prop. 9, note)

Of note here is the manner in which Spinoza tightly associates will with *conatus* (the 'endeavour to persist in being'). Will is no longer the judge presiding over sensory data in the court of the Cartesian cogito (only God or Nature as *causa sui* possesses 'free will'). With Spinoza there is a sense in which ideas are in themselves forms of judgement (Gilbert, 1991). If an idea is part of mind then it is already affirmed to some degree. Now, leaving aside for now the question of truth and falsity, Spinoza places this affirmation in the context of mind and body as manifolds. Human physical being consists of a 'complex body' made up by the alliance of many simple bodies. In parallel fashion, mind, as idea of the body, consists of the ideas of all these simple bodies, as well as the modifications that may befall them. Thus what is 'affirmed' in an idea is some actual modification, which has its effect upon the power of the individual to persist in being. Will is therefore *conatus* viewed with 'reference to the mind alone.'

Modifications occur in encounters between the individual and other finite things (themselves manifold). As such, the precise kind of modification experienced depends upon the exact nature of relations that are possible between two individuals qua complex bodies. Spinoza describes the outcome of encounters in terms of emotion or *affect*:

> By EMOTION (*affectus*) I understand the modifications of the body by which the power of action of the body is increased or diminished, aided or restrained, and at the same time the idea of these modifications. (E. III. def. 3)

Affect, as an emergent property of the encounter, takes the form of either an increase or diminishment of the finite individual's power to act. This is described in the basic distinction between affects of 'joy' or 'euphoria' (*laelitiae*) that increase power, or those of 'sorrow' or 'dysphoria' (*tristitiae*) that decrease power. What takes place as an affect (an emotion) is an ordering of the relations between bodies and between ideas that shows forth as a decision or a determination for action:

For each one manages everything according to his emotion, and thus those who are assailed by conflicting emotions know not what they want: those who are assailed by none are easily driven to one or the other. Now all these things clearly show that the decision of the mind, and the appetite and the determination of the body, are simultaneous in nature, or rather one and the same thing, which when considered under the attribute of thought and explained through the same we call a decision (*decretum*), and when considered under the attribute of extension and deduced from the laws of motion and rest we call a determination (*determinatio*). (E. III. prop. 2, note)

Although affect seems here to be the prior term ('for each one manages according to his [*sic*] emotion'), Spinoza avoids what we moderns would understand as the opposition of emotion and cognition, by insisting that affects are emergent orderings of the relational field made up in the encounter between manifold finite beings. His project is thus perhaps closer to those contemporary explorations of the production of order from disorder in physical and social worlds (Cooper, 1990; Hetherington & Munro, 1997; Law, 2002; Massumi, 2002; Latour, 2005). Following this line, we will proceed to explicate Spinoza's system of affects as processes of ordering, and describe how this transforms psychological understanding of specifically human emotions.

What is an Encounter?

By describing affect as all modifications of finite things, which result in increases or decreases of the potential to act, Spinoza dislodges the emotions from the realm of responses and situations and ties them firmly to action and encounters. Affects occur between finite things on the basis of their mutual relations, in the context of an infinitely productive Nature. This placing of emotions in the broadest possible context carries with it the obligation to consider the intersection of multiple chains of causation. Encounters and the modifications in which they result are complex events, complex productions of order. Here Spinoza's 'geometric method' serves as a tool to 'diagram' each encounter, demonstrating precisely which relations are at issue and the orderings of the bodies and ideas they call forth. The first step in analysing encounters is to maintain the parallelism of body and mind. This involves, for Spinoza, a separate explication of how affects order relations between bodies and between ideas. Proximate causes are sought *within* each attribute. The body cannot act as the cause of changing order within ideas, nor do ideas directly bring about modifications in bodies.

With respect to the attribute of extension, for example, one could trace causal connections between, for example, neurotransmitters from the presynaptic membrane of one neuron to the postsynaptic membrane of another, or one could trace the process by which a chemical molecule in the bloodstream activates neural sensors in, say, the hypothalamus. *Within* a given body one can follow nerve fibres from the nervous system to the musculature of the face and show the causal connection between brain activity and facial expression, and vice versa.

One can cut these links and show that the musculature can no longer be affected via this route. Symmetrically, under the attribute of thought it is perfectly possible to trace the connectivity between, say, the experience of reading a love letter which might set in motion a whole train of thoughts and feelings that flow one into another: Can it be true? If the sender of the letter is serious, what next? What shall I say at our next meeting? And so on. We might also *perceive* that the encounter makes our pulse race. In this case, however, the effects of our rapidly beating heart become an element of our 'mind' (it is conscious *experience*). This experience might in turn lead us to think that we, too, are in love, leading to further thoughts and feelings that continue the unfurling stream. Spinoza evocatively refers to this self-referential *concatenation* of mind as a 'spiritual automaton'. Thus the proximate cause of a finite thought is another thought and the proximate cause of a finite mode of extension is another extended mode. Our circulatory system *as such*, however – i.e. as a biological mode of the attribute of extension – cannot enter into the attribute of thought, just as a thought or a memory or a feeling cannot enter into, for example, the circulation of the blood. The body cannot act as the proximate cause within the order of ideas and ideas cannot directly bring about modifications in bodies. Both systems, however, are subject to modification through ongoing encounters.

What is sought is the dual expression of the encounter as it presents under each attribute. Spinoza then proceeds by examining the registering of an image or an impression of something by the body (that is ordering under extension). Images are understood here as literal intrusions by external causes upon the body of the individual:

> [T]he images of things ... are the very modifications or modes by which the human body is affected by external causes and disposed for doing this or that. (E. III. prop. 32, note)

Images result in modifications whereby the body becomes disposed for action in a particular way. For this to occur it is not even necessary for the other who brings about the image to be present. Images of absent persons may, for example, be at the root of affects of love or hate. Indeed, it is sufficient merely to perceive some evil occurring to the image of the absent loved one to then experience sorrow or despair.

What is also important in this process is the link made by Spinoza between *being affected* (through the image) and the *capacity to affect* (as the result of modifications). It is this dual aspect of affection that links ordering to power. Affects of dysphoria determine the person in such a way that their abilities are diminished. This occurs in encounters between bodies that do not agree in some way, such as when one body adversely affects, dominates or even, in extreme cases, destroys another by *decomposing* the relations through which it is constituted. Opposed to this are affects of euphoria which are marked by an increase in power when 'agreeable' bodies unite into a new form of composition that extends the abilities to act of one or both. What matters, then, is how bodies (as manifolds) come together in the encounter to compose either harmonious or disharmonious relations:

> The power of any particular thing, and consequently the power of man, by which he exists and works, is determined only by another particular thing whose nature must be understood through the same attribute, through which human nature is conceived. Therefore our power of acting, in whatever way it may be conceived, can be determined, and consequently aided or hindered, by the power of some other particular thing which has something in common with us. (E. IV. prop. 29, proof)

The phrase 'something in common with us' or 'common notions' plays a pivotal role in Spinoza's ethical system. Suffice it to say here that there is a great deal in nature that is 'disagreeable' to the human, and thus the source of dysphoria or worse. Such things are obviously to be avoided, and it is one of the central propositions in Spinoza's political theory that the role of the state is to provide the conditions under which disagreeable encounters and accompanying affects of dysphoria may be minimized (see Hardt & Negri, 2000; 2004 for recent developments of a Spinozist political theory).

Spinoza then moves on to consider the *idea of images*, or the finite aspects of thought. Seen in terms of this other attribute, the encounter shows forth as a series of modifications arising from the relations between ideas, some of which currently constitute the mind (as idea of the body, divisible into ideas of the simple bodies constituting the manifold complex body), others of which are the ideas of external bodies (themselves manifold). For Spinoza, the passage to greater or diminished abilities in euphoria or dysphoria is paralleled by a movement toward 'adequacy' or 'inadequacy' with regard to ideas. An 'inadequate' series of ideas (the effect of a disagreeable encounter) is one that does not contain *the cause of the effect*. In other words, it is a failure to have the 'idea of the external body' as 'clearly and distinctly' part of mind. Whether adequate or not, the resultant ordering of ideas acts as the ideational form of the affect:

> [T]his idea, which constitutes the form (*forma*) of the emotion, must indicate or express the constitution of the body, or some part of it, which constitution the body or that part possesses by reason of the fact that its power of acting, or existing is increased or diminished, aided or hindered. (E. III. gen. def.)

It is important to consider exactly what this 'form' means. Spinoza's parallelism means that, in effect, bodies cannot be the cause of ideas, nor can the ideational be reduced to, made to correspond with, or be explained by the physical. The demand to explicate ideas solely in terms of their standing as a finite mode of the attribute of thought lends no purchase to a correspondence theory of truth (Wilson, 1996). Equally there is no support for the view of ideas within affects as the simple mental registration of physical events.

On Deleuze's interpretation, ideas receive their form from a relation to a wider ordering, in other words a 'system' or 'series' within which individual ideas gain recognisable standing as components or elements. Here Spinoza is read as offering a kind of semiotics. This system or series must logically surpass any individual 'psychological consciousness', much as communication goes beyond the personal being of any particular speaker (see Chapter 4). This interpretation is reinforced by considering that what is at stake in the 'material' of an idea is the expression of a cause (the idea of the external body), which is in turn related to God or Nature as *the formal cause of any effect*. Hence what is explicated is a whole chain or series of ideas, all of which refer to and have their sole standing in terms of one another. And the process of this explication expresses a certain power of understanding, which emerges when the individual, as a manifold, is able to grasp an adequate ordering of ideas:

> By IDEA (*idea*) I understand a conception of the mind which the mind forms by reason of its being a thinking thing ... I say conception rather than perception, for the name perception seems to indicate that the mind is passive in relation to its object, while conception seems to express an action of the mind. (E. II. def. 3)

Now with regard to affects, it is the series of ideas that circulate around the idea of the image of the external cause itself, which comprise what Damasio would call 'feelings' but what Deleuze's followers have called 'emotion' (e.g., love, hate, hope, jealousy). As long as the individual fails to explicate the idea of the cause, that is, fails to place this idea clearly and distinctly within the series of ideas currently constituting mind, he or she may be said to be passive with regard to the encounter. Passivity expresses inadequate thought and a diminishment in the power to act. By contrast, an ability to grasp the external cause is an expression of the individual becoming active, since what was external to the individual is now, in a sense, part of their constitution (as the idea is adequately placed within mind).

How does this occur? It is at this point that Spinoza's beginning with the body becomes explicable. In passive encounters, modifications are wrought by some external mode. However, as Spinoza notes, it is rare that the individual does not contribute something to the encounter, and inasmuch as she does make some contribution then she herself is a part of the cause of subsequent effects (modifications). Now, it is by considering how bodies combine in the cause that the individual is able to grasp what is common to both, and on what they disagree. Ideas of commonality and difference, or 'common notions', are the result. Common notions are always adequate orderings of ideas and present themselves to mind as such. They emerge fortuitously during agreeable or euphoric encounters, which is to say that rudimentary common notions accompany joyful affects. From which it follows that by maximising encounters marked by euphoria the individual begins to develop the means to exercise adequate ideas.

To summarise briefly, affects are, for Spinoza, modifications of bodies and ideas, indexed to agreeable and disagreeable encounters, which result in determinations to action and the expression of a certain power of understanding. Grasping how affects emerge from encounters, and, more importantly, organising one's conduct so as to maximise joy and minimise sorrow is the basis for an ethical performance of becoming active. It is around this ethical account that Spinoza is able to analyse each of the particular affects. In order to clarify this further, we will now turn to a brief discussion of how Spinoza treats some specific emotions.

Love, Hate, Sympathy, Antipathy, Jealousy, Despair, Hope, Confidence, Disappointment ...

As we have shown, at the core of Spinoza's 'definitions of the emotions' (E. III. def.) are the three primary affects of desire, pleasure (joy or euphoria), and pain (sorrow or dysphoria). Desire, as 'appetite with consciousness thereof' is the endeavour to persist in being (*conatus*) seen under the attribute of thought. It is through desire, as the essence of the individual that the terms 'good' and 'bad' are in any ways applicable to affects:

> The knowledge of good and bad is the emotion of pleasure or pain in so far as we are conscious of it: and therefore every one necessarily seeks what he thinks to be good, and turns from what he thinks to be bad. But this appetite is nothing else than the very essence or nature of man. Therefore every one, from the laws of his nature alone, necessarily seeks or turns away from, etc. (E. III. prop. XIX, proof)

> Desire leads the mind to endeavour to conceive (to place within itself) those things that improve the individual's power of understanding. Things that reduce this power lead the mind to conceive ways of excluding or avoiding those things. (E. III. props. XI–XIII)

Hence we love whatever increases our power and perfection (i.e., whatever gives rise to euphoria), and hate those things that decrease it. To hate is to endeavour to remove or exclude the hated thing, and to love is to endeavour to have and to keep the loved thing. All encounters, even those where only the image is actually present, lead to modifications and determinations for action. The euphoria resulting from an encounter with a loved thing, for example, configures the body as a lover disposed to love. All things may now be encountered according to this *sympathetic* disposition, and things which may previously have been encountered as neutral – or even dysphoric – may accidentally or incidentally become causes of further pleasure:

> From the fact alone that we have regarded something with the emotion of pleasure or pain, though it were not the efficient cause of the emotion we can love or hate that thing. (E. II. def. XV, corollary)

The inverse is true in cases of *antipathy*, were the thing becomes regarded as hateful. Of course sympathy is not the only possible effect of a modification involving euphoria. If through satiation or familiarity the loved thing ceases to produce euphoria, then it may be said that, effectively, the thing is no longer loved. For example:

> [W]hen we imagine something which is wont to delight us with its flavour, we desire to enjoy it, that is, to eat it. But as soon as we enjoy it the stomach is filled and the body is disposed differently. But if while the body is in this condition the image of this food ... be stimulated, and consequently the endeavour or desire of eating it be stimulated, the new condition of the body will be opposed to this desire or endeavour, and consequently the presence of the food which we sought will now be odious to us. (E. III. prop. LIX, note)

The wider import of this note is to indicate that it is not the properties of what is encountered that are decisive in emotions, nor the qualities of the affected individual. What is at issue is the *composition* of an affective relationship. So euphoria and dysphoria are not the ground or foundation of any given emotion any more than musical harmony is the ground of the simultaneous tones which give rise to it. The names of the many emotions we experience are merely the names given to differently assembled euphoric or dysphoric relations, akin to musical chords. Hence Spinoza does not build a hierarchical structure upon them as if they were foundations, but points instead to the lack of any essential connection between affected body, encountered body, and quality of affection:

> The human body is affected by external bodies in many ways. Therefore two men can be affected in different ways at the same time, and therefore they can be affected in various ways by one and the same object. Again, the human body can be affected now in this way and now in that, and consequently it can be affected by one and the same object at different times in different ways. (E. III. prop. LI, proof)

If the same person is affected simultaneously in different ways by the same external body, then they are subject to *vacillation*. This is the result of an unstable relation that admits simultaneously of modifications according to euphoria and dysphoria. The vacillation between the two forms of ordering gives rise to the ambiguity or doubt of dissonance. Hence in jealousy a loved thing whose faithfulness is questioned may acquire hateable qualities. Another way of putting this is to say that, in vacillation, two opposing images of the external body vie with one another for certification (e.g. the image of the lovely object that brings me joy and that of the hateful deceiver). Vacillations may also result from the fact that:

> A man is affected with the same emotion of pleasure or pain from the image of a thing past or future as from the image of a thing present. (E. III. prop. XVIII)

To anticipate an encounter that will affect us in some way is to be already affected by the image of a thing that is not yet present. If we are certain of this future encounter, then we may *despair* or helplessly resign ourselves; despair being the name of the sorrow felt when uncertainty about a future painful encounter is removed. But if some doubt remains, then our affection will be *fear* if the encounter is anticipated as disagreeable, or *hope* if we fasten on to an image of some more agreeable encounter actually occurring. Fear is here the name given to inconstant dysphoria, and hope inconstant euphoria, both of which arise 'from the image of a thing future or past of whose event we are in doubt' (E. III. prop. XVII, note II). If we subsequently become certain that the future event will not bring dysphoria, and perhaps will even result in euphoria, then we experience this latter scenario as *confidence*. If that certainty proves misplaced, then *disappointment* is the name of the affect that follows. In all these examples what occurs are substitutions as one image takes the place of another. Once a certain affective relationship has been composed by the encounter between individuals, this may be conceived as establishing an extended individual or alliance. If a loved object is harmed or a hated object benefited, this will then be experienced as pain by the lover/hater. In contrast, they will feel euphoria if a loved object is itself affected with joy or a hated object harmed. This process extends the possibilities for alliance such that we are inclined to love whatever loves what we love and hates what we hate (this type of euphoria is called *approval*), and, contrariwise, we are inclined to hate whatever hates what we love and loves what we hate (*indignation*).

In the course of describing the emotions, the components of Spinoza's ethical system begin to fully operate. Now, whilst it is certainly possible to take issue with the precise content of some of his characterisations (particularly around such complex affects as 'shame' or 'consternation'), there is much to recommend the method by which they are drawn. It is, first and foremost, a way of exploring affects as *ways of being*. This much is clear from the association of *conatus* with desire. What is at stake in an affect is nothing less than how the person should 'go on' or proceed forth on the basis of their emotion. Moreover, Spinoza is presenting a process account of affects as the unfolding of personal powers to act and understand within a complex web of forces made up by a world of finite beings and things *affecting* one another.

Although Spinoza makes repeated reference to 'individuals', it is clear from his conception of bodies and minds as manifolds that the prior ontological category is the 'alliance' or 'relationship'. Affects occur in an encounter between manifold beings, where everything depends upon what form of composition they are able to enter into. Thus the method begins from a point that exceeds individualism (as we moderns would understand it), concerning itself instead with the 'necessary connections' by which relations are constituted. Spinoza challenges us to begin not by recourse to biology or culture, or indeed any of the great dualist formulations, but with the particularity proper to an encounter, such as 'common notions', 'proximate causes', or 'resultant modifications'. Indeed it is a substantial part of this challenge to be able to understand or explicate affects as ultimately part of a single analytic frame or 'plane of composition', known as God or Nature.

Damasio's Error

Damasio shares Spinoza's dissatisfaction with Cartesian dualism and shares his concern to rethink the powers of the body. Although it does not correspond to Spinoza's terminology, Damasio's distinction between emotion and feeling maps neatly onto Spinoza's attributes, according to which emotion would be a mode of extension (and hence a modification of the body), and feeling a mode of thought (and hence a modification of the mind). This enables Damasio to do two important things. It enables him to take feelings seriously rather than to consign them to the status of scientifically inaccessible epiphenomena. Yet it also enables him to give due weight to the amazing capabilities of organic processes. In the context of the mainstream of twentieth- and twenty-first-century psychology and neuroscience, these are promising steps forward. On the other hand, however, Damasio cannot resist raising the Cartesian question of the causal relationship between thought and extension that, as we have seen, Spinoza was so articulate in refusing. This latter tendency perhaps explains the extent to which Damasio's account remains resolutely *foundational*. Indeed, it is foundational in a double sense. 1) 'Emotions and related phenomena are the foundation for feelings' (2004, p. 28), and 2) feelings are 'the foundational component of our minds' (ibid., p. 79). Damasio ends up, for all his sophistication, violating Spinoza's parallelism by positing biology as the foundation for psychology and hence – via feelings – for society.

Damasio relates the idea that emotions are the foundation for feelings to the thirteenth proposition in part II of Spinoza's *Ethics* that we briefly examined above and which he translates into the notion that the '*human mind is the idea of the human body*' (ibid., p. 12). He is attracted by the foundational priority that this proposition gives to the body, and he wonders whether Spinoza might have intuited the findings of contemporary neuroscience. He states that nothing 'could be more comforting than coming across this statement of Spinoza's and wondering about its possible meaning' (ibid., p. 12). He lets himself wonder whether, after all, Spinoza's resolute insistence on the strict 'parallelism' of thought and extension and corresponding emphatic rejection of the attempt to form causal links between mind and body might not actually be a ruse designed to cover up what is in reality a bold attempt at 'penetrating the mystery' of how the body generates the mind (ibid., p. 210).

Without for a moment doubting the relevance of interoceptive perception to feeling states (on this, see Langer, 1988) we think it wise to reflect further on these matters of the relation between thought and extension. Indeed, we think that Spinoza's thought is ultimately discomforting to those who hold that emotions and feelings are explicable solely in terms of the brain representing the state of the rest of a living body to itself. There is a paradox here. Damasio's error, or so it seems to us, is to re-entrench Spinoza's philosophy in exactly the kind of materialist ontology that it should give us the resources to supplant. This materialist ontology holds, as we saw in Chapter 2, that ultimate nature is made up of material stuff. If we understand the ultimate foundational stuff, then we understand reality. Anything that does not have the appearance of material stuff must then be explained away by recourse to the stuff that can be posited as giving rise to it. In this way mysteries can be penetrated and illusions, even useful ones, dispersed (feelings, for example, can be explained away as emotions).

Now, although Spinoza continues to use the long-traditional concept of *substance* in his philosophy, he does so in a way that makes it clear that what matters is not matter as such but the relations between material forms (which are themselves relational compositions of smaller elements). As we have suggested, if there is a basic concept, then that concept is the relation or, more specifically, the *encounter*. Far from being a materialist ontology, this is a relational ontology that presupposes the temporal notion of forms of knowing and forms of physical engagement that take place simultaneously in unfolding scenes of encounters. Spinoza's 'one substance' is not a realm of passive materiality, but a constant underlying activity of realisation involving an interlocked plurality of modes. This underlying activity can be 'conceived' either physically or mentally, but it always and already involves both physical and mental aspects. Damasio's implicit materialist ontology paradoxically has the effect of removing affect from the temporally unfolding scene of encounters in which, according to this relational ontology, it has its being. In so doing he risks misrecognising emotion as a set of artificially abstracted biological mechanisms and misrecognising feeling as consciousness of the operations of these mechanisms at play in a given individual's body. Abstract functions are then posited for these abstracted mechanisms (Damasio, p. 137). In short, Damasio commits the error of abstracting existence from process and assuming that process can be decomposed into discrete mechanisms that constitute actual biological reality. Damasio, we fear, will never find Spinoza where he is looking. A further change of perspective is required.

Spinoza's account of affect must therefore be understood in a relational context in which the ongoing process of being affected by and affecting others in an ongoing stream of concrete activity assumes decisive analytical importance. An affect, whether understood physically or mentally, is first of all the outcome of an encounter that follows a previous encounter and that presages yet another encounter (actual or potential). What matters is that one being is affected, and thus modified or 'moved', by another. Affects thus occur between finite things on the basis of their mutual relations, in a broader temporal and spatial context whose relevance should never be overlooked (see Hardt & Negri, 2000).

This means that a given affect can never be adequately understood by reference to the inner experiences of an isolated individual alone, or by way of the physiological mechanisms that mediate such experiences. Rather, the affect is the way in which such an individual is modified (qua body) and perceives themselves to be modified (qua mind) through the event of an encounter. Our affects announce the relevance of our connection to a world beyond ourselves, and they are the means by which we articulate a relationship to that world. Naturally, the specific constitution or powers of an entity limit the ways in which that entity can be affected in an encounter, as do the qualities of whatever is encountered. A snail may be unmoved by a poetry recital, but retreats soon enough when touched on the tentacle by an overly inquisitive human finger. The retreating snail is affected by that particular snail/finger encounter. It is one of many ways in which a snail can be affected by the others it encounters. A dead snail would lack this particular capacity to be so affected.

If affect is inherently relational, then we should be very cautious about conflating 'it' with the material structures that mediate it and make it possible. Naturally, those material structures complexify as one moves up the evolutionary scale, but one must never lose affect amongst this complexity. Damasio makes an important contribution in highlighting the interoceptive basis of feelings. The intimate experiences that constitute affects are indeed closely entangled with the physiology of the body of the biological organism, and that body is indeed an exquisitely adjusted and interconnected society of parts in which the brain acts as a central organiser. For its owner, the body is a bit of the world radically distinct from any other region since it alone is intimately experienced in a flux of feelings. But there is a world of difference between recognising the close entanglement of experience and body and asserting the body as the foundation of experience, and this is a distinction we wish to insist upon since it has far-reaching implications.

Affects, in short, concern the ways in which entities enter into mutual relations. Damasio mistakes the medium for the message and in so doing decreases our powers of sensibility in the name of increasing them. In making his case that emotions are discrete biological mechanisms for homeostatic regulation, Damasio reports various clinical cases. We will examine two of these to illustrate our critical point.

The first involves a 65-year-old woman with parkinsonian symptoms that resisted treatment. Electrodes designed to modify the operation of relevant motor nuclei were implanted in her brain stem. When one of the contact sites in the left side of the brain stem was stimulated the woman quite unexpectedly displayed clearly recognisable signs of sadness, including sobbing, tears and what appeared to be depressive utterances. If the stimulation stopped, so did the display of sadness, leaving the woman bemused as to her inexplicable comportment.

The second example involves a patient of Itzhak Fried known as A.K. whose supplementary motor area in the left frontal lobe was subjected to electrical stimulation as part of a procedure related to the treatment of epilepsy. In this case the unexpected result on the part of the patient was unmitigated laughter and, so we are told, a related feeling of great merriment. When stimulated in this manner, the patient would find much to laugh about, including the doctors: 'You guys are just so funny… standing around' (Damasio, p. 75). The doctors in turn confessed to finding the laughter rather contagious.

The conclusion Damasio draws is that here we have examples of fully fledged emotions that happen to have been mistakenly evoked through the artificial stimulation of what are effectively neural 'switches'. Such switches belong to complex and multi-layered neural mechanisms and can function as trigger, executor or moderator switches. In the first case it seems we are dealing with an emotion execution 'switch', namely, one of the brain stem nuclei that controls the full repertoire of responses that characterise the emotion that we subsequently experience as the feeling of sadness. In the second case we are dealing with a trigger switch. Namely, the medial and dorsal prefrontal regions appear to trigger activity in other regions (such as the brain stem nuclei) that in turn execute the emotion of joyful laughter. The implication is that whatever is executed at the terminus of such processes *is* the emotion proper: a highly coordinated but purely biological set of responses. Since the mind is the idea of the body, these emotions are the foundation of the feelings of sadness and merriment that the patients subsequently (i.e. secondarily) experienced. The fact that all of this occurs despite the absence of any actual 'sad' or 'merry' encounter is taken as proof of the distinct and autonomous physical nature of emotions. 'The evidence', concludes Damasio, 'speaks both to the relative autonomy of the neural triggering mechanism of emotion and to the dependence of feeling on emotion' (Damasio, p. 70).

It is not our place to take issue with the nature of the neurological findings that Damasio discusses here. These concern the neural media that enable a highly complex organism to be affected by its surroundings by way of sensitivity to its own multiply relayed bodily expressions. But we may observe that although some details are new – thanks to the careful work of scientists such as Damasio – such theoretical ideas have been familiar to psychologists since at least the work of Silvan Tomkins in the late 1960s. Within any higher animal, a given experience expresses itself throughout the body in complex internal relays involving multiple interconnecting centres of experience, which are in turn coordinated and integrated via a more general centre. Such an animal is multiply affected by the expressions of its own body, but this body is of course itself a part of, and continuous with, broader nature. Our problem is hence not with the details of the material structure of the body. Our problem is that, in making his case, Damasio strips the phenomenon of emotion down to a decontextualised mechanism that is then mistaken for an explanation of the mediating process the mechanism makes possible. Emotions – through which we are in fact connected to the world – are disconnected from the world in Damasio's account.

To draw a deliberately simple analogy, the sails of a windmill are indeed connected via a shaft to a wheel which turns a mill stone which grinds out flour. A canny experimenter could easily demonstrate that, even in the absence of wind, a strong pull on the sails can serve to turn the shaft and hence set in motion the whole flour-generating process. In our analogy, this experimental intervention would be akin to electrical stimulation of a 'trigger switch' in, say, the dorsal prefrontal region of the brain. Or, our windmill scientist might go direct to the main wheel that drives the mill stone, turn this 'artificially' by force, and note that the ground flour is produced in this way too. This would be akin to electrical stimulation of an 'execution switch' in the brain stem. Clearly the sails affect the main shaft which in turn affects the main wheel which in turn affects the mill stone, and so on. But it would be an error to abstract one or more of these mechanisms and to imagine that one could thereby explain the windmill. It would be an error to identify the windmill with the mechanisms abstracted from it, as if these were its foundations. It would be a particular error to imagine that because one has excluded the variable of the wind from its operations (and shown that the process can continue in its absence) one can therefore conclude that the phenomenon of the windmill has nothing to do with the wind. Such erroneous conclusions forget that the point of the windmill is to mediate the wind and convert it into energy that can in turn affect other bodies. The windmill, we might say, parasitises the wind and in so doing invents a new type of exchange, much in the way of the fable Michel Serres describes (see Chapter 3).

In the same way, affect should not be identified with an abstracted component of a physiological mechanism (Damasio's 'emotion') or with its subjective experience (Damasio's 'feeling'). Rather, the mechanism, when operating in its concrete context in a living body alongside a multitude of others, is one of the things thanks to which a range of affects can occur (Stenner, 2005). If the artificiality of this process of abstraction is apparent in the case of a windmill, then the error must be even more obvious when considering something that actually lives.

In a sense, Damasio's connection to Spinoza lies simply in his recognition of the need to acknowledge the embodied nature of the brain. Damasio is rightly alarmed at the increasing neo-Cartesian tendency to abstract brain processes and to bestow on these abstractions the miraculous powers of generating a 'mind'. But Damasio is equally enthralled with the Cartesian idea of an abstraction called 'mind' emerging from an abstraction called 'the brain'. He simply allows a little more into his abstraction: namely the relations between the brain and what he tellingly calls the 'body-proper'. Damasio's perspective shift is effectively 'the understanding that the mind arises from or in a brain situated within a body-proper with which it interacts' (Damasio, p. 191). His complaint that the body-proper has become scientifically invisible in the context of neuroscience is quite correct, but it needs to be supplemented by the equally important recognition that the body-proper is but one body amongst a manifold of others (themselves manifold) that together, in their mutual co-determinations, make up what we like to call 'nature'. One must talk not just of the invisible body but of the ways in which the world is rendered invisible by contemporary neuroscience and psychology. The brain is part of the body-proper of a higher animal, and this body-proper must be situated in the context of those other bodies – of numerous kinds and each multiple and complex – with which it interacts. Damasio gives the brain its body back, but still denies it its relations with other bodies. We must take more care with our abstractions, since it is through them that we render vast swathes of nature invisible. Bergson puts this Spinozist warning neatly:

> But is it possible to conceive the nervous system as living apart from the organism which nourishes it, from the atmosphere in which the organism breathes, from the earth which that atmosphere envelopes, from the sun round which the earth revolves? More generally, does not the fiction of an isolated material object imply a kind of absurdity, since this object borrows its physical properties from the relations which it maintains with all others, and owes each of its determinations, and, consequently, its very existence, to the place which it occupies in the universe as a whole? Let us no longer say, then, that our perceptions depend simply upon the molecular movements of the cerebral mass. We must say rather that they *vary with* them, but that these movements themselves remain inseparably bound up with the rest of the material world. (Bergson, 1908/1991, pp. 24–25).

We bring this critique full circle by reframing the proposition from Spinoza's *Ethics* that most appeals to Damasio. As we indicated above, the proposition must in turn be situated in the context of the following statement: 'The human mind has no knowledge of the human body, nor does it know it to exist, save through ideas of modifications by which the body is affected' (E. II. prop. XIX). It is the body as affected through its encounters that is the source of mind and its knowledge and not the body as such. Viewed under the attribute of extension, an affect is a modification of a body. Viewed under the attribute of thought, an affect is an idea of such a modification. It is not 'the body' that is 'the *origin* of the perceptions that constitute the essence of feeling' (Damasio, 2004, p. 87), and neither is it some cognised external entity; rather it is the affects wrought in a body by way of an encounter. We applaud Damasio's attempt to give the brain back its body, but he is not yet a Spinozist until he returns that body to the matrix that is its world.

Note

1. In citing passages from the *Ethics*, we have referred to part (E), proposition (prop.), definition (def.), note or proof. Hence the note to the second proposition in part two is E. II. prop. 2, note.

SEVEN

Bergson and Memory

[Without memory] life would consist of momentary experiences that [would] have little relation to one another. Without memory we could not communicate with other people for we could not remember the ideas we wished to express. Without memory, we would not have the sense of continuity even to know who we are. (Loftus and Ketcham, 1994, p. 18)

It began, apparently, in October 1991 during a car journey to Atlanta airport. Elizabeth Loftus imagined a scenario where a false memory might be implanted in a participant (see Ashmore, Brown & MacMillan, 2005 for full analysis). Two weeks later, at a party, she oversaw an 'instant experiment' based around the scenario. The following week she tried it as a classroom exercise (Loftus & Ketcham, 1994). The procedure became known as 'Lost in the shopping mall'. It goes something like this: the researcher (Loftus) recruits a confederate (Jim) who has a younger sibling (Chris). Jim interacts with Chris in the course of which he asks Chris, 'Do you remember the time when you got lost in that shopping mall?' – an event that, according to Jim (and Jim's and Chris's mother; and thus Loftus) never occurred. Eventually, after more interactions, Chris agrees that he did indeed get lost in the mall; moreover, he elaborates on the details, and is disappointed and doubtful when later debriefed. This basic design was subsequently modified and formalised, Human Subjects Committee permission was sought and gained, a 'proper' experiment was run, and its results were published as *The formation of false memories* (Loftus & Pickrell, 1995). Meanwhile, replications appeared, which were both positive (e.g. Hyman, Husband & Billings, 1995) and negative (e.g. Pezdek, Finger & Hodge, 1997).

'Lost in mall' (LIM) is conceived within a tradition of experimental studies of memory that uses analogues of real-world situations to investigate the processing of memories. It builds upon Loftus' findings in her studies of eyewitness testimony, where participants viewed and then reported on different features of a video recording of a traffic accident (Loftus & Palmer, 1974). Participants sometimes 'remembered' details, such as broken glass, that had not actually been present in the original recording. From this Loftus concluded that by some mechanism it might be possible for participants to recall memories of events that they had not actually experienced as such. The kinds of events that Loftus subsequently became interested in were so-called 'recovered memories' of child sexual abuse. This occurs when adults report memories of traumatic events in their childhood for which they have previously expressed little or no awareness of having taken place. The experience of being 'lost in the mall' was chosen by Loftus because as a mildly traumatic childhood experience involving adults it was considered to be a suitable analogue. That is to say, not really the same thing, but having features which are similar enough (trauma, powerlessness, fraught adult interaction) to suggest that any effects produced in the study might be extrapolated to comment on the intended real-world phenomenon.

What does LIM show? What sorts of claims can be made on the basis of the study? For Loftus it is a clear demonstration that if the information given to a target individual is manipulated by others who can pass themselves off as being 'in the know', then this creates the conditions for 'imagination inflation' (Loftus, Coan & Pickrell, 1996). This is an increase in confidence of the veridicality of some remembered event which arises when the person concerned is asked to speculate about their personal history. The analogy that Loftus makes is with therapy.

Recovered memories are usually, although not always, uncovered during the practice of psychological therapies. During the 1980s and early 1990s in the USA and Northern Europe, the number of clients claiming to have recovered memories of this sort rose exponentially (Pope & Brown, 1996). To some extent this phenomenon went hand in hand with the growing awareness and cultural prominence of debates around child sexual abuse, which had hitherto been subject to little formal public discussion (Haaken, 1998). For some commentators the links between these two phenomena were clear. Because child sexual abuse now had a recognisable 'name' and was now publicly considered a matter which could be openly discussed, adult survivors of abuse could feel confident in discussing their traumatic experiences with their therapists. More significantly, adults who had 'repressed' or managed to dissociate these memories from their daily consciousness might now find other ways of managing their ongoing trauma and begin to re-confront their past.

A movement of advocates claiming to speak on behalf of those with recovered memories emerged around this time (see Campbell, 2003). It involved therapists who were concerned to advise their peers on how best to help clients identify and cope with recovered memories (see Bass & Davis, 1988). It also included women's and children's rights activists, lawyers and adult survivors themselves. This movement made some notable accomplishments, such as supporting survivors in bringing legal cases against their abusers, who were usually, but not always, a parent (see Commonwealth vs. Landon Carter Smith, 1990). Some changes were even temporarily made to the US legal system to recognise the unique circumstances involved, such as suspending the automatic limitation placed on reporting such crimes.

By 1992, a counter-movement coalesced with the formation of the False Memory Syndrome Foundation (FMSF). Set up by Pamela Freyd, whose husband had been accused of childhood abuse by their daughter (Jennifer Freyd, a cognitive psychologist who later published *Betrayal trauma*, 1998). The FMSF claimed that recovered memories were actually fictitious and were invented by vulnerable clients under the systematic influence of therapists. For the FMSF, therapists were centrally responsible for the rise in 'false memories'. They referred to the phenomenon using the medical-sounding term 'syndrome', although no medical authority had actually defined it as such (see Campbell, 2003). The board members of the FMSF consisted of an eminent body of mainly academic psychologists, including Elizabeth Loftus. FMSF board members acted as legal experts, usually for the defence, in cases of abuse accusations following recovered memory, and wrote a number of powerful critiques including Richard Ofshe's *Making monsters* (1995) and Loftus & Ketcham's *The myth of repressed memory* (1995).

LIM is a strategic piece of research. It is designed to demonstrate the possibility of a counter-phenomenon: rather than consider reports of abuse as stemming from 'repressed' memories, they might instead be considered as arising from 'implanted' memories. The power of this demonstration depends upon how far one is convinced by the analogy. Some of Loftus' critics have forcefully argued that the analogy is entirely insufficient:

> The nature of trauma, the reason why it causes memory disturbances, is that it is so overwhelming it can't be taken in. We're not talking lost in a shopping mall here. We're talking about the agony of anal rape on a little boy, about the weight of a father's body on a small girl, the tearing pain of penetration, and the fear evoked by the words, 'If you tell, I'll kill you'. (Mason, 1995)

The critique is that what goes on in a laboratory is of no consequence, because with regard to recovered memory the trauma in question is so extreme, so violent in character, so utterly corrosive of normative social relations that it cannot be adequately modelled (nor perhaps understood) in the usual disinterested manner of experimental psychology. In this sense, recovered memory as a phenomenon becomes for some of its proponents a challenge to the very authority of experimental psychology as an epistemic practice: 'Trauma sets up new rules for memory. You can't replicate trauma in an experimental lab' (Terr, 1994, pp. 51–52).

What though if the experiment were not understood as seeking to create an analogue of false memory? What instead if it were seen as a more straightforward analogue for the power relations which are present in family recollection? Isabelle Stengers (2000) makes a similar point in relation to Milgram's infamous studies of obedience. She accuses Milgram of acting 'in the name of science' rather than adhering to a solid principle of scientificity in his studies. What Milgram does, Stengers claims, is demonstrate how institutions work through the domination of individuals:

> 'In the name of science' Stanley Milgram has taken on responsibility of 'repeating' an experiment already realized by human history, and has shown that torturers could be fabricated 'in the name of science' just as others have done so 'in the name of the state' or 'in the name of the good of the human sciences'. (Stengers, 2000, pp. 22–23)

In other words, Milgram tells us what we already know through bitter historical experience: torturers can subcontract their business to others when the conditions favour it. Extending this argument, we might observe that in its procedures LIM demonstrates precisely the kinds of strategies that are deployed by abusive family members to get their child victims to remain silent. Kenneth Pope (1996) makes this point clearly:

> Is it possible that older family members can rewrite younger relatives' memories in regard to traumatic events at which they were present? Might this occur in the context of sexual abuse when the repeated suggestion is made by a perpetrator that 'nothing happened' and that any subsequent awareness of the abuse constitutes a false memory? (Pope, 1996, p. 963)

LIM, Pope argues, is an experimental demonstration of the way in which adults who have control over a social setting can influence and intervene in the memory processes of children. In this sense the study is 'rescued' for the Recovered Memory side – Loftus has indeed demonstrated something important, but she has not adequately grasped just what that is.

A more apposite characterisation of LIM might be made by drawing on what Chertok and Stengers (1992) conclude about studies of hypnosis. Psychology and psychoanalysis have long sought to get a firm grasp of the ways in which a person may act upon another indirectly, yet effectively. Chertok and Stengers observe that psychologists have used the notion of 'suggestion' as a way of dismissing the problem – as in the idea of something being 'mere suggestion'. But these attempts at denying that there is a real phenomenon to be understood often rebound, since psychologists have found it difficult to adequately account for the very mixed results they gain from studies. The phenomenon they wish to study is then barely under their control – it tends to overspill or exceed the limits which are set for it within the experimental procedure.

One example is provided in Johanna Motzkau's (2007) work on child witnesses. She describes a study conducted in Germany where researchers attempted, much in the same way as LIM, to implant memories in children. This involved the false event of being stung by a bee or falling from a bicycle, which was confirmed by parents as having not occurred in children's lives. The researchers did indeed manage to satisfactorily demonstrate that children could recall these false events. However, when they contacted the parents a second time, many voiced a concern – they could not now be sure that their children had not in fact experienced the events in question. Motzkau piquantly observes that in this instance 'suggestion' seems to migrate beyond the experimental setting and into relations between children, parents and researchers. The experiment itself becomes suggestive.

Understood in this way, LIM is an experiment which is not able to control the forces, the phenomena it brings together. It is unable to explain away why Chris might have been so disappointed to learn that the experience he has so enthusiastically endorsed was false. It has nothing to say about why Jim committed himself to an act which involved deceiving his brother and potentially compromising their relationship. It is silent on what the effects of its publicity might be on people who have to deal with either the trauma of abuse or the social disaster of false accusation.

This last point is perhaps the most important. Pope (1995), for example, in his highly critical review of *The myth of repressed memory* (Loftus & Ketcham, 1994), comments that 'the story of "Chris" has appeared in *American Psychologist, The New Yorker*, newsmagazines, newspapers, books, scholarly articles, television shows, courtroom testimony, lectures, work-shops, and countless informal discussions'. It is a 'critical', 'pivotal', 'historic' experiment in which the subject Chris 'will likely become as well known as Anna O' (Pope, 1995: 310). If that is so, the relationship between LIM and the broader cultural effects – the understandings and ways of being that it either makes possible or problematises – becomes a central concern. LIM's combination of high renown, critical resistance and relatively low 'surface scientificity' fits the pattern described in Brannigan's analysis of the mythic character of famous social psychological experiments:

> Many landmark experiments survive otherwise fatal questioning of their validity because of their moral, ontological or pedagogical relevance. ... As a result, the history of the discipline tends to comprise studies that are morally pertinent but scientifically ephemeral. (Brannigan 1997, abstract)

In this chapter we will try to address what the 'moral, ontological and pedagogical' significance might be of the questions that LIM raises. We will be concerned with the relationship between the psychological approaches to memory that are embedded in LIM and how they translate into the broader cultural and social problems of memory. We have chosen to frame our questions around a discussion of the work of Henri Bergson because his work presents a shock to how memory is typically thought of in psychology (see Middleton & Brown, 2005 for an extended treatment).

Representation and Action

Matter and memory (1908/1991), Bergson's best known text, has been described as one of the most significant challenges to psychology in modern philosophy (Deleuze, 1986, 1989). In this work Bergson uses the 'definite example' of memory to challenge the 'theoretical difficulties which have always beset dualism' (1991, p. 9). Specifically, Bergson is concerned with the doctrine of psychophysiological parallelism, where mind is seen as an autonomous entity in relation to the body, and the attendant metaphysics of representation. The peculiarity of Bergson's argument, however, is that it is as he puts it 'frankly dualistic' (p. 9) in itself. He offers an apparent dualism of 'pure perception' and 'pure memory' in its place. However, as we will try to outline briefly, the implications for psychology of this alternative division prove to be very different.

Under Cartesianism, the body is treated as a material entity, part of the broader matter or 'substance' which makes up the physical world. Like all forms of substance, the properties of the body are that it has extension in space and enters into causal relationships with other bodies, following Newtonian laws. Mind, by contrast, is immaterial, consisting of pure ideas. Mind has no extension in space, although it may be said to have intensive or qualitative relations between its various components. The split between body and mind appears to give to each a kind of autonomy – bodies being affected by and affecting other bodies, ideas combining together in mind. As we saw in the last chapter, the key difference between Descartes and Spinoza is that the Cartesian division is absolute, mind and body being completely separated, whereas Spinozism is technically a dual-aspect monism, where body and mind are treated as dual attributes or two sides of the same fundamental substance.

Cartesianism confronts the central problem of deciding how to sew together mind and body, having first sutured them apart. What Bergson objects to is the way in which this is typically done:

> That there is a close connection between a state of consciousness and the brain we do not dispute. But there is also a close connection between a coat and the nail on which it hangs, for, if the nail is pulled out, the coat falls to the ground. Shall we say, then, that the shape of the nail gives us the shape of the coat, or in any way corresponds to it? No more are we entitled to conclude, because the psychical fact is hung onto a cerebral state, that there is any parallelism between the two series psychical and physiological. (Bergson, 1908/1991, p. 12)

There must, of course, be a connection between mental states and brain states. To claim otherwise would be to fly in the face of all reason. But it does not follow from this that we can impute the form which mental states take on the basis of the physical properties of the brain. This assumption is a type of reductionism that Bergson saw as common in the psychology of his day. It is arguably still with us in the recent resurgence of brain imaging studies (i.e. functional Magnetic Resonance Imaging), and in the sort of neuroscientific approaches which we discussed in relation to Damasio's work. Here, too, the tendency is often to seek to explain the shape of the coat on the basis of the shape of the nail.

Bergson offers a deceptively simple retort to such thinking: it suggests that the brain is more important than the immediate world with which it engages.

For instance, the notion of representation typically takes the following form in psychology. Stimuli are perceived by the body, resulting in sensation. This sensation is fed through to the brain where it is converted into mental images (i.e. cognitive representations). These images are then processed in such a way that likely responses can be put into action, if required. This involves the reverse movement, where images are transformed into motor responses. The problem with all of this is, as Bergson sees it, that the absolute separation of mind and body makes it almost impossible to grasp how representation occurs. At what point does sensation stop being the physical reception of stimulation and transmute into a mental image? And conversely, when we remember some scene from the past, how is it that this mental event can be effectively re-experienced physically in the present? Bergson describes the standard view of representation as depicting a 'transformation scene from fairyland' (1908/1991, p. 39), since it describes a process whereby the intimate relations between 'the material world, which surrounds the body; the body, which shelters the brain [is] abruptly dismissed' (p. 39) in favour of this immaterial entity – the representation – which is taken to be the dominant term.

The alternative that Bergson proposes is to see the brain as a complex 'centre of action':

> [T]he nervous system is in no sense an apparatus which may serve to fabricate, or even prepare, representations. Its function is to receive stimulation, to provide motor apparatus, and to present the largest possible number of these apparatuses to a given stimulus. (Bergson, 1908/1991, p. 31)

The brain is considered here first and foremost in its relations to the body rather than to the mental. If the body is a part of nature, and the brain enveloped in turn by the body, then we may see perception as a process entirely dedicated to linking motor responses to stimuli without the intervention of mental images as the central point of coordination. We stay then purely at the level of bodies and action, rather than invoking mind. This sounds an awful lot like the behaviourist or stimulus–response psychology which was just beginning to emerge in the USA at the time *Matter and memory* was first translated there into English (1911). However, as we shall see, it is not that Bergson wants to abolish consciousness altogether; he merely begins by clarifying what must be involved in perception in its 'pure' state.

A representational view of the brain sees perception as a process of elaboration. Sensation is transformed into mental image which is then layered with subjective elements. For instance, I see someone walking out of the crowd towards me, I compare his features with various social prototypes and impute likely characteristics and motives. I steel myself and watch him closely as he approaches. Here a simple event is transformed into a massive information processing operation using a large number of cognitive representations. It is as though mind 'adds' something to the world. Bergson takes the contrary position:

There is nothing positive here, nothing added to the image, nothing new. The objects merely abandon something of their real action in order to manifest their virtual influence of the living being upon them. Perception therefore resembles those phenomena of reflexion which result from an impeded refraction; it is like an effect of mirage. (1908/1991, p. 37)

Pure perception is a process of *subtraction*. Nothing is added, rather a part is isolated and extracted from the whole. To react to someone walking towards us is to already have performed a work of focusing on one particular bit of the environment. Out of the myriad of behavioural possibilities they may be engaged in, we narrow the field of likely action as 'walking towards me'. It is more accurate to say that perception selects aspects of the world through a process of reduction or concentration at a particular point.

Bergson's account of perception is utterly realist in the sense that what we respond to is not some impression of the world which has been transformed into a subjective mental image. Rather, we selectively focus upon one aspect of what is already there, which affords certain possibilities for our engagement. There are resonances here with J.J. Gibson's (1966) theory of 'direct perception', which similarly argues that perception operates with 'affordances' provided by the world without needing the addition of cognitive processes for elaboration. Yet if Bergson is a realist, then he is a very special sort of realist. Understood in the usual sense, realism is a commitment to an ontology that prioritises 'things in themselves'. Our knowledge either is or ought to be built around the qualities of these things as they actually are in and for themselves, rather than around our subjective impressions or ideas. A fundamental feature of this position is the assumption that things (i.e. entities, including living beings) have stable properties which can be determined more or less accurately. Hence realism belongs to the philosophical tradition of 'ontologies of being'.

By contrast, Bergson, like the majority of thinkers we discuss in this book, works in the tradition of 'ontologies of becoming' or 'philosophies of difference'. As we saw with Whitehead, the key feature of this philosophical tradition is that change and process are considered primary in relation to stability and identity. Bergson refers to the physical world as 'undivided flux' or a 'fluid continuity of the real'. Here there is no other reality than that of a continuous, ongoing flow of change: 'what is real is the continual change of form: form is only a snapshot view of transition' (1911/1998, p. 302). Those forms that we perceive are akin to 'snapshots' or provisional viewpoints on the 'open whole' of a ceaselessly changing world. Although fundamentally we exist in a 'fluid continuity of the real' we are nevertheless able to actively 'cut out' or 'isolate' discrete forms within that flux. The crucial point, for Bergson, is that these forms are products or outcomes relative to our particular perspectives – they are not reality itself:

From our first glance at the world, before we even make our *bodies* in it, we distinguish *qualities*. Color succeeds color, sound to sound, resistance to resistance, etc. Each of these qualities, taken separately, is a state that seems to persist as such, immovable until another replaces it. Yet each of these qualities resolves itself, on analysis into an enormous number of elementary movements. Whether we see in it vibrations or whether we represent it in any other way, one fact is certain, it is that every quality is change. In vain, moreover shall we seek beneath change the thing which changes: it is always provisionally, and in order to satisfy our imagination, that we attach movement to a mobile ... In short, the qualities of matter are so many stable views that we take of its instability. (1911/1998, pp. 300–302)

What seems real to us are qualities: sounds, colours, the feel and weight of objects. But these qualities are themselves condensations or snapshots produced by our intellect, and which reflect our concerns ('satisfy our imagination'). For example, when we stare into the eyes of another the colours we see are not a fundamental property of their body, but rather an effect of the complex reflection of light waves and the way we apprehend this process. If this is so, Bergson argues, we would be mistaken to imagine that it is possible to arrive at a once-and-for-all definition of the essential qualities of some thing, because those qualities are entirely relative to our current viewpoint (including, in this case, the relationship between us that had afforded our desire to hold a look). And if we properly consider what this relativity implies, we must conclude that rather than there being 'things which change', properly speaking there is 'change provisionally grasped as a thing'. Consider, for example, the relationship between two siblings as they grow up. Each notices changes in the other, but in all likelihood assumes that these changes are secondary to core characteristics: 'he is just like he was when we were little'. Yet over the course of one's life, everything changes: one's relationships, one's knowledge, the physical state of one's body, the transitory ebb and flow of thought and emotion. It would then be more accurate to say that these changes are primary, and the attributions of stability are secondary: 'the qualities of matter are so many stable views that we take of its instability'. In formal philosophical terms this is a reversal of the way so-called primary (core) and secondary (transitory) qualities are considered. In Chapter 2 we saw how Whitehead made a similar reversal, but how is it worked out by Bergson and how might this inform the study of memory?

The Virtual and the Actual

Bergson describes perception as akin to a kind of 'foothold' that we establish in the changing flux of the real. This foothold is always limited, provisional and structured around a subtraction of possibility. What we take to be *actual* – i.e the states of affairs in which we find ourselves – arises from limiting and selecting the immediate potential of the world. Although we may artificially isolate some aspect of the world, it still remains connected to the whole that is the 'fluid continuity of the real'. Beneath the 'crust' of what we perceive the ceaseless movement of 'real action' remains present. Bergson argues that any objectivity we might be tempted to attribute to what we see – that is, what some aspect of the world contains 'over and above what it yields up' to perception – consists 'precisely in the immense multiplicity of the movements which it executes, so to speak, within itself as a chrysalis. Motionless on the surface, in its very depth it lives and vibrates' (p. 204). What we perceive is then not this movement in its totality, but rather, properly speaking, a 'virtual image' that is projected back onto the world.

Bergson's use of the term 'virtual image' is consistent with his reference to 'images' throughout *Matter and memory*. By 'image' Bergson means 'a certain existence which is more than that which the idealist calls a *representation*, but less than that which the realist calls a thing – an existence placed halfway between the 'thing' and the 'representation' (pp. 9–10). An image is what we see when we open our eyes, it is the stuff of the world implicated in perception. But since what we see is not the entirety of what might be concretely considered, being only a limited and provisional selection, the image is neither 'subjectively' nor 'objectively' determined. Put another way, an image is always relational. It has a concrete existence within this relation (I see the stranger coming out of the crowd towards me) but this does not exhaust the possibilities or fully express the 'fluid continuity'. Although images are the basis of our experience, they emerge from the 'undivided flux' consisting of 'innumerable movements' or 'vibrations'. An image is then a 'snapshot' or provisional 'stable view' that is artificially 'cut out' of this ongoing flow. Bergson speaks of images as being 'contracted', 'selected', 'discerned', 'isolated' or otherwise 'cut out from' reality by perception in accord with our needs:

> Our needs are … so many searchlights which, directed upon the continuity of sensible qualities, single out in it distinct bodies. They cannot satisfy themselves except upon the condition that they carve out, within this continuity, a body which is to be their own and then delimit other bodies with which the first can enter into relation, as if with persons. To establish these special relations among portions thus carved out from sensible reality is just what we call *living*. (Bergson, 1908/1991, p. 198)

Our engagement with the world is structured through our ongoing needs and concerns. It is these that direct our perception, and play a role in guiding the selection of images through 'carving out' or 'delimiting' portions of 'sensible reality'. But what is carved out is not a mere reflection of those needs, being instead a concrete *actualisation* of a potential relationship we might have to some aspect of the 'fluid continuity'. The difference could not be starker from a weak constructionist argument where our ability to represent the world in one way or another passes for reality. Nortjes Marres (2008) comments that this version of constructionism remains committed to the idea that there is an elevated principle – a 'logos' – which is doing the work of organising things – 'ontos'. Typically this is considered to be language (see Gergen, 1982), conversation (Harré, 1983/4) or talk-in-interaction (Edwards, 1997). There is no such principle in Bergson's work. The relationships between images are in a constant process of self-articulation and elaboration, there is nothing which stands behind or moves this process beyond its own movements. The human body is one image amongst myriad others. Whilst it certainly has its own distinctive modes of engaging with the world, the 'special relations among portions thus carved out from sensible reality' are not thereby automatically placed under our control or rendered fully intelligible. There is always more to the 'fluid continuity of the real' than that which we imagine we have caught in our sensibilities. Bergson thereby insists on subsuming human sense-making practices within general processes of articulation and elaboration. This amounts to a strong constructivism.

The key terms that Bergson uses to do this are *virtual* and *actual*. As we have seen, the actual or actualisation refers to a definite state of affairs indexed to a particular vantage point or mode of experience. For example, if I say my keys are now in the same place there on the table where they were yesterday then this is said from the perspective where this object, 'my keys', remains a reasonably enduring part of my daily existence and their location a routine matter of concern. By contrast, the virtual is the set of potentials expressed by the state of affairs, or the broader relations implicated in our situated apprehension of them. One way of grasping this distinction is to see the actual as a 'solution' to a 'problem' posed by the virtual. For instance, we might ask what it is that makes where we have left our keys an intelligible matter. Presumably this involves a relationship to a particular kind of space – a home perhaps – along with the others who share that space, and others still whom we might welcome or want to deny access. More than this, it implies a whole set of felt relations between bodies or ways of being affected and affecting others, as Spinoza would put it (see last chapter). Did I remember to lock the house? Is that her key in the door? Will he still be there when I get back?

We will show in Chapter 9 how Gilles Deleuze's work develops Bergson's work in directions that make its value for social science more apparent. But it is worth noting for now the connection Deleuze makes between Bergson and Proust. In *The creative mind*, Bergson (1933/1992) emphasises the difference between possibility and potentiality. To say that some state of affairs is 'possible' is to already have a fixed notion of what might come to pass, and thus to see its future emergence as somehow latent in some current state of affairs. For Bergson this is problematic since it suggests a mechanistic view of change where the present can be so thoroughly known that all future developments can be predicted. It is more likely, he suggests, that such claims are made after the event and projected backwards in a 'retrograde movement of the truth' (Bergson, 1933/1992) (I say now that I always knew I would have to leave, but this being a possibility all along only became clear to me after I had left). Understood in this way, it becomes difficult to think 'possibility' without working out its exact terms. Hence the term potential is preferred since it implies an appropriate degree of openness and indeterminism. Deleuze points to Proust's succinct summary of this in his phrase 'real without being actual, ideal without being abstract' (1994, p. 208).

By way of summary, we can say that if perception involves selection and 'cutting out' then there must be a point at the limits of perception where there is some vague awareness of the alternatives, the possibilities which are not actualised but are nevertheless real potentials. A 'virtual image' is then the image considered in terms of these vaguely sensed possibilities. Bergson notes that 'the objects which surround my body reflect its possible action upon them' (1908/1991, p. 21). But some actions are only vaguely anticipated, half-sensed, indeterminate. They are nevertheless 'real' in the sense that they might come to be enacted in the relational engagement between my body and that of another. Hence what we call perception is not stretched between the objective (what is there) and the subjective (what I believe to be there) but rather between the actual (the concrete possibilities for how two bodies/images might relate) and the virtual (the indeterminate field of potential in which this relation emerges, the full range of vaguely sensed relational engagements which might come to be).

Memory as Duration

In *Matter and memory*, Bergson argues that the images we perceive do not produce automatic responses on our part. There is a gap, or delay. Bergson describes this as akin to a 'central telephonic exchange'. Actions directed at our bodies are coordinated, sorted and held in a waiting pattern, like so many incoming calls, before being redirected to 'this or that motor mechanism' which is 'chosen and no longer prescribed' (p. 30). Hence the body is a 'zone of indeterminism' opened up between action and reaction. Bergson characterises the capacity to open this gap as being due to the evolution of intellectual capacities. For the 'lower organisms' perception resembles a 'mere contact' (p. 32), a brush or immediate engagement with the world which leads to automatic responses. Humans, by contrast, are able to prolong and sustain perception in such a way that they create a wider latitude for selecting responses. Bergson sums this up with the general law that 'perception is master of space in the exact measure in which action is the master of time' (p. 32).

This law introduces the other side of Bergson's 'frankly dualistic' approach: his treatment of memory. In order to grasp this adequately we must first understand a little of the unique approach that Bergson takes to the philosophy of time. The approaches that philosophers take to this topic can be crudely schematised as type A and type B (see Mullarkey, 1999). Type B approaches understand time as structured by objective relations of succession and simultaneity, where there are clear causes and effects shared between linked states of affairs (e.g. I gave him the key last week and this Friday he will let himself in). By contrast, type A approaches see time as a dynamic passage of future into present based on one's ongoing experience (e.g. she seems a little quieter and less engaged than when I saw her last). Bergson's philosophy of time resembles a type A approach in that it emphasises the ongoing flow or stream of time as we experience it, whilst reserving questions of objectivity for his philosophy of space.

This does not mean that Bergson's view of time is subjectivist, in the sense of there being a clearly bounded consciousness which moves through time. In *Time and free will*, Bergson argues that in order to have something like a consciousness, living beings must be able to synthesise past with present. The past must, in effect, be extended and prolonged beyond its immediate occurrence in such a way that the organism can compare its immediate circumstances with those that occurred previously. The ability to do so marks the transition between a purely reactive or instinctual mode of existence, where time and its passage is relatively unimportant since it has no significance for the organism, to a mode of living characterised by what Bergson calls *endurance*. To endure is to experience time as irreversible, as marking and shaping one's ongoing existence. Although the past is 'done' in the sense that there is no returning to the previous state of affairs, it extends into the present in that the organism is still involved in, or has an ongoing memory of its own past. Bergson names this extension of the past as *duration*:

> Pure duration is the form which the succession of our conscious states assumes when our ego lets itself *live*, when it refrains from separating its present state from its former states. For this purpose it need not be entirely absorbed in the passing sensation or idea; for then, on the contrary, it would no longer *endure*. Nor need it forget its former states: it is enough that in recalling these states, it does not set them alongside its actual state as one point alongside another, but forms both the past and the present states into an organic whole, as happens when we recall the notes of a tune, melting, so to speak, into one another. (1913/2001, p. 100)

Duration is the passage of time where one state 'melts' into the other, such that, whilst there is a real transition, the former is never really abolished by the latter. Bergson likens it to the unfolding of a tune. We know that there are different notes, but in the playing these notes become subsumed in the unwinding of the melody. The advantage of viewing the temporal succession of conscious states in this way is that it no longer becomes necessary to explain how one state replaces another. Experience is, for Bergson, a continuity which consists of qualitative rather than quantitative differentiation. Consciousness is an 'organic whole' where states have intensive rather than extensive relations to one another: 'we are thus compelled to admit that we have here to do with a synthesis which is, so to speak, qualitative, a gradual organization of our successive sensations, a unity resembling that of a phrase in a melody' (p. 111).

Bergson contrasts this view of the temporal structuring of experience with the commonsense notion that time consists of a series of instants or interval, where one follows the other in regular metric fashion (i.e. 'clock time'). To think time in this way is, Bergson claims, to transpose notions of spatiality onto the temporal, and thereby think time through its precise opposite. He illustrates this point by using the example of astronomy:

> [W]hen the astronomer predicts, e.g. an eclipse, he does something of this kind: he shortens infinitely the intervals of duration, as these do not count for science, and thus perceives in a very short time – a few seconds at most – a succession of simultaneities which may take up several centuries for the concrete consciousness, compelled to live through the intervals instead of merely counting the extremities. (Bergson, 1913/2001, p. 117)

The astronomer is in the business of making predictions. She needs to treat time as a simple metric against which the movement of astral bodies can be plotted. What matters is precision and the ability to calculate when some event may occur, whether or not it falls within her own lifetime. But the 'intervals' are not merely mathematical points. Conscious beings are 'compelled to live' through these intervals. The time of the astronomer is then fundamentally 'inhuman', it is a 'pulverised time' which cannot instruct us as to the real, qualitative experience of enduring as a living, acting being. Bergson's point applies to the most basic aspects of psychological life, as in the following example:

> Take for example the simplest feeling, suppose it to be constant, absorb the whole personality in it: the consciousness which will accompany this feeling will not be able to remain identical with itself for two consecutive moments, since the following moment always contains, over and above the preceding one, the memory the latter has left it. (Bergson, 1933/1992, p. 164)

Time, Bergson claims, is not something that happens *to us*, against which we might clearly mark, at any given moment, our particular state of mind. Rather time is *within us*, such that 'no two moments are identical in a conscious being' (p. 164). The transitory feeling of, say, anxiety, is not constituted by the rapid succession of anxious instants, but is rather a 'continual winding', subject to infinite variations, like a melody subject to innumerable arrangements. When one feels anxiety, the immediate consciousness of what has just happened, and of may be about to happen, lends the moment a unique character. It is implausible that we could ever feel precisely the same way again, not least because any future occasions of anxiety will include, and so gain their own unique tenor from, the memory of this current experience: 'there is no mood, however, no matter how simple, which does not change at every instant, since there is no consciousness without memory, no continuation of a state without the addition, to the present feeling, of the memory of past events' (p. 179).

If we approach psychological life as the kind of mobile continuity that Bergson outlines, then the traditional concerns of the psychology of memory are to some extent inverted (see Brown, 2008). It is no longer necessary to explain 'how' the past is stored since 'the past preserves itself automatically' (Bergson, 1933/1992, p. 153). Which is to say that if time is not a succession of instants, then it is no longer necessary to imagine that human memory has as its principal function the storing away of instants of past experience to make them fit for future retrieval. To see human life as structured by duration is to attend to:

> the continuous life of a memory which prolongs the past into the present, whether the present distinctly contains the ever-growing image of the past, or whether, by its continual changing of quality, it attests to the increasingly heavy burden dragged along behind one the older one grows. (Bergson, 1933/1992, p. 179)

What Bergson points to here is that if time, as duration, is of itself indivisible, then similarly memory must be treated as a continuous thread or 'burden' that is automatically built up and coextensive with ongoing experience. The past continuously 'gnaws into' (Bergson, 1911/1998, p. 4) the future, imbuing our current perceptions with a patina of recollection. What Bergson is arguing for, in psychological terms, is an understanding of memory as 'always on', as automatically recording the entirety of our experience, and, simultaneously, as informing our current actions at every turn. In addition, Bergson demands that we think of memory not as the preservation of individual events or episodes, but an indivisible whole where the totality of past experience is prolonged into the present (for broader discussion, see Middleton & Brown, 2005).

If the relationship between past and present is an indivisible whole, then our relation to the past is not set or stable. The meaning and significance of the past is continually restructured by the unfolding of duration itself. This 'reconstructive' view of memory is shared by experimental psychologists (see Schacter, 1996; Engel, 2000) and socio-cultural psychologists (see Middleton 2002; Wertsch, 2002). However, there is a real difference in how each handles questions around the nature and form of this reconstruction. For experimental psychologists it remains the case that it is possible in theory to establish the relative degrees of accuracy present in a given memory, even if it is often difficult to do so in practice. For socio-cultural psychologists, reconstruction is a more thoroughgoing matter since it involves a broader set of cultural and social forces. For example, the ways that Russians tell the history of their own nation is dominated by a narrative of 'expulsion of invading forces'. Individual memories are then shaped and contextualised by this overarching narrative (Wertsch, 2002).

Bergson adds another sense of reconstruction. If we have an indivisible bond with the entirety of our past, then clearly we do not consciously relate to every aspect of it at every moment (to do so would be to find ourselves in the frankly terrifying delirium of the Mnemonist 'S' studied by Luria (1962), or of the central character in Borges' short story, *Funes the Memorious*). Indeed, seen from this perspective the problem is not that of how the past is retained, but rather how it is held back 'from pressing on the portals of consciousness':

> [I]f we take into consideration the continuity of the inner life and consequently of its indivisibility, we no longer have to explain the preservation of the past, but rather its apparent abolition. We shall no longer have to account for remembering, but for forgetting. (1933/1992, p. 153)

'Forgetting' here means not to abolish something from experience, but to make less relevant, to background the greater part of the 'heavy burden' of the past so that it does not overwhelm our every act. Instead, only selected aspects of our past are made relevant at any moment in the unfolding of experience. The idea that duration 'swirls' or 'gnaws' its way into the present suggests that it is possible for novel ways of turning around on experience to emerge ('I listen to her voice and hear in it a trace of the accents from my old home town. I recall exactly why I wanted to never go back there'). In other words, whilst the past remains 'the same', it can be brought into novel juxtapositions with present events that allow for creative and transformative experiences to emerge.

Deleuze describes this idea in relation to Marcel Proust's conception of a 'time in a pure state' (Proust, 2003). When Marcel recalls his childhood town of Combray, in the famous scene with the tea-infused madeleine near the opening of *Swann's way*, what is interesting is the contingent relation between what is remembered and the process of recollection. Deleuze notes that we cannot understand this scene if we think of it in terms of associations between sensation (i.e. taste) and ideas (i.e. those of Combray and its inhabitants), since there really is no direct link between the tea and what Marcel subsequently recalls. What there is instead is a play of similarities and differences. The taste of the madeleine is the same both now and then. But the Combray that 'rises up' within that taste is not constituted in episodic terms. What Marcel recalls is a *set of qualities* that make up Combray – an array of colours, a sense of the temperature, the shape of the madeleines displayed in the patisserie window and so on. This, Deleuze argues, is a recollection of Combray that is dislocated, different in kind from either past or present moment:

> Combray rises up in a form that is absolutely new. Combray does not rise up as it was once present; Combray rises up as past, but this past is no longer relative to the present that it has been, it is no longer relative to the present to which it is now past ... Combray appears as it could not be experienced ... Combray rises up in a pure past, coexisting with the two presents, but out of their reach ... 'A morsel of time in the pure state'. (III, 872) (Deleuze, 2000: 61)

Deleuze then claims, drawing on Bergson, that what Marcel recollects is a 'past that never was'. This is most certainly not a 'false memory'. What is at issue is the structure of memory itself (see also Haaken & Reavey, 2009). This follows directly from Bergson's approach to memory in terms of duration. If all of our past experiences are by definition part of our unfolding duration, and if duration is organised in a qualitative, undifferentiated 'virtual' fashion, our memory for events then involves reconstruction; we artificially extract or dissociate past events from the otherwise interconnected tissue of duration in order that they can be re-inserted into the demands of current circumstances by 'actualisation'. So what we recollect is technically not exactly what we experienced at the time. Moreover, since duration is the condition of any sort of experience whatsoever, it is simply impossible that we could ever bring these conditions as such directly to consciousness (this would be rather like attempting to lift ourselves up by our own shoe laces). So, again, we must necessarily say that what we recollect is a past 'that never was' (see also Lawlor, 2003).

What Marcel recollects is a set of qualities that are extracted from his unlimited 'virtual' prior experience of Combray. This includes not only his former direct experience, but also his experience of all the times that he has since reflected upon Combray. So these qualities, whilst grounded in the totality of his experience, are not really relative to any particular event. Hence what he recollects is strictly speaking relative to neither past nor present. It is Combray 'as it could not [have been] experienced'. So the overwhelming sense of joy which Marcel feels arises from his sense of a difference in kind between this 'new' Combray and the one that was recollected on other occasions. Proust refers to this as the experience of a 'morsel of time'.

Bergson's notions of reconstruction and forgetting in memory allow us to approach the 'memory wars' in a slightly different way (for empirical illustrations see Reavey & Brown, 2006, 2007, 2009). Reconstruction is acknowledged by all sides, including the FMSF, who claim on their website that 'some of our memories are true, some are a mixture of fact and fantasy, and some are false – whether those memories seem to be continuous or seem to be recalled after a time of being forgotten or not thought about' (fmsfonline.org). For the FMSF, these differences in the truth value may be resolved by external corroboration. However, as the feminist philosopher Sue Campbell (2003) observes, this implies that all accounts of the past are given equal merit and subject to fair test. This is simply not the case. Some groups of rememberers – notably women, children, persons with mental health issues – find their testimonies subject to systematic mistrust and suspicion. They tend not to be regarded as 'reliable rememberers'. The idea that their accounts of their own past, whether 'continuous' or 'recalled after a time of being forgotten', would automatically be taken seriously and on that basis allowed to seek external corroboration is often not the case. Moreover, as Janice Haaken (1998) describes at length, this also fails to acknowledge the way that claims about abuse may serve as 'master narratives' for all manner of routine, casual oppression suffered by women. From Bergson's perspective, reconstruction in memory is always relational. It arises from the juxtaposition between that part of our experience which is being mobilised in the present and the circumstances, the 'selectivity' or 'foothold' we have in relation to the world around us. Under these circumstances we may turn around on our experience in novel ways, in the same way that Marcel experiences Combray in a way that is 'new'. But the elements that make up this experience are not themselves invented – they are real parts of our 'ever-growing' duration. The question then becomes that of understanding the juxtaposition, the precise ways in which our duration becomes inserted into the ongoing action, and at the same time has to confront the duration of others.

Lost in the Past

Jim persuades his brother that he was once lost in the shopping mall as a child. Chris comes, apparently, to believe this. From our Bergsonian perspective, the first thing we might observe is that if such an event did happen, Chris's experience of being lost would have little to do with any subjective beliefs on his part. Our engagement with the world is not driven by our ability to represent it in one way or another. Because Bergson refuses to accord any determinate role to mental images or cognitive representations in human action, we will be unable to sort out what happens in LIM by appeal to a superordinate layer of mental processing which intervenes either at the time of the original events or in the process of their subsequent recollection. The concept of 'imagination inflation' will be of little use to us.

LIM predicts that Chris will include the false event suggested to him by Jim to produce a different story about their joint past. But it does so without taking into account anything about their relationship so far, other than the effects of the suggestion procedure itself, as though this were something like a chemical reaction rather than one interaction situated with respect to the broad and deep history shared by two brothers. The experiment hypothesises that a given state of affairs will come about (the participant will recall something that did not happen), irrespective of the particular circumstances in which the experiment is conducted (a party, a classroom, a laboratory) and the specific unfolding of the interaction between the confederate and the participant. LIM seeks to abolish time and place in the name of predicting a determinate change in the subjective qualities of its target participant – Chris will develop a false belief.

In *Time and free will*, Bergson discusses a thought experiment used by physicists to consider the temporal paradoxes which occur as physical movement approaches the speed of light. There are two brothers – Peter and Paul. One agrees to travel through space at a faster-than-light speed. The other remains on earth. A seeming eternity passes until Peter returns. During this time Paul has become an old man. His brother, however, has not aged due to the paradoxes of faster-than-light travel. For physicists the point of the story is the paradox and the relation between time and the speed of light. Bergson emphasises instead that the lived time of Paul's ageing is not incidental to the experiment, it is a central feature. It really matters that Peter has lived a whole life before he greets his brother again. Similarly, in LIM the shared history between Jim and Chris is also important. It is significant that at this particular point in their lives together Jim asks Chris to turn around on his own past. That they reflect on this particular (false) episode jointly also has implications for the way their futures might unfold. Duration, time as it is lived, is not something that can be excluded. It is utterly essential to understanding both experiments and experiences. Consider the following example that Bergson provides in *Creative evolution*:

> If I want to mix a glass of sugar and water, I must, willy nilly, wait until the sugar melts. This little fact is big with meaning. For here the time I have to wait is not that mathematical time which would apply equally well to the entire history of the material world ... It coincides with my impatience, that is to say, with a certain portion of my own duration, which I cannot protract or contract as I like. It is no longer something *thought*, it is something *lived*. (1911/1998, pp. 9–10)

In a simple act, such as mixing sugar with water, time is important because it is lived. We cannot simplify time – 'prolong or contract it as I like' – since to do so is to simplify the very nature of experience itself. We must wait for the sugar to dissolve. Our own duration becomes hooked into that of another (in this case, the time of the sugar dissolving). The impatience that we feel is an emergent property of this interdependency between our own lived time and that of the other. Being made to wait then involves a form of 'uncertainty' in relation to the unfolding of time: 'time is this very hesitation, or it is nothing' (1933/1992, p. 93). Jim and Chris must experience something similar during the LIM procedure. Each is hooked into and comes to depend upon the time of the other. Jim is made to wait until Chris comes to affirm the false memory. Chris is made to wait in whatever he is doing by Jim's insistence that they discuss this particular episode from their childhood. What is in fact crucial to LIM is this simple fact of Jim's and Chris's shared childhood. It is because Jim's duration, his lived time, includes that of Chris that he is able to discuss the childhood episode. It is less that they share a common duration, than that their durations are overlapping, interdependent with one another. Bergson describes this phenomenon using the following example:

> When we are seated on the bank of a river, the flowing of the water, the gliding of a boat or the flight of a bird, the ceaseless murmur in our life's deeps are for us three separate things or only one, as we choose. (1922/1999, p. 36)

Sat on the river bank, the observer can become involved with any of the movements they see and hear around them. These movements can come together, being folded into our 'rhythm of living'. This experience is not so much one of losing oneself, as becoming synchronised with other pulses and undulations in the unfolding of their and our lived time together. Bergson (1992) speaks of this synchronisation as akin to two trains running at similar speeds on parallel tracks. One might lean from the window and try to greet a passenger on the opposite train, since it feels like there is no movement. In truth it is simply that two moving trains are for that moment synchronised following similar patterns of movement. In LIM Jim plays on an apparent synchronisation of his duration with Chris. Like the passenger who extends her hand to greet another on the opposite train, Jim asks Chris to look back from the conversation they are having to the childhood experience. But Jim's folding of Chris's duration into his own is not a greeting, a mutual envelopment of one duration by another. It is a form of betrayal. Jim is attempting to discredit Chris's relationship to his own past.

It turns out then that LIM is an extremely important experiment for the psychology of memory, and for the 'memory wars' themselves. It tells us about the complexities of relations and the ways in which memory, as duration, comes to be 'inserted' into the present. Our foothold in the present is always limited, selective. As such it is structured by the relations we have to others and the forms of mediation which allow us to extract or abstract the bits of the world that appear most useful to us. This is accomplished relationally in tandem with others. Chris struggles to make sense of the peculiar circumstances in which he finds himself through interaction with his brother, and with the setting itself. Both of them turn around on their past, on their individual durations, which overlap and envelop one another. Again, this is a relational matter – how does our past show up when it is juxtaposed with that of another, when my experience becomes folded into yours and yours into mine, in a kind of grasping, enveloping, intensifying and unfolding? This is where we need to start, and indeed where our lives always begin and end, in the immersion of our duration into the immensity of others, and theirs into ours.

EIGHT

Foucault and Subjectivity

We are at the admissions department of the Sainte-Anne Psychiatric Hospital in Paris in 1952, from where the mentally ill, whom the Paris police have picked up the night before, are distributed. 'How many do you want for the clinic this morning?', the charge nurse asks psychiatrist Pierre Deniker. Normally, these patients were not 'particularly welcome' on the wards. Jacques Thuillier ... tells us 'It was not much of a gift when one received a maniacal patient who for weeks would shriek, and injure other patients; who had to be put in a straight-jacket and even tied to the bed with straps'. Nonetheless, Deniker, who normally would have taken just one or two to demonstrate in his clinic, tells her he will take them all. He says to the nurse, 'We've found a trick that works'. (Shorter, 2000, p. 89)

The trick that Deniker describes was a new drug treatment – Chlorpromazine (CPZ). Derived from a class of drugs originally intended as anaesthetics, CPZ was one of the first pharmacological anti-psychotics to be widely used. The team at Sainte-Anne, including Pierre Deniker and his senior colleague Jean Delay, were the first to use the drug for the treatment of patients with psychotic symptoms (i.e. persons usually diagnosed as 'schizophrenic'). It is important to grasp not merely the perilous state of the mental health service provision in which they operated, but also the nature of the rival treatment then available, principally Electro-Convulsive Therapy (ECT) and Insulin-Coma Therapy (ICT) (see Healy, 2002 for overview). The former involved either repeated electric shocks to the patient to bring about seizures, as endured by Artaud at Rodez, or application of insulin to lower blood sugar levels to induce stupor and coma. Both treatments, developed in Europe in the 1930s, were initially considered progressive inasmuch as they replaced a system where psychotic symptoms were simply contained by confining patients (e.g. physical restraint and literal imprisonment). ECT and ICT aimed to arrest symptoms by putting the body into such a state of arrest that it could no longer function. The embodied ground is cut from under the psychotic episode.

Although initially considered as treatments of last resort, the rapid results that could be gained from these methods ensured their spread across Europe and to North America (Doroshow, 2007).

Despite initial successes, ICT and ECT were surrounded by controversy. Not only was the actual means by which they 'worked' not fully understood, but also their relative crudeness, along with the high risks associated (mortality in patients who received ICT can vary from 1–10 per cent, Doroshow, 2006), made them both unpleasant to endure and dangerous to administer. Set against this, Deniker's enthusiasm for his new 'trick' is understandable. CPZ treatment appeared to offer a reliable, comparatively safe method of treating psychotic symptoms. More than this, it promised to transform the psychiatric ward from a prison *manqué* to a genuinely therapeutic environment. As Jean Thullier describes it:

> The hemp waistcoats were put back in the cupboards, and the hydrotherapy pools were used only for personal washing ... One no longer passed patients walking with their straightjackets open with straps undone on the way to the toilets ... The most evident sign of this extraordinary therapeutic result could be appreciated even from the outside of the building of the men's clinic – there was silence. (1999, p. 113)

The 'silence' both literally and metaphorically around CPZ would not last for long. From the late 1950s onwards, driven by the work of R.D. Laing in the UK, Franco Basaglia in Italy and Kees Trimbos in the Netherlands, an 'anti-psychiatry' movement rapidly developed around a powerful critique of psychiatry as an institution of social repression (see Sedgewick, 1982). There were numerous aspects to this critique, including a demolition of the concept of schizophrenia (elaborated again recently in the comprehensive work of Richard Bentall, 2003, and Mary Boyle, 2002), a political analysis of psychiatry as an agent of state power (see Cooper 1978; Guattari, 1984), and a critique of the role of the pharmaceutical industry as having a vested interest in developing mental health as a market for consuming new drug therapies (Newnes, Dunn & Holmes, 1999; Newnes, Holmes & Dunn, 2001). For the anti-psychiatry movement, CPZ amounted to a 'chemical cosh', a way of ensuring that mental health service users were docile and manageable in psychiatric settings. The adverse effects of this management practice have been detailed at length in the writings of mental health service users (e.g. Shaugnessey, 2000), ranging from constipation, weight gain, disrupted sleep patterns, chronic sedation and the accompanying sense of general impairment, lack of agency and utter inattention to the social context of 'madness' (see Bentall et al., 2009). If it ever did 'work' as such, Deniker's 'trick' can most certainly no longer be described in such simplistic terms.

The work of Michel Foucault is often described against the background of the psychiatry/anti-psychiatry debate. His *History of madness* offers a grand story of the emergence of 'confinement' as the preferred social technology for managing mental health. But it does considerably more than this. It also traces an ambiguous relationship between madness and reason which unfolds in accord with the major historical shifts in Western Europe (i.e. the changing social fabric following the Black Death; industrialisation and Enlightenment; the opening of modernity). The treatment of madness is then continuous with shifts in forms of reason, as that which serves as its limit and opposite. Foucault's concerns in this book are apparently very removed from the specific struggles around mental health in the late 1950s/early 1960s, being lodged at a level of philosophical analysis that seems to play fast and loose with actual historical details (see Sedgwick, 1982; Porter, 1990).

Foucault had, however, both studied and taught psychology, with a particular orientation to the clinical. He also claimed to have served an informal internship in a psychiatric setting (see Macey, 1993), and published his first work on the relationship between categories of mental health and the phenomenology of madness (Foucault, 1987). His choice to position madness within a historically informed philosophical analysis of the transformations of reason and truth in Western Europe was therefore grounded in some experience of the practicalities of mental health treatment that were routine for Deniker. In later years, Foucault would describe the logic of his project in the following terms: 'My objective ... has been to create a history of the different modes by which, in our culture, human beings are made subjects' (Foucault, 2002, p. 326). There is a gap – or as Heidegger would put it an 'ontological difference' – opened here between 'human being' and 'subject'. We can grasp this as the difference between questions of what it is to be human, and the various historical and cultural renderings of humanness as particular kinds of 'subjects' that differ in kind to the entities that make up the rest of the natural world. This is the difference between asking 'what is it to be human?' and studying the historically specific means of what Ian Hacking (2000) calls 'making up people' – i.e. establishing what is relevant and meaningful about human conduct and how it ought to be best organised. Although it might appear to be the case, the one question does not negate the other. Rather, what Foucault points to, following Heidegger, is that at every point in history, there are specific bodies of knowledge and techniques through which the abstract, universal question of humanness is posed and explored. At their point of intersection there is what could be called a faultline (Curt, 1994), or better perhaps a membrane, across which the two questions – 'what is it to be a human?' and 'how in this time, at this place is the human subject constituted?' – come into contact with another. A psychology of the second order (see Chapter 1) takes this membrane as its subject matter.

Mental health has always been a highly contested faultline along this ontological difference. Many of the psychologists and psychiatrists who were responsible for the care of Artaud, for example – whose number included Jacques Lacan – were involved in the literary and arts scene of pre-war Paris. Jean Delay himself had studied under the great philosopher/psychologist

Pierre Janet, whose work had been rediscovered as a conceptual resource by proponents of the 'Memory Wars' (see Haaken, 1998). The man who would introduce the treatment that would so effectively compromise the sense of agency and self in generations of mental health service users had completed a doctorate on the 'dissolution' of memory under Janet's direction. In his later years, Delay dedicated himself to producing a 'psychosociobiography' of his own family (Etain & Roubaud, 2002), displaying a level of acuity to the contextual shaping of the personal that he appeared to be unwilling to accord to his own patients.

Raising the ontological difference in psychology seems, then, to be problematic. On the one hand we have a figure such as Foucault who prepares a philosophical analysis that seems to stand in an ambiguous relation to the actualities of daily practice, despite his close understanding of the latter. On the other, we have someone like Delay who appears to leave behind his philosophical roots in the discovery of a 'trick' that renders his wards orderly. And yet surely it is the business of psychology to ensure that the difference, the gap, between 'what it is to be a human' and 'how subjects are practically formed', remains under constant questioning. Can Foucault's work allow us to do so, or does it bequeath a problematic legacy to psychology?

Foucauldian Psychology

The initial reception of Foucault's work in British psychology was through the writings of the editorial collective (Diana Adlam, Julian Henriques, Nikolas Rose, Angie Salfield, Couze Venn, Valerie Walkerdine) of the journal *Ideology & Consciousness* (later *I&C*) in the late 1970s. In a seminal article, Adlam et al. (1977) argued that the 'subject' of psychology was an ideological construct premised on the systematic decoupling of the individual from the broader social order. This subject is built up out of a set of liberal-humanist, male, bourgeois Western assumptions, but is passed off as though it were a universal model of selfhood. What is studied by psychologists is a convenient fiction that bears little resemblance to concrete lived experience. But, perniciously, the institutional power of modern psychology invites its clients and consumers to view this fictitious subject as though it were the best route to self-understanding.

This work drew upon a mixture of Althusserian Marxism and psychoanalysis to critique modern psychology and theorise alternative models of subjectivity. In a subsequent co-authored book, *Changing the subject*, Henriques, J., Hollway, W., Urwin, C., Venn, C. & Walkerdine, V. (1984) drew Foucault's work more centrally into this heady theoretical brew to elucidate the power/knowledge couple at work in psychology as a diverse set of institutional and cultural practices. Psychology is viewed as intertwined with the governance of everyday life, where it seeks to promote itself as the principal authority on self-knowledge. Drawing heavily on Foucault's (1977) notion of the shift from 'sovereign' to 'pastoral' power relations, Henriques et al. argue that psychology is critical to modern techniques of subjectification, i.e. the forging of a relationship to self through prescribed techniques of self-knowing that is accomplished with reference to particular images or models of selfhood.

This notion is drawn out at greater length in Nikolas Rose's (1985; 1989; 1996) historical sociology. Rose proposes that the power relations that mediate psychological knowledge go far beyond academic or clinical psychology. They have extended deep into social welfare practices (e.g. social work, professional child care), into education and criminal law. To capture this deep dispersion of interrelated psychological power/knowledge, Rose offers the term 'the psychological complex' (typically shortened to 'psy-complex'). Central to Rose's analysis are the twin Foucauldian notions of 'normalisation' and 'confession'.

Normalisation is the promotion of a moral code which comes to serve as the standard for deciphering a given aspect of human conduct. Thus, in Foucault's early work (1961/2005), a key moment in the cultural archaeology of madness arises when 'reason' becomes the moral standard. Madness is then construed as either being excluded from or refusing reason – it becomes defined as 'unreason'. Similarly, in the *Will to knowledge* volume of the *History of sexuality*, the emergence of a 'science' of sexuality creates a new hegemonic relationship between sex and truth – 'Not only did it speak of sex and compel everyone to do so; it also set out to formulate the uniform truth of sex' (1979, p. 69). This 'compulsion to speak' of sex in a particular way, or 'incitement to discourse' as Foucault sometimes expresses it (1979), is a new twist on the ancient cultural practice of *confession*. Foucault (2000a) notes that in ancient Rome, the confessing of one's weaknesses or transgression was seen as critical to self-improvement. However, within the subsequent Christian tradition, confession comes to be seen as involving a renunciation of self. To confess is to disavow one's conduct and seek reparation. For Rose, following Foucault, the psy-complex transforms confession again, such that what is renounced is one's former self-knowledge, whilst reparation comes from following the explicit guidance of the psychologist. Confession draws persons into speaking and thinking of themselves entirely with reference to the liberal-humanist subject. As a consequence, the key values of modern capital (entrepreneurship, self-reliance, personal growth) are inculcated in the many and varied sites through which the psy-complex operates.

Although Rose's work is mostly historical analysis, concerned with very specific topics such as the emergence of the Tavistock School of Human Relations (Rose & Miller, 1986), it has given inspiration to an empirical approach dubbed Foucauldian Discourse Analysis (see Willig, 2001). The reasoning behind this approach is that if modern subjectivities are formed through processes of normalisation and confession, then close textual analysis ought to be able to reveal how the moral codes of the psy-complex are mobilised and contested in interactions (e.g. counselling sessions; relationship talk) or texts (e.g. official documents; formal instructions and advice) where psychological issues are at stake. Erica Burman and Ian Parker's work has done most by way of demonstrating the normalising effect of the psy-complex in areas such as psychopathology

(Parker, Georgaca, Harper, McLaughlin & Stowell-Smith, 1995) and child development (Burman, 2007). What is most striking about this approach is its ability to show the sheer ubiquity of normalisation – as in Parker's analysis of the moral codings at work in the instructions on a tube of toothpaste (see Banister, Burman, Parker, Taylor & Tindall, 1989).

Foucauldian Discourse Analysis also accords a central place to the notion of *resistance*. Foucault uses resistance as a methodological device from which to view power relations from the perspective of the strictly local and particular points where opposition develops. He describes this operation in the following way:

> It consists in taking the forms of resistance against different forms of power as a starting point. To use another metaphor, it consists in using this resistance as a chemical catalyst so as to bring to light power relations, locate their position, find out their point of application and the methods used. Rather than analyzing power relations from the point of view of its internal rationality, it consists of analyzing power relations through the antagonism of strategies. (Foucault, 2002, p. 329)

This methodological use of the term accords it a peculiar status – instances of resistance are the 'odd term in relations of power; they are inscribed in the latter as an irreducible opposite' (Foucault, 1979, p. 96). In other words, not only is resistance assumed by the analyst, it is also, Foucault claims, logically assumed within power relations themselves. Thus in an oft-cited phrase from the fifth methodological proposition of *Will to knowledge*, Foucault declares 'Where there is power there is also resistance, and yet, or rather consequently, this resistance is never in a position of exteriority in relation to power' (1979, p. 95). There are two distinct epistemic 'horrors' (cf. Woolgar, 1988) contained here. First, from a methodological perspective, if we make the analytic assumption that resistance is present in any empirical material, then to some extent we risk the lure of seeing what we want and confirming our own prior perspective. Second, in theoretical terms, positioning resistance as interior to power skirts a certain kind of nominalism. Power can have no outside at all. It is literally the fabric of social life itself. If this is so then analytically the concept becomes quite impoverished, since it provides no differentiation and acts as a universal given (see Brown, 2007). In fact, Foucault himself came to view his theory of power as an obstacle to his own thought (Marks, 2000).

These twinned methodological and theoretical horrors mean that a Foucauldian psychology often finds itself in the rather difficult-to-sustain position of providing a relentless and repetitive auto-critique of the normalising role of the psy-disciplines without being able to offer much by way of an alternative. Take, for example, the following description of the psy-complex given by Rose:

> On the parade ground, in the factory, in the school, and in the hospital, people are gathered together en masse, but by this very fact may be observed as entities both similar to and different from one another. These institutions function in certain respects like telescopes, microscopes, or other scientific instruments: they establish a regime of visibility in

which the observed is distributed within a single common plane of sight. Second, these institutions operate according to a regulation of detail. These regulations, and the evaluation of conduct, manners, and so forth entailed by them, establish a grid of codeability of personal attributes. They act as norms, enabling the previously aleatory and unpredictable complexities of human conduct to be conceptually coded and cognized in terms of judgements as to conformity or deviation from such norms. (Rose, 1996, p. 105)

What Rose describes here is a process where persons are brought together in order to be collectively compared and assessed with respect to one another. In so doing, each individual is brought into a common frame of reference and evaluation. This enables her or his conduct, which was hitherto 'unpredictable' and 'complex', to be rendered as knowable in terms of how far it follows or diverges from the common reference points or 'norms'. In one sense, this appears to be a straightforward gloss on Foucault's (1977a) description of the disciplining of 'docile bodies'. But it overlooks a crucial additional meaning to the sense of the normal in which Foucault was well versed.

Georges Canguilhem, who acted as internal examiner on Foucault's doctoral work, was a philosopher of science who specialised in studies of the life sciences. Canguilhem's studies treat science as the exploration of normative rational judgements constituted within a historically grounded discourse. In so doing, science necessarily divides and evaluates its given field and objects of enquiry to produce statements about norms (i.e. tendencies, generalities, laws). But the actual practice of accomplishing this work has its own contingent, historical character according to its own internal norms of progression and good judgement, which are sometimes subject to wholesale crises and revisions. To study science, then, is to study the interdependence and interplay between two sorts of normativity – norms which arise from the division and manipulation of scientific objects and norms which define the forms of rationality driving such scientific activity at any given historical moment. Foucault's description of his own work as examining the historicity of 'games of truth' which construct the very objects of which they speak through their own practices is deeply indebted to Canguilhem.

The interplay between norms that Canguilhem points to is rather different from Rose's description. Rose talks of the standardisation and codification of norms as means of transforming a previously unknown and unpredictable object into a clear target of evaluation and management. Norms become inscribed, laws of truth are imposed on the object. But for Canguilhem, norms are not only applied in such a 'top-down' fashion. Norms do not emerge entirely within the discursive framework of a given practice. It is rather the case that the object of the practice has its own capacity to 'bear' certain kinds of normative activity. The practice then procures or recruits this prior capacity for normativity on the part of the object in the formulation of its own norms. For example, in Canguilhem's key work *The normal and the pathological*, these two terms are interrogated closely. Typically we assume that pathology involves a departure from the norm, from usual functioning. Ill health is then judged to be'abnormal'. However, Canguilhem argues that this treatment of health flies in the face of biological reality. To be healthy is to be adaptive, to be able to respond to the challenges of the environment flexibly and changeably. This variability in response is the capacity for normativity – the ability to become attuned to a range of possible norms. By contrast, pathology is typically characterised either by a lack of adaptive responses, or by becoming locked into a single response despite changes in conditions. When interpreted in this way, health is related to the prior capacity for normativity of the organism, whilst pathology becomes the reduction of this capacity, for whatever reason, to a single norm.

Monica Greco (2004; 2005; *in press*) discusses this theme in relation to Canguilhem's particular brand of 'vitalism', according to which normativity is associated with a form of *creativity* resonant with our conception of creative foundationalism. That is to say, with regard to health 'normativity' refers to an indeterminate surplus of vital possibilities available to an organism; a surplus with respect to those that are actualised in response to any given situation (Greco, 2004, p. 3). As Canguilhem put it:

> [b]ehind all apparent normality, one must look to see if it is capable of tolerating infractions of the norm, of overcoming contradictions, of dealing with conflicts. Any normality open to possible future correction is authentic normativity, or health. Any normality limited to maintaining itself, hostile to any variations in the themes that express it, and incapable of adapting to new situations is a normality devoid of normative intention. When confronted with any apparently normal situation, it is therefore important to ask whether the norms that it embodies are creative norms, norms with a forward thrust, or, on the contrary, conservative norms, norms whose thrust is toward the past. (1994, p. 351–352)

If we apply Canguilhem's distinction to psychology we rapidly see that normalisation per se is not the problem. It is simply not the case that the psy-disciplines have historically imposed norms on persons who were until that point blessed with unknowable and unpredictable attributes. Rather, the psy-disciplines engage selectively with the normative capacities of persons, elaborating and promoting certain aspects of these capacities which become elevated into their own disciplinary norms, leaving the others at the periphery of their field of concern. For example, the well-known human capacity to affect concrete changes in the physical state or behaviour of another through sub-physical means (i.e. words, rituals) is routinely ignored by psychologists as 'mere suggestion' and hence deemed unworthy of attention (see Chertok & Stengers, 1992). In other words, it is the ontological difference between the capacity for normativity and the local practices of 'norming' that ought to be of central concern for psychology.

The difference between Canguilhem's and Rose's account of the psy-complex is subtle but significant. For Rose, the psy-disciplines are a disaster. They have constituted and fostered forms of subjectivity that are governed by norms fitted to the demands of late capital. This description is quite close to the image of the 'general rationalisation' of the social field envisaged by the

Frankfurt School. But whilst they could at least find solace in the idea of the liberation of desire, Rose sees only limited opportunities for 'breaking the diagram' of modern governance by way of the psy-disciplines, most notably through the new technologies of neuropsychological manipulation, such as Prozac use (see Rose, 2001). For Canguilhem we may say, contrastingly, that he finds the psy-disciplines to be a relative disappointment. Their failure is not that of having forged norms for human conduct, but rather that they have failed to be sufficiently normative. In an article pithily entitled 'What is psychology?' Canguilhem argues that psychology will not be a science so long as it is content with an impoverished view of human capacities based around a few norms which are selected for their ideological resonance with modern governmental practices. A scientific psychology would multiply and proliferate normative criteria to express the adaptive powers of the human organism. Against the common claim that psychology is normative and reductive because it is enamoured with the biological sciences, Canguilhem would retort that psychology does not draw enough inspiration from biology, that it fails to appreciate the complex nature of biological modes of normativity.

In summary, Foucault's work has typically been adopted within psychology as a means of conducting an auto-critique of the psy-disciplines. Modern subjectivities are wrought through practices of normalisation, with alternative modes of relating to self having only just started to emerge through the rise of techniques of bodily manipulation and modification (see Rose, 2001, and Hardt & Negri's 2000 deeply unlikely list of 'modern primitive' revolutionary subjects). However, as we have seen, such a reading misses other tendencies and meanings in Foucault's work – such as Canguilhem's normativity – that might serve as more productive starting points for considering subjectivity. In the remainder of this chapter we explore the extent to which Foucault's later work offers an alternative to this relative neglect of ontological difference and enables us to see normativity as a source of creative foundationalism.

The Art of Living

In the last few years of his life, Foucault embarked on a series of changes to his working practices (see Macey, 1993). In 1979, Foucault announced that his annual course at the Collège de France would be concerned with 'the government of the living'. This marked a departure from previous years in that the focus was no longer on the 'biopolitical' forms of governance that emerged in the eighteenth and nineteenth centuries. Foucault proposed, instead, to study how in Western Christian culture the 'government of men' (*sic*) demands that the subject not only tells the truth, but more importantly 'tells the truth about himself, his faults, his desires, the state of his soul and so on' (Foucault, 2000b, p. 81). This would be accomplished through an examination of confessional practices in early Christianity.

Confession had, of course, been one of the major concepts in Foucault's work during the mid-1970s and in the first volume of *The history of sexuality*. But in the 1979 course Foucault makes not just a historical but also a conceptual shift. Confession is no longer seen solely as instrumental to relations of power, instead it is accorded a kind of autonomy as a practice. Foucault is particularly concerned with the twin concepts of *exomologēsis* (the act of revealing the truth about oneself and affirming one's commitment to doing so) and *exagoreusis* (an obligation to produce exhaustive self-descriptions of one's thoughts and conduct). Whilst these twin practices certainly become adopted by the psy-disciplines – most notably in psychoanalytic therapeutic practice – Foucault intimates that their role in early Christian culture is not one of normalisation, but of creating a different kind of relationship to self.

The 1980 course on 'Subjectivity and truth' provides further clarification. Here Foucault introduces the term 'technologies of self' to refer to the variety of ways that 'the subject [was] established at different moments and in different institutional contexts as a possible, desirable or even indispensable object of knowledge' (Foucault, 2000c, p. 87). 'Technologies of the self' is one interpretation Foucault offers of the ancient term *tekhnē tou biou*. Foucault's use of the term technology here accomplishes several things. It enables him to locate these practices of relating to self as a distinct domain of enquiry alongside his previous work. In a seminar at the University of Vermont in 1982, Foucault divided his work to date into four themes:

> 1) technologies of production, which permit us to produce, transform or manipulate things; 2) technologies of sign systems, which permit us to use signs, meanings, symbols, or signification; 3) technologies of power, which determine the conduct of individuals and submit them to certain ends or domination, an objectivising of the subject; 4) technologies of the self, which permit individuals to effect by their own means, or with the help of others, a certain number of operations on their own bodies and souls, thoughts, conduct, and way of being, so as to transform themselves in order to attain a certain state of happiness, purity, wisdom, perfection or immortality. (Foucault, 2000a, p. 225)

Technologies of self sit with the other technologies described here in so far as each represents a sort of 'practical rationality'. Each technology comprises a body of knowledge and a simultaneous field of application that constructs and elaborates its own objects (i.e. what is commonly referred to in Foucauldian work as the inseparability of power-knowledge). Hence the self that is the object of the fourth technology is no less a product than the values produced by the first, the signs constituted by the second or the ends defined by the third. Moreover, the technical project of effecting a 'certain number of operations' on the person is one that is without end. In the same way that technologies of power are perpetually active in the social field, so technologies of the self form a kind of life project, a working on oneself that defines a certain mode of existence.

Foucault's translation of *tekhnē* as technology is consonant with Heideggerian scholarship (a permanent thread throughout Foucault's work). In an apocalyptic lecture given in 1955, Heidegger (1977) had proposed that the ultimate end of modern technology was the complete instrumentalisation of the human subject (cf. Stenner, 1998). We would come to think of ourselves as calculable objects to be deployed or disposed of in the same way that nature had been rendered as a pure 'resource'. Once set in train, Heidegger claims, there is no end to modern technology. But there is the possibility that a 'saving power grows within', since what we call 'technical' remains in its essence the modern development of ancient *tekhnē*. The statement about a 'saving power' derives from the poetry of Hölderlin who wrote *'but where the danger is, grows the saving power also'*. Hölderlin also wrote the following line: *'poetically dwells man upon the earth'* (cited in Heidegger, 1977, emphasis not in original). For Heidegger, the potential saving power of ancient *tekhnē* flows from the fact that it was characterised as a mode of *poiēsis*, where *poiēsis* denotes a mode of revealing that 'brings forth' (p. 29) or that 'lets what presences come forth into appearance' (p. 27) and that 'has the character of a destining'. This is the same *poiēsis* that is at play in Maturana and Varela's (and by extension, Luhmann's) notion of *autopoiesis* – a self-foundationing creativity whose present actuality calls into being its own future from out of its own past. Heidegger contrasts this *poiēsis* in which presencing bursts forth from within the thing itself with the mode of revealing and destining that characterises modern instrumental technology. Heidegger names this *das Ge-stell* which is translated as 'Enframing' but which also evokes a sense of a bare skeleton of existence. Heidegger thus contrasts *tekhnē*-as-*poiēsis* with modern technology-as-enframing:

> As compared with that other revealing [i.e. *poiēsis*], the setting-upon that challenges forth [i.e. *Ge-stell*] thrusts man into a relation to that which is, that is at once antithetical and rigorously ordered. Where Enframing holds sway, regulating and securing of the standing-reserve mark all revealing. They no longer even let their own fundamental characteristic appear, namely, this revealing as such. (Heidegger, 1977, p. 27)

Meditating on the difference between the ancient and the modern may, Heidegger announces, provide a means to reorient our understanding of technology from within. Foucault adopts a similar strategy. If modern subjectivities are dominated by normalising techniques, then searching for the ancient origins of *tekhnē tou biou* may provide a way to reactivate a 'saving power' within their contemporary use. Foucault then turns to ancient Greece and Rome, in part because he hopes to find alternative modalities of normativity for fashioning selfhood rather than extreme normalisation (see O'Leary, 2002). As he puts it: 'I don't think one can find any normalization in, for instance, the Stoic ethics' (Foucault, 2000d, p. 254).

The return to antiquity also marks a shift in *The history of sexuality* series. In *Will to knowledge*, Foucault had been concerned with the emergence of the science of sexuality and the way this reconfigured sexual relations through confessional technologies. But in resituating confession as a technology of self, Foucault folds the genealogy of sexuality back into a broader project of the 'history of the different modes by which, in our culture, human beings are made subjects' (Foucault, 2002, p. 326). Foucault shifts his attention to the way in which the Greeks considered sensuality – the pleasures of the body. He becomes concerned with 'self-mastery' as the basis for an ethics of subjectivity, which includes sexual ethics. In *Discipline and punish*, Foucault had tended to consider the body as a 'docile' object which was managed and arranged within technologies of power. These technologies treat the body as a passive 'recording surface' on which norms and subjectivities are inscribed. But in ancient Greece, what appears to matter is the active relation one has with one's own body. This is in turn mediated by the application of physical and spiritual exercises or *askēsis*. Self-mastery, taking charge of one's own pleasures, is accomplished through the ongoing application of these exercises.

Foucault (1988) notes that the relative neglect of *askēsis* in studies of subjectivity has arisen because of a gradual separation between two key Greek terms – *epimeleisthai sautou* ('to take care of yourself') and *gnōthi seauton* ('know yourself'). It is the latter edict, the search for self-knowledge as the basis for living the good life that has been retained and made central to modern subjectivity. Yet for the ancient Greeks, self-knowledge could only come about through 'taking care', that is, the use of exercises and techniques performed in relation to oneself. Knowledge of self emerges from active efforts to master embodiment. O'Leary (2002) emphasises that care of self should not be understood as a purely physical concern for the state of the body or one's health. It is better grasped as an attention to self, or an ongoing project of lending form to oneself through careful inspection of one's thoughts and acts. This is captured in Foucault's alternative translation of *tekhnē tou biou* as 'aesthetics of existence' or 'art of living'. The stress here is on the constitution of subjectivity as an aesthetic project, which aims to give 'style' to life, or rather to mark one's life out as one's own (see Brown, 2001). What matters is not so much the nature of the individual acts one engages in, but rather the work of creating a sort of aesthetic consistency in one's conduct by absorbing actions into a coherent and highly stylised ethical orientation:

> Putting it schematically, we could say that classical antiquity's moral reflection concerning the pleasures was not directed towards a codification of acts, nor towards a hermeneutics of the subject, but toward a stylization of attitudes and an aesthetics of existence … It was this attitude – much more than the acts one committed or the desires one concealed – that made one liable to value judgements. A moral value that was also an aesthetic value and a truth value since it was by aiming at the satisfaction of real needs, by respecting the true hierarchy of the human being, and by never forgetting where one stood in regard to truth, that one would be able to give one's conduct the form that would assure one of a name meriting remembrance. (Foucault, 1987, pp. 92–93)

On Foucault's reading, the attitude or aesthetic value common in ancient Greek culture was one of moderation and precision in one's acts, aiming at a form of self-mastery accomplished through the domination of others. Whilst Foucault sees in this aesthetic project a clear alternative to the Christian ethics of self-making through confession and personal renunciation, he also acknowledges that this art of living was confined to a small class of privileged (and slave-owning) males. The choice of adopting a relative austerity in relation to their pleasures was also a means of consolidating and justifying their own personal standing ('the true hierarchy of the human being'). By contrast, when Foucault moves forwards several hundred years to explore Roman stoicism in the third volume of *The history of sexuality*, he finds that it becomes 'dominated by self-preoccupation' (1988, p. 238). The concern with domination of others through self-mastery was replaced, he claims, by a desire to develop all the practices 'by which one can maintain self-control and eventually arrive at pure enjoyment of oneself' (p. 238). In other words, the aestheticisation of existence (which admittedly is still limited to a small group of men) becomes an end in itself.

Foucault's reading of ancient stoicism is not uncontroversial, as classicists such as Pierre Hadot, widely credited with reinvigorating the implications of stoicism for modern philosophy in his key work *Philosophy as a way of life* (1995), have taken issue with Foucault's relative prioritisation of the aesthetic (see O'Leary, 2002). Whether or not this is the case, what Foucault demonstrates is the intimate relationship between the constitution of self as an ongoing project and the range and complexity of the techniques/exercises (i.e. *askēsis*) through which this is accomplished. This is well illustrated in a letter sent by the Roman Marcus Aurelius to his mentor and lover, Fronto, which Foucault cites on several occasions:

We are well. I slept somewhat late owing to my slight cold, which now seems to have subsided. So from five AM till nine I spent the time partly in reading some of Cato's *Agriculture* and partly in writing not such wretched stuff, by heaven as yesterday. Then, after paying my respects to my father, I relieved my throat, I will not say by gargling – though the word *gargarisso* is I believe, found in Novius and elsewhere – but by swallowing honey water as far as the gullet and ejecting it again. After easing my throat I went off to my father and attended him at a sacrifice. Then we went to luncheon. What do you think I ate? A wee bit of bread, though I saw others devouring beans, onions, and herrings full of roe. We then worked hard at grape-gathering, and had a good sweat, and were merry … After six o'clock we came home.

I did but little work and that to no purpose. Then I had a long chat with my little mother as she sat on the bed … Whilst we were chattering in this way and disputing which of us two loved the one or other of you two the better, the gong sounded, an intimation that my father had gone to his bath. So we had supper after we had bathed in the oil-press room; I do not mean we bathed in the oil-press room, but when we had bathed, had supper there, and we enjoyed hearing the yokels chaffing one another. After coming back, before I turn

over and snore, I get my task done ... and give my dearest of masters an account of the
day's doings and if I could miss him more, I would not grudge wasting away a little more.
(Marcus Aurelius, cited in Foucault, 2000e, p. 220)

In the letter a whole series of techniques and attitudes towards self are
present. First of all there is an exhaustive account of what appears to be a relatively uneventful day. All aspects of one's day-to-day existence are deemed
important. To take care of self is to examine one's acts and thoughts at the
closest possible level. Hence, Foucault remarks, the very fact that nothing
appears to happen is morally significant because it indicates that Marcus
Aurelius was not disturbed in his task of self-attention on this particular day.
There is also an equal attention between body and soul, act and thought. The
state of the body is integral to an evaluation of one's self. The 'slight cold' and
the 'relieving of the throat' are indexes of the extent to which one is monitoring and taking hold of oneself in response to daily exigencies. The 'wee bit of
bread' is important since it provides a way of contrasting one's own self-discipline
in dietary matters from the conduct of others. Similarly, the place and time
where one bathes is significant because it exemplifies the continuity of giving
a particular form to one's daily existence in the smallest details. An aesthetics
of existence demonstrates care of self, attention to how one lives, in all aspects
of daily affairs.

The addressee of the letter is important. Although Marcus Aurelius is concerned in the main with his own thoughts and acts, he recounts them to Fronto
as a significant other. This act of self-revelation to another is multi-layered.
When Marcus Aurelius writes of getting his 'task done', he is describing the
process of recording the day's events in a journal, where he can compare his
prior plans with what actually occurred. This daily review of one's activities is
an important technique for examining conscience. In the Christian Jesuit tradition, for example, recording and reviewing one's acts serves as a sort of spiritual accounting (see Quattrone, 2004). The letter to Fronto is then a
reproduction of this other exercise. But in doubling the exercise in this way,
Marcus Aurelius is engaging in a form of confession, a laying open of oneself
to a master or authority. Yet as a form of confession, the letter has no sense of
the element of self-renunciation that would become important in the
Christian use of the technology. Rather, revelation to another serves to elevate
and elaborate one's own self-attention, particularly when, as in this case, there
is an erotic dimension to the relationship to the confessor.

In this and in the other classical sources he works with, Foucault shows a practice of self-invention that adopts an entirely different normative basis from those
which have been enshrined in the psy-complex and modern political technologies of individualisation. Nevertheless there are some commonalities and important points of transformation (e.g. around confession, the role of the mentor,
orientation to pleasure and desire). In order to capture these genealogical threads,
Foucault proposes a fourfold scheme which can be used to plot the 'manner in

which one ought to form oneself as an ethical subject' in relation to a given 'code of actions' (Foucault, 1987, p. 26). The scheme comprises:

1 *The determination of ethical substance* – 'the way in which the individual has to constitute this or that part of himself [*sic*] as the prime material of his moral conduct' (p. 26). Or, what aspects of my self ought I to work upon?

2 *Mode of subjection* – 'the way in which an individual establishes his relation to the rule and recognizes himself as obliged to put it into practice' (p. 27). Or, what attitude ought I to strike in adopting this rule of conduct?

3 *Forms of elaboration* – the 'ethical work that one performs on oneself, not only in order to bring one's conduct into compliance with a given rule, but to attempt to transform oneself into the ethical subject of one's behaviour' (p. 27). Or, what techniques and exercise can I use to transform my conduct?

4 *Telos of the ethical subject* – 'the establishing of a moral conduct that commits an individual not only to other actions always in conformity with values and rules, but to a certain mode of being' (p. 28). Or, what ultimate goal or endpoint, what sort of self do I aspire to become?

Applying these distinctions to the kinds of subjectivities promoted within the contemporary configuration of the psy-complex, one might observe the following. The ethical substance is typically the biographical development of one's desires. That is, the reasons, to be found buried in one's own past, why one wants the sorts of things one feels one wants, whether this be sexually, economically, pharmaceutically, dietetically. The corresponding mode of subjection that must be adopted is a profound mistrust of one's current self-understanding or what Karl Mannheim once called an 'unmasking turn of mind' (1952/1985). This consists of treating self-knowledge as potentially erroneous or covering over the truth. Suspicion is then enacted in forms of elaboration which are dominated by the application of specialist 'objective' knowledge derived from the figure of the expert, and the teleological aspirations tend to be restricted to the drama of a 'self-contained' individual, and vary from mere restoration of 'normal functioning' to humanistic notions of 'self-actualisation' with their promise of personal advantage.

Subjectivity and Resistance

In psychology, the reception of Foucault's work has primarily been in terms of his theory of power and the corresponding critique of how the psy-complex constitutes modern selfhood through normalisation. In his final works, Foucault finds a new sort of normativity in the active relationship or 'care' of self in ancient Greece and Rome. But what sort of 'self' is this that is cared for? And how does this help us to raise the question of ontological difference? It is most certainly not a self that is developed when values and truths are imposed on persons by technologies of power. That is to say that self is not socially constructed, in the classic sense of the term. But neither is self a pure ontological given. Foucault's return to the Greeks does not seek to revivify a humanist conception of self as prior to social relations or some transcendent entity. O'Leary (2002, p. 120) notes that it is important not to be misled by the English translation of '*souci de soi*'. Rather than 'care of *the* self', the phrase is better rendered as 'care of self' or 'self-care'. Self is here a reflexive pronoun; it does not imply that there is a clear entity which is either doing the work or being substantively modified. Self is merely a convenient phrase for marking this ongoing process.

Until the end, Foucault remained avowedly anti-humanist. In an interview given a few months before his death in 1984, Foucault offers the following definition of self:

> It is not a substance. It is a form, and this form is not primarily or always identical to itself. You do not have the same sort of relationship to yourself when you constitute yourself as a political subject who goes to vote or speaks at a meeting and when you are seeking to fulfil your desires in a sexual relationship. Undoubtedly there are relationships and interferences between these different forms of subject; but we are not dealing with the same type of subject. In each case, one plays, one establishes a different type of relationship to oneself. And it is precisely the historical constitution of these various forms of the subject in relation to games of truth which interests me. (Foucault, 2000f, pp. 290–291)

Self is a form, a pattern, a type of ongoing relationship that a person has with herself or himself that is continuously varying – 'not primarily or always identical to itself'. What is more, this form is not singular. It is, Foucault states, variable across the settings where it is seen to matter (e.g. voting, fulfilling one's desires). If it is possible to speak of a subject at all then it must be done with reference to the 'various forms' subjectivity takes and the multiplicity of relationships and connections that pertain between these forms. A close image to what Foucault sketches here is to be found in Bergson's depiction of consciousness as duration, the qualitative enmeshing and unfolding of thoughts and affects which resembles a musical performance – 'we are thus compelled to admit that we have here to do with a synthesis which is, so to speak, qualitative, a gradual organization of our successive sensations, a unity resembling that of a phrase in a melody' (Bergson, 1913/2001, p. 111). Another close image is found in Whitehead's description of the self as constituted by the personal occasions of experience which were our self …

> … between a tenth of a second and half a second ago. It is gone and yet it is here. It is our indubitable self, the foundation of our present existence. Yet the present occasion while claiming self-identity, while sharing the very nature of the bygone occasion in all its living activities, nevertheless is engaged in modifying it, in adjusting it to *other* influences, in completing it with *other* values, in deflecting it to *other* purposes. The present moment is constituted by the influx of *the other* into that self-identity which is the continued life of the immediate past within the immediacy of the present. (Whitehead, 1933/1935, p. 233)

To view self as a form in flux which is never identical to itself is also to deliberately blur the ontological difference between what we are, as humans, and what we can make of ourselves, as subjects. It is not simply that one serves as the content for the 'work' of the other, rather that there is a continuous elaboration or 'becoming' of our capacities for normativity which are realised – or as Bergson would say *actualised* – in the shifting relationships to self that make up our lives. In the next chapter we will turn to Deleuze to say something more about this difference between the capacity or endeavour to live and the specifics of our actual, lived experience. But for now it is worth making one last connection to Artaud. As we saw in Chapter 5, Foucault devoted an early essay to the study of Artaud's work.

Foucault writes there of the difficulty of establishing Artaud's relation to his own oeuvre – the life-work, or general project constituted by Artaud's fragmented forays into diverse forms of expression. This is life-work as continuous negation, as refusing to render the keys to its own intelligibility, thereby achieving a kind of singularity since it becomes impossible to readily categorise or situate with respect to the proper intellectual traditions. Foucault (1995) calls this a kind of 'anti-work' that he proposes might serve as a useful heuristic device for thinking about madness itself – madness here understood as the 'absence of work'. In that essay he talks of the 'absence' of work, or the failure to instantiate one's thoughts and writings as an oeuvre or life-work. However, the phrase 'absence of work' or 'anti-work' has another genealogy, which encompasses Gaston Bachelard, one of the most prominent French epistemologists of the early twentieth century. Bachelard (1934/1962) sought a way of characterising the productivity of scientific knowledge outside of established logical criteria (e.g. the application of sound deductive principles). For Bachelard, what made science distinctive was its orientation to the natural world, understood in the classic Greek sense as *physis*. What defines physis is the productive capacities of the world directed by itself and for itself. The natural world functions as it does irrespective of our human desires or needs. However, we may, as humans, direct our own labour towards modifying these natural capacities, such that they be channelled and steered towards the fulfilment of our own particular projects. Human labour or more simply 'work' is thus *anti-physis*, against nature, or properly speaking the act of transforming nature to create novel and singular alignments with human interests.

It is in this sense that Artaud's oeuvre is 'anti-work', or 'anti-anti-physis'. Artaud rails against traditional practices, in either the theatre, art or the cinema. He sees development in any of these areas as arising from a continuous turning around on performance and practice. It will not do to enshrine the 'work' or the 'working practice' of any particular director or author. All must be continuously questioned, interrupted, dismantled and reconstituted (see, for example, his re-imagining of Matthew Gregory Lewis' *The Monk* [Artaud, 2003]). Anti-anti-physis is the very condition of the evolution of work. The theatre can only go on, only become what it ought to be if it destroys its own heritage and opens itself out to a continuous reformulation of its own practice. Artaud's argument here prefigures Deleuze and Guattari's gnomic claim that 'desiring machines only work when they break down' (1992, p. 8), which we will attempt to decipher in the next chapter. Artaud will then introduce ruptures into tradition which are every bit as powerful as the 'epistemic breaks' which Bachelard saw as the markers of good science, since it involves the overturning or reversal of accepted reason in the name of an intensified engagement with the world.

For Foucault, an art of living occurs across the ontological difference. It is a cautious and prolonged examination of 'self', or rather of one's normative capacities as a 'self' and the variety of ways these might take on a form in one's life. Such an art involves both 'work', in Bachelard's sense of elaborating on life, pushing it into productive directions, and 'anti-work', in Artaud's sense of making breaks or continuously modifying this productivity in order to turn one's capacities into novel and unexpected directions. We will return to mental health to illustrate how this might differ from the interpretation of Foucault which often dominates psychology. The following extract comes from Ian Tucker's (2006) study of the daily routines of mental health service users (see also Brown & Tucker, 2008). In this particular extract Graham, a mental health service user, is describing the effects of some of the medication he has been prescribed:

Ian: Have you ever had any, sort of side effects have you had things that you think may have been caused by your medication?

Graham: Um, when I was on the Chlorpromazine my skin used to burn and I used to feel er, like a tingling in my legs and it was *ever* so bad like, a er a restless feeling in my thighs on the Chlorpromazine. They gave me Procyclidine for that but um, they eventually put me on Benzexhol which stopped the er restless feelings, but my sk..skin still used to burn. They gave like a cream to put on and that but but I didn't really like it on my fa.. you know skin and that … (lines 231–238)

Graham demonstrates here a close attention to the body. He self-monitors the sensations which he sees as emerging from the medication, and provides a clear taxonomy of experiences: being on Chlorpromazine made his skin 'burn', his legs 'tingle' and his thighs feel 'restless'. It is worth noting the precision with which Graham makes these distinctions in his experience. He refers not to the general state of his body, but to concrete aspects. In Foucault's terms we would see the 'substance' which Graham is working on here is the specific modes through which his body responds to medication – his particular experience as a 'medicated body' (see also Tucker, 2006). These experiences are in turn mediated by his interactions with his Community Psychiatric Nurse (CPN), General Practitioner (GP) and Psychiatrist. Drawing on formal medical knowledge about the potential side-effects of the cocktail of medication Graham takes, they make further prescriptions and recommendations. Here the 'restlessness' was managed through Bezexhol and the 'burning' through a prescribed cream. The 'tingling' however was evidently not followed through.

Now although this is but a small fragment of Graham's daily life reported here, it still raises the problem of how to analytically grasp the management of side-effects. It would be very easy to mobilise a Foucauldian account of psychiatric knowledge as a technology of sign systems that lays down a grid of intelligibility through which Graham is obliged to view his experiences. Equally, we might see here a straightforward instance of relations of domination produced by technologies of power. In choosing to turn to Foucault's latter work and invoke technologies of self, we are certainly not ignoring these other analytic possibilities. In fact, to call what Graham describes here 'care of self' is to recognise that such care is utterly interdependent with these other technologies and forms of knowledge. But, by virtue of his ability to monitor and reflect on the specific modes through which he experiences himself as a 'medicated body', Graham has access to forms of normativity which exceed the norms and canalisations of experience demanded by psychiatric consultation. It may well be that these normativities do not help much, since, as we have seen, experiences like the 'tingling' appear to be ignored by the CPN and GP. But focusing on them here serves as a means of demonstrating that normalisation does not have the monolithic character we might be tempted to ascribe to it. There are always other normativities in play.

This is also apparent in an extract from another mental health service user. Here Roy discusses the regimen he has adopted for taking his medication:

Ian: How often do you have to take that then?

Roy: Oh I take it every day

Ian: Once a day or twice a day?

Roy: Supposed to take it twice a day but I always take it in the evening. I'm supposed to take four in a day, but because I take other medication as well, I sort of limit that to the evening, and the rest of the ones I do in the morning. So it sort of evens out in the same way. I know you're not supposed to do that but it does what it's supposed to do for me anyway.

Ian: So do you kind of, um how did you kind of work out that that was the best way to do it for yourself?

Roy: Well I noticed, I was doing that for a while and while I was doing that I thought I don't think it really matters. So long as I'm taking the four a day you know what I mean? Clozipine, and er, while I was doing that I found that it didn't really make much difference so long as I was just taking the same amount of medication.

Ian: So you had previously taken them in the morning and then in the evening? Like perhaps the CPN would say to do?

Roy: I was getting confused when I was taking them that way. When I found my own way of taking them it was it was doing the job, if you know what I mean?

Roy makes a contrast between the way he is 'supposed' to take a particular prescribed drug and the actual way he includes it in his daily routine. Roy takes a range of substances that he refers to as 'medication' (only some of which is prescribed). The prescribed drug in question is meant to be taken twice a day, but Roy has developed a pattern of taking the full daily dose in the evening – this, he claim 'evens out in the same way'. When asked how he developed this practice, Roy describes falling into the habit and then self-monitoring the effects in order to conclude that 'it didn't really make much difference'. We ought perhaps to modify this slightly. Clearly changing the timing at which medication is taken will make a pharmacological difference. What Roy is then saying is that this difference was not sufficient to find it to be a reportable matter to his CPN. This is significant because as a mental health service user the key criterion for maintaining good standing with medical services (and hence his liberty) is to be able to demonstrate continuous 'adherence' with his prescribed medical regimen. We might say that 'adherence' is the telos, the ethical horizon that is necessary to the constitution of a subjectivity as a 'good mental health service user'. Again rather than see adherence as purely an instance of normalisation (which of course it most certainly is), we can view it as an open-ended telos which can be oriented to through a variety of forms of elaboration (e.g. specific ways of taking medication and monitoring their effects). At the same time, we might see that the orientation Roy strikes to the work he is required to do under the sign of this telos – the mode of subjection – is itself open to being respecified and transformed. Through self-experimentation, Roy can take his medication in his own preferred way whilst still being able to claim that it is 'doing the job, if you know what I mean'. Self-care, an ongoing attention to the minor details of living, enables Roy to tailor and lend form to a subjectivity which, whilst not of his own choosing, can nevertheless be rendered as ethically coherent.

In the cases of both Graham and Roy we see subjectivity being enacted as a form-giving activity. The subjectivity of a mental health service user is, we want to argue, like any other in so far as it is grown along the surface of one's daily activities and interactions. It comes from the mundane practices of attending to one's experiences and lending them a consistency and cohesion within a general ethical horizon. But within this horizon there is a variety of forms of normativity – of potential experiences which the body is 'able to bear' – which can become objects for elaboration. Hence, rather than see subjectivity in the way Foucault appears to do in the mid-period work which has been so influential for psychology as something 'implanted' or 'inscribed' on the body, we think it more apposite to see subjectivity as the shifting form which both contains our sense of self and continuously interacts with and is marked by the forces which sustain living.

We are, then, positioning psychology along the ontological difference or boundary between 'human' and 'subject'. This might appear to be a strange place to occupy, since it seems off to the side of both philosophy and social science, stuck awkwardly between metaphysical questions and densely empirical questions. To claim that psychology ought to operate in this terrain resembles the situation of the medical doctor who chooses to specialise in the care of skin. Whilst skin may be interesting in terms of what it shows about the insides of the body, or the ways in which it reflects the influences of the environment, it is scarcely the most important aspect of either. Doctors who choose this specialism are typically denigrated as pursuing merely 'cosmetic' rather than proper medicine. It may then seem that we are calling for a cosmetic or *dermatological psychology*.

But as Robert Cooper (1990) argues in a remarkably powerful exploration of basic terms in social science, the boundary, the 'non-place', is precisely where enquiry needs to begin because that is where everything happens. Boundaries provide the means of circumscribing and thereby rationalising and rendering intelligible that which is thereby contained within its bounded domain. The boundary is what Derrida often referred to as an 'enabling limit'. That is, the means by which a horizon is established for meaning, which acts back to designate the appropriate forms of enquiry and interpretation. The kind of psychology we have in mind is neither then solely an investigation of the techniques for 'making up people', nor a metaphysics of being, but rather a study of the enabling limit between these two distinct projects.

For Artaud, subjectivity is to be continuously dismantled, unmade as part of the process of rejecting the premature settlement of what we are as persons. What Artaud calls 'cruelty' is this perpetual monitoring of self, an exposure of what one is to extreme force – 'cosmic strictness'. If subjectivity is akin to skin, then Artaud seeks to render it porous, to attack it and fill it with holes, to examine what the *subjectile* will bear. This is what it means to be against work, to be anti-anti-physis. In Foucault's final work, his return to the Greeks and the rediscovery of self-care also uncovers a sort of freedom that remains imbricated within contemporary technologies of self. But this freedom is not some classical version of personal liberation. It is the freedom to make oneself through a continuous exposure – to put some holes in the 'skin' stretched between the various technologies that afford selfhood.

Perhaps in this dermatological version of subjectivity there is also a way to reformulate the problematic conception of resistance. One of the most visible aspects of skin is that it ages, it literally bears the marks of experience. Skin offers a sort of hermeneutics of memory – 'When did she get that scar?' 'Doesn't he look young in that picture?' Memory becomes increasingly important in Foucault's final work. His investigations of self-care begin with his observation that some of the earliest forms of *askēsis* are known as *hupomnē mata* – or 'memory aids' (Foucault, 2000e). Self-writing, for instance, is originally a practice which is used to gather together and synthesise the variety of readings which a person might have made. Recall that Marcus Aurelius's letter begins with just such a description of his daily reading. This synthesis is necessary because the ancient Greeks considered *logos* or truth to exist in a scattered or dispersed state. It is to be found threaded across the great works. Foucault observes that this scattering is then extended further as *hupomnē mata* becomes transformed into tools for examining how one's life becomes a repository for what one has learned, a 'kind of book one rereads from time to time' (2000e, p. 101). However, what is meant by memory here differs completely from the classical or Platonic notion of reminiscence as a means of connecting the subject to an original truth, nor the later notion of finding the truth in oneself (which still dominates the psy-disciplines). Instead Foucault speaks of arming 'the subject with a truth it did not know, one that did not reside in it; what is wanted is to make this a learned, memorized truth, progressively put into practice, a quasi subject that reigns supreme in us' (Foucault, 2000e, pp. 101–102).

The memory that Foucault speaks of here is closer to the 'reconstructive' form of recollection that we described in the last chapter. To put 'memorized truth' into practice is to find ways to orient to and deploy the past in the present, much as Bergson described. It is to render the past as significant and a practical concern for one's ongoing subjectivity. And yet the past which is so rendered finds its truth not in some objective or veridical accuracy, but in relation to how it is lent form by practices of self-making. What we call memory is then perhaps best characterised as a stretching of the skin of subjectivity back into the past, to allow it to bear the marks of past events and to reconfigure and rework these markings within the aesthetic consistency one lends to self.

NINE

Deleuze and Life

anyone lived in a pretty how town
(with up so floating many bells down)
spring summer autumn winter
he sang his didn't he danced his did
(e.e. cummings, *anyone lived in a pretty how town*)

The idea has got about that in speaking of a text it is no longer necessary to make reference to the personal qualities of the author. One of the main sources of this idea is the small fragment written by Roland Barthes entitled *The death of the author*. Barthes wants the author to be no longer a symbol of authority, the hermeneutic hook around which the decipherment of the text must proceed, the 'final signified' which closes the writing (1977, p. 147). Once the author is disposed of we see a text as 'made of multiple writings, drawn from many different cultures and entering into mutual relations of dialogue, parody and contestation' (p. 148). This multiplicity becomes focused around the reader, she or he who acts as the space in which these entangled threads can be arranged and given a kind of provisional unity. It is the work of reading, of engaging, seeking interlocution, the activity in which a given text is activated, opened out and connected to innumerable other texts that demands attention. Reading is an event, an activation of the text along unforeseeable lines. Writing is just presenting the pieces.

The death of the author as she or he who authorises or underpins the text rapidly gives way to the death of subject, understood as the self-possessive individual who governs and determines their own behaviour. The subject has always been the central puzzle of psychology – how is it that the biological, the social and the psychic come together in human thought, feeling and action? However, as work in critical psychology has demonstrated at length, the work of sewing together body, mind and society need not be approached with reference to a bounded subject as such. Early work reached out to culture and history as organising principles which stood behind human action (e.g. Gergen, 1982; Shotter, 1994). Later, Foucauldian-inspired work drew on notions of power (Adlam et al., 1977; Henriques et al., 1984; Rose, 1989). A separate thread developed a micro-analysis of talk-in-interaction with particular reference to linguistic tokens treated by speakers as 'psychological' (Potter, 1996; Edwards, 1997). Finally, a return to psychoanalysis under the general rubric of 'psychosocial' research has placed the figure of the unconscious back in place as hidden centre of gravity of the psychological (Frosh, 2003; Hollway, 2004).

We have both been extensively schooled, in the many senses of that term, by critical psychology, which has been a formative influence upon us. And yet we have both found ourselves progressively turning from our schooling. If we had to sum up as simply as possible why that has been, then it would be because critical psychology has no concept of life. The promise of psychology – and, we would venture the reason for its ongoing success as a teaching and research endeavour – is that it will find a way of speaking to the vitality of living, of what it is to be involved in the creative, dynamic evolution of the modes of existence which make up personal and collective lives lived together. Whilst it is undoubtedly a serious diminution of life to reduce it to the notion of a subject, it is equally so to treat it as reducible to the trading of interactional tokens or the all-enmeshing web of unconscious identifications.

The problem we face within psychology is not, then, as is commonly assumed, the problem of 'the subject', but rather that of 'life'. Or more precisely, of understanding how particular lives are extracted from the modes of existence, relations, normativities and processes which comprise life-in-itself. In this chapter we will draw on the work of Gilles Deleuze to explore this difference. Deleuze spoke of the philosophy as providing an 'image of thought' (see Deleuze, 1994, pp. 129–167). But this image is problematic in that to represent thinking with a clear set of axioms or a priori statements is already to have denuded thinking of all that is vital and creative, an act which 'profoundly betrays what it means to think' (1994, p. 167). Thought cannot be adequately represented directly, or given a formal determination in the way that Descartes, for example, seeks to found all thinking on the singular experience of doubt. Deleuze sees the task of philosophy as being the invention of concepts which articulate and express thought in different ways, whilst never exhausting the multiplicity of potential images that might be given to thought (see Deleuze & Guattari, 1994). Our own particular project of reflexive foundationalism around psychology – continuously reinventing what the psychological can be in the course of following its complex patterns of mediation – clearly takes direction from Deleuze.

Immanence: a Life ...

The small text entitled *Immanence: a Life...* (2006a) has a particular place in Deleuze's writing. It is the final text he wrote before his suicide in 1995. The Italian philosopher Giorgio Agamben (2004) suggests that the force of the entire piece is already prefigured in the title. The colon between the terms 'immanence' and 'life' is deliberately chosen: 'Deleuze could have written "Immanence Is a Life", or "Immanence and a Life" ... and, furthermore ... "Immanence, A Life". Deleuze instead used a colon, clearly because he had in mind neither a simple identity nor a logical connection' (Agamben, 2004, p. 153). The colon suggests that 'a Life' is not equivalent to, the same as, 'immanence'. Nor is 'immanence' the precursor or the progenitor of 'a Life'. From his very first book on Hume, Deleuze (2001) had opposed the logical principle whereby one term can be deduced from the properties of another. He continually reiterated that empiricism demands that relations be seen as external to the terms they relate. The implication being that to grasp a relationship one must explore or experience it rather than logically posit it in advance. The relationship between 'immanence' and 'a Life' is therefore not one that can be defined through analytic logic. Readers must come to experience, to sense the relationship for themselves.

We will say something about each term before considering what sort of experience the text might afford. Immanence is a technical term which is usually associated with Spinoza, as we described in Chapter 6 (see also Whitehead, 1927–8/1985). Spinoza uses it primarily to describe how he views the relationship between cause and effect:

> Everything that is, is in God, and must be conceived through God ... and so ... God is the cause of things, which are in him. That is the first. And then outside God there can be no substance ... that is, thing which is in itself outside God. That was the second. God, therefore, is the immanent, not the transitive cause of all things. (Spinoza, E. I, prop 18, demonstration)

As we discussed earlier, Spinoza holds that there can be no fundamental divisions, no dualisms in metaphysics. There is a single substance that can be called 'God, or nature', which divides within itself to create the distinctions that we come to know as 'bodies' and 'minds'. Since there are no dualisms or external divisions it follows that 'God, or nature' cannot be the cause of any effect in the usual or transitive sense (where cause and effect are logically distinct entities) because 'God, or nature' is implied equally in both cause and effect, there being no outside to it as substance. However this does not mean that there is an identity between cause and effect, rather the effect is a qualitative transformation, or change in intensity of the cause. Moreover, Spinoza holds that this transformation is not predictable in advance, since this would mean that he would be unable to account for change and novelty. Spinoza argues instead that causes can be adequately ascertained only after rather than in advance of the event.

Hence substance is *autopoietic*, in the sense in which we discussed this term in earlier chapters, and as a whole 'God, or nature' is seen as *causa sui*, or 'cause of itself'. Following Spinoza, Deleuze positions 'absolute immanence' as the substance or plane from which all else is seen to derive as autopoetic or internal modifications – 'absolute immanence is in itself: it is not in anything, nor can it be attributed *to* something; it does not depend on an object or belong to a subject' (2006a, p. 385).

Rather confusingly, Deleuze also introduces the notion of a 'transcendental field'. This is a term usually associated with Immanuel Kant's critical philosophy and with its twentieth-century successor, Edmund Husserl's phenomenology. Crudely put, the problem raised in both philosophical systems is how the subject gains access to phenomenological reality (i.e. a particular experience of the world), whilst being fundamentally unable to grasp things are they are in-themselves. The solution which Kant and Husserl adopt, albeit in very different ways, is to posit a set of a priori conditions or fundamental capacities which define any given subject. Since these conditions transcend or underpin the particular life or experience of any living individual, they define a *transcendental ego* (Kant) or *transcendental field of consciousness* (Husserl). This transcendental field then structures consciousness, but cannot, of itself, be inspected by or known directly to consciousness. This kind of notion is absolutely central to the project of psychology as a science which dedicates itself to revealing the common mechanisms that underpin the capacity for and diversity of individual experiences.

Deleuze's statement that immanence does not depend upon an object, nor belong to a subject clearly indicates that this Kantian/Husserlian scheme is not what he is proposing. He defines the transcendental instead as a 'pure a-subjective stream of consciousness, as pre-reflexive impersonal consciousness, or as the qualitative duration of consciousness without a self' (2006a, p. 384). The explicit nods to William James ('stream of consciousness') and Bergson ('qualitative duration') situate this description within process metaphysics. David Lapoujade (2000) points to the explicit links here. James spoke of 'pure experience', in the same way that Deleuze talks later of 'pure immanence'. As we saw in Chapter 7, Bergson refers similarly to 'pure duration'. The common thread in all these descriptions is of the world understood as process, as an ongoing dynamic flux of differentiation. Such a world cannot be contained by and continuously exceeds the usual categories and forms deployed by consciousness (see also Whitehead on the extensive continuum, 1927–8, part II, chapter II). But – and here is the crucial difference from the Kantian/Husserlian scheme – this does not mean that it is outside of experience. We can and do have an experience of pure immanence, but it is a form of experience that is had entirely without reference to a bounded subject.

This returns us to the apparent contradiction that we discussed with respect to Whitehead in Chapter 2: the notion of experience which is outside of the modes of subjectivity we associate with consciousness. Lapoujade (2000, p. 193) suggests that we must understand experience here 'in a very general sense: pure experience is the ensemble of all that which is related to something else without their necessarily being consciousness of this relation'. Whilst Whitehead (e.g. 1927) grasps this issue in relation to his distinction between the affective perception of 'causal efficacy' and the sensory perception of 'presentational immediacy', for Deleuze, this is a kind of experience of immanence itself, of the multiplicity of relations that can be unfolded within substance, without there being a rational, conscious grasping of the particularities themselves. We might call this instead an affective involvement in the world that is not bound by the conscious subject. Lapoujade goes on to illustrate this with the French phrase *'faire une expérience'*, which means both to 'have an experience' and 'to conduct an experiment'. Anyone who sets up an experiment with chemical agents certainly has an experience, either of success, failure or sheer boredom. But the chemical agents are not simply the objects of the experimenter's experience, they also have their own form of experience in that they undergo the procedure. Here experience is not divided up along subjective and objective lines but rather denotes the plurality of relations which come together in the 'event' of the experiment.

What is meant by experience here is not first of all the recognition of something by consciousness, but rather an orientation, an involvement, a process of being affected by and affecting others that belongs equally to conscious and instinctual organisms or to organic and inorganic beings. In a chapter entitled 'What is an event?', Deleuze describes the unification of this plurality of relations as a '"concrescence" of elements', and he elaborates on the nature of their connection or conjunction in Whiteheadian terms as 'a *prehension* ... the eye is a prehension of light. Living beings prehend water, soil, carbon, and salts' (Deleuze, 1993, p. 78). It is these prehensions, states Deleuze, 'that somehow anticipate psychic life'. In this respect, Deleuze follows Whitehead in avoiding the bifurcation of nature into subject and object by multiplying the subject/object and discovering it in every event at every scale: 'The vector of prehension moves from the world to the subject ... the event is inseparably the objectification of one prehension and the subjectification of another; it is at once public and private, potential and real' (ibid.). Bergson anticipated this prehensive experience in the following way:

Hydrochloric acid always acts in the same way upon carbonate of lime whether in the form of marble or of chalk yet we do not say that the acid perceives [i.e. rationally experiences] in the various species the characteristic features of the genus. Now there is no essential difference between the process by which this acid picks out from the salt its base and the act of the plant which invariably extracts from the most diverse soils those elements that serve to nourish it. Make one more step; imagine a rudimentary consciousness such as that of an amoeba in a drop of water: it will be sensible of the resemblance, and not of the difference, in the various organic substances which it can assimilate. In short, we can follow from the mineral to the plant, from the plant to the simplest conscious beings, from the animal to man [sic], the progress of the operation by which things and beings seize from their surroundings that which attracts them, that which interests them practically, without needing any effort of abstraction, simply because the rest of their surroundings takes no hold upon them: this similarity of reaction following actions superficially different is the germ which human consciousness develops into general ideas. (Bergson, 1908/1991, pp. 159–160)

For Bergson, the involvement of hydrochloric acid with carbonate of lime does not differ in kind from the assimilation of substances by an amoeba, nor from the conscious efforts of humans to 'seize their surroundings'. Hence it is not necessary to invoke consciousness to describe what Deleuze refers to as 'powerful, nonorganic vitality' (1998, p. 131), or impersonal, preconscious experience. The example of the tick, drawn from Jakob von Uexküll, which Deleuze uses on several occasions, also illustrates this (see opening to Chapter 6). Although the tick engages with the world by the sole means of three affects, 'in the midst of all that goes on in the immense forest' (Deleuze, 2005, p. 59), this still constitutes a sort of experience – albeit one which is entirely im*personal* (cf. Whitehead's definition of a *personal* society discussed in Chapter 2) – off to the side of what we would call the bounded consciousness of 'personality'.

If pure immanence can be described as 'impersonal experience' then what is 'a Life' such that the terms are worth distinguishing? Deleuze offers this apparently unhelpful gloss:

We will say of pure immanence that it is A LIFE, and nothing more. It is not immanent to life, but the immanence that is in nothing else is itself a life. A life is the immanence of immanence, absolute immanence: it is complete power, complete beatitude. (Deleuze, 2006a, pp. 385–386)

Pure immanence is not immanent to life – that would be to repeat the Kantian/Husserlian scheme where transcendental consciousness serves as the formal conditions for experience. As the Bergson example demonstrates, conscious experience is a development, an elaboration or qualitative intensification of impersonal experience rather than the product or effect of transcendence. The personal is a twist in the impersonal, another unfolding or complication of its intrinsic plurality. Hence the colon in the title, which indicates a pausing, or slowing down of one term into the other without suggesting either their equivalence, or their fundamental difference in kind. To say that life is the 'immanence of immanence' is to say that it is the dynamic, the vitality which expresses pure immanence. Agamben (2004) notes that 'a Life' is a kind of striving within immanence, a force that attempts to express the potential of pure immanence.

Spinoza referred to this striving as *conatus*, or 'endeavour to persist in being' (see Chapter 6). *Conatus* is not bounded consciousness or something like a self. It presupposes the impersonal power of 'picking out' or the operation of 'seizing' described by Bergson which is expressed by organic and nonorganic life when it selects 'that which interests them practically' from the environment (which for Whitehead is the operation of prehension grounded in the basic structure of concern, whilst for Heidegger it is the event of appropriation or *ereignis*,

grounded in basic care structure). *Conatus*, as Spinoza views it, strives to preserve itself, but does so not by seeking to govern itself in isolation from the world
around it, thereby seeking to become an *imperium in imperio* ('sovereignty within
the sovereign'). Rather it preserves itself by continuously seeking new connections and by entering into relations which enable it to better extend its capacities to act and be acted upon. In Canguilhem's terms (see last chapter), *conatus*
attempts to develop its capacity for normativity to the highest degree, rather
than take shelter in clearly defined norms and distinctions. In Whitehead's terms
it is the basic *eros* oriented to living, living well, and living better. For Neitzsche
it is *will to power* and for Bergson it is the *élan vital* (see Brown 2005).

The highest degree of development of the capacity for normativity is called
'beatitude' by Spinoza. It is the serenity that arises from having pushed the
expression of potential to its highest degree. At first glance this may appear close
to the humanistic psychology notion of 'self-actualisation' (cf. Maslow, 1962),
with its bourgeois elitist platitude to 'become all one that can be'. However,
humanistic psychology not only bounds this self-development into a clear (and
ideologically narrow) version of the self, it also promotes a prescribed set of
stages through which one ascends to this dizzy height of self-expression. By contrast, beatitude is impersonal – it is an expression of a striving that may, in part,
be articulated as a given individual biography, but is not reducible to that individual's life, since it refers to the recognition of a thorough relationality
grounded in the affirmation of a unity amidst diversity. Beatitude also has
no direction, no clear course. It is a *becoming* or a continuous process of re-
elaboration and involvement in wider sets of connections rather than a set of
stages in the personal evolution of a given being. Becoming has no necessary
direction since, as Spinoza says, 'no one has thus far determined the power of the
body, that is, no one has yet been taught by experience what the body can do'
(*Ethics*, III, prop. 2). Becoming expresses pure immanence since we do not yet
know what kinds of unfoldings or relations are possible on this impersonal plane
of experience and affection. We do not know what we are capable of becoming.
In Spinoza beatitude is also termed the 'intellectual love of God' (see part V of
Ethics), a 'third kind of knowledge', or 'the love of God as God loves men [*sic*]'.
Since knowledge and love in Spinoza consist of embodied connections to others,
then the secular translation of beatitude is to have participated in the maximal
number of connections which expand one's capacity to affect and be affected.
Or, put another way, to have striven to have involved oneself in as many relations as possible, and to have therefore shed a clearly bounded identity along the
way. Deleuze and Guattari (1988) refer to this as 'becoming imperceptible',
defined as the 'immanent end of becoming, its cosmic formula' (p. 279).

There is then a distinction between 'a Life' as an impersonal striving 'composed
of virtualities, events, singularities' (Deleuze, 2006a, p. 388) and 'the life' of a
given individual. Deleuze often plays on the difference between personal and
impersonal pronouns, definite and indefinite articles as part of an ongoing project
to disrupt attributions of identity:

Proper names belong primarily to forces, events, motions and sources of movement, winds, typhoons, diseases, places and moments, rather than people. Infinitives express becomings or events that transcend mood and tense. The dates don't refer to some single uniform calendar, each refers to a different space-time ... Together, these elements produce arrangements of utterance: 'Werewolves swarming 1730' ... and so on. (Deleuze, 1990b, p. 34)

For Deleuze, proper names are not indicators of persons. Rather they are expressions of forces or bundles of affects. To say one's own name is not then to lay claim to an identity but rather to direct a force, make a move in an inter-action, to draw particular kinds of relations ('Yes, I am...'; 'Do you know my name?', 'They call me...'). We assume and relate to a range of proper names continuously – Mummy, Professor, Patient Number 37, The Lady Next Door – a process which Deleuze and Guattari (1983) call, after Whitehead, *conjunctive synthesis*. Each time we speak the name we situate ourselves in relation to a set of impersonal forces or affects. There are things that follow, that become possible when we say the proper name 'Professor', but there is no fundamental difference between this act and the affects of the tick, or the picking out of carbonate of lime by hydrochloric acid. They are all modes of selective concern, of becoming involved with the world in a particular way. In this sense Deleuze's view of language sits in the tradition of linguistic pragmatics (see, for example, Austin 1962; Levinson, 1983), where utterances are studied in terms of their capacity to bring about effects in the course of interaction, rather than in relation to some referential meaning (see Chapter 4, in partic-ular of Deleuze & Guattari, 1988). The conjunctive synthesis of speaking the proper name need not constitute the speaker as a particular kind of subject. It is an illegitimate use of the conjunctive synthesis to 'own' or become fixated on the name as though it had referred to some subjective attribute or essence. This is why Deleuze and Guattari praise Artaud's lines in *Here lies*: 'Me, Antonin Artaud, I am my son, my father, my mother and me' (p. 193). 'I believe in neither father nor mother, ain't gotta daddy-mommy' (p. 237). Artaud releases the force of the proper names 'son', 'father' and 'mother' by first laying claim to them (a legitimate conjunctive synthesis) and then reject-ing their referential status (avoiding the illegitimate conjunctive synthesis).

The infinitive – 'the horse', 'the child', 'the day', 'the life' – equally has no fundamental referential function for Deleuze. What is does instead is tie the statement in which it appears to a *collective assemblage*. We will discuss this concept in more detail later on, but for now we may define an assemblage as an arrangement of bodies, relation and affects. Or, as Deleuze and Guattari put it, a 'longitude and latitude, a set of speeds and slownesses between unformed particles, a set of nonsubjectified affects' (1988, p. 262). The use of the infini-tive expresses this assemblage by opening it out onto the world without deter-mining its identity (contrast with 'this horse', 'that child', 'yesterday', 'her life'). It marks the potential of the assemblage rather than its current state of affairs.

This contrast is central to the example from Dickens' *Our Mutual Friend* that Deleuze describes. The 'rogue' Riderhood is saved from drowning by onlookers, and for a few moments is between life and death. In these moments, there is a separation between the living being, the 'sign of life', and the actual, nefarious individual. It is this 'sign of life', or rather the potential for living, the singular and impersonal force of what a human body can do, that attracts Riderhood's 'benefactors'. For a few moments 'a life' and 'the life' are distinct from one another. But as Riderhood begins to breathe, so the one becomes 'incarnated' in the other, pure immanence becomes individuated as 'the man' and the onlookers correspondingly lose interest. Although this example allows Deleuze to express the difference between immanence and individuation, the two are never really separated: 'A life is everywhere, in every moment which a living subject traverses and which is measured by the objects that have been experienced, and immanent life carrying along the events or singularities that are merely actualized in subjects and objects' (Deleuze, 2006a, p. 387).

What Deleuze means by 'a Life' is then close to both Spinoza's 'conatus' and to what Agamben calls 'bare life' (Agamben, 1998; 2004). It is the potentiality, the striving, the absolute capacities of a body understood outside of the particular acts and arrangements that the body comes to enact. There is nothing abstract in all this. In a sense, 'a life' is the most precise and realistic way of characterising a body, since it implies the full range of the body's capacities for acting and being acted upon rather than its transitory states. Nor does this potentiality ever transcend the concrete way in which it is 'actualized in subjects and objects'. 'A Life' is immanent to 'the life'. Or as Deleuze puts its, 'the singularities or the events which constitute a life coexist with the accidents of the life which corresponds to it, but they are not arranged and distributed in the same way' (2006a, p. 387).

The relevance of all this for psychology is a critique of the tendency to focus on that portion of experience which appears to be bound by reflective consciousness. The greater portion of experience transcends 'self' without ever ceasing to be immanent to it. In other words, our subjectivity emerges from the impersonal forces that our bodies can express, whether this be in the form of affects, the power of proper names, or in the speeds and slownesses of the relations and connections to the world that we can make, without our being able necessarily to reflect them within consciousness. We experience affects, forces, speeds and relations outwith a 'personal', rational-conscious framework. The question then becomes that of grasping the passage between the impersonal and the personal, a life and the life.

The Actual and the Virtual

The principal connection between the work of Deleuze and Michel Serres is that both are philosophers of multiplicity and pluralism. As Serres makes clear in his writing (see *Genesis* (1998) and *Rome* (1991) in particular), the challenge of thinking multiplicity is to think it in a way which does not reduce it to a singular 'thing'. Nothing could be further from the spirit of such an endeavour than simply applying the label 'multiple' to a collection of individual things. The parallel in social science would be defining society as simply an accumulation of citizens. Clearly there is something more, something which is irreducible to the notion of the individual in the collective – the 'collectivity' of the collective, or the 'multiplicity' of the multiple. Our thinking has to confront a paradox of inevitably referring to the multiple as though it were a singular entity, whilst retaining the idea that there is a plurality beating within it. This is what Whitehead grapples with in his discussion of the patterning of the many into the one by way of conjunctive synthesis, and in his notion of endurance as entailing the assembling of actual occasions into societies (such that a rock, an amoeba and a 'stream of consciousness' are equally 'societies' – see Chapter 2). It is an attempt to think differentiation outside of either foundational dualisms (what Whitehead calls 'bifurcations in nature') or representational notions of identity. This is what Deleuze and Guattari describe as the search for the 'magic formula' of 'PLURALISM = MONISM' (1988, p. 20).

Deleuze's piece *The actual and the virtual* is a set of notes written roughly around the same time as *Immanence: a Life...* It is thought that both pieces were preparation for a speculative project called *Ensembles and multiplicities* in which Deleuze would expand upon the concept of the virtual (see translator's note, Deleuze, 2006a, p. 410), which he had originally derived from Bergson (see Deleuze, 1991), and then elaborated in *A thousand plateaus* (Deleuze and Guattari, 1988) and in his later work on cinema (Deleuze, 1986; 1989). In two audacious books, Keith Ansell-Pearson (2002) and Brian Massumi (2002) explain at length why Deleuze's elaboration of the concept of the virtual is so central to his work and holds such promise for contemporary social and cultural theory. Both argue that the virtual is a way of considering the indeterminacy and openness of systems with respect to the individual agents who serve as the focal points through which they act. In other words, the virtual is a way of thinking the relationship and passage from multiplicity to individuation.

Like much of his writing, Deleuze's piece appears to start in the middle, without adequate definition of the problem. He states that 'Philosophy is the theory of multiplicities, each of which is composed of actual and virtual elements. Purely actual objects do not exist. Every actual surrounds itself with a cloud of virtual images' (Deleuze, 2002, p. 148). The phrase 'virtual images' clearly locates this argument with respect to Bergson (see Chapter 7). In this sense 'actual' refers to a concrete set of relations which is experienced in the course of action, whilst 'virtual' refers to an overall set of potentials which appear to surround the actual like 'a cloud'. For example, I catch sight of a sudden bolt of lightning through the window of the car in which I am travelling. The lightning is actual – an electric discharge produced by the atmospheric conditions at this particular time and place. I see the flash, I am startled. What then do we mean by its potential? This is the range of possible relations that might be opened up in the arrangement of car-flash-passengers-startle. For instance, I may turn to my daughter and tell her that the car is the safest place to be. The lightning is folded into our relationship. Or the cars in front may swerve, the traffic being momentarily gathered into the progress of the coming storm. Or I may feel a rising dread, an omen of bad fortune which overtakes me, with consequences for the rest of our journey.

All of these potentials are there, constituted alongside the lightning bolt, but they have a peculiar status. They are not causal possibilities – there is nothing in the lightning that 'causes' dread, swerving cars or parental reassurance. It would be better to say that these are ways in which the lightning might be potentially elaborated, or loaded up into the very specific relations arranged around it (car-passengers). Moreover, these potentials are not purely subjective, nor fully recognisable to consciousness. The cars really might swerve. My daughter might become alarmed. Virtual elements then continuously track or follow actual events, such that for every successive state of affairs there is a corresponding 'emission' of new potentials: 'the virtuals, encircling the actual, perpetually renew themselves by emitting others, with which they are in turn surrounded and which go on in turn to react upon the actual' (Deleuze, 2002, p. 148).

The crucial point is that states of affairs are not first virtual and then become actual. Rather, the actual is that aspect of the movements, forces and relations that we are able to grasp at a particular point. It is the rendering of the virtual as a specific state of affairs in which we are implicated. The actual is extracted from the virtual, it 'falls from the plane like a fruit' (p. 150). But whilst our involvement is critical to actualisation, it not done by us as subjects who render the virtual as actual through their conscious efforts alone. Rather, actualisation constitutes subjects and objects, it lays out their relation: 'the actual itself is individuality constituted' (p. 149). Out of the myriad of relationships which might obtain between this body, travelling in a car, caught in the storm, what became actual was the realisation of dread. In this sense the subject is less the originator than the result of actualisation: the 'superject' (see Chapter 2) of its own experience.

This all sounds very strange, as though Deleuze were attempting to delete not only causality but also any sense of agency, as though the world were an entirely random set of occurrences. This is simply not the case. Deleuze, following Bergson and Whitehead, has no problem speaking of causality when it refers to the relationship between actual states of affairs (i.e. bodies occupying 'simple locations' in bounded systems). In *What is philosophy?*, Deleuze and Guattari write at length about how science necessarily actualises the virtual as a 'plane of reference' that can be mapped using 'a system of co-ordinates' that includes sophisticated determinations of causes. But such notions do not assist when it comes to thinking the becoming of relations or the expression of potentials in open systems (Deleuze, like Serres, draws inspiration from some branches of the exact sciences such as Georg Riemann's mathematics of multiplicity and René Thom's morphogenesis). Equally, although Deleuze wants to avoid bifurcating nature into a distinct subject/object dualism, he sees something like agency in his Nietzschean inspired vision of impersonal forces which express themselves in the course of the encounters and confrontations in which they are continuously involved. From Nietzsche, Deleuze drew the key idea that impersonal forces are 'active' when they go as far as they can in the expression of potentials, and 'passive' when they are subjugated by and solely express other forces (see Deleuze, 1983). What we call a 'subject' or an 'object' is always a complex coming together of these impersonal forces:

> What is the body? We do not define it by saying that it is a field of forces, a nutrient medium fought over by a plurality of forces. For in fact there is no 'medium', no field of forces or battle. There is no quantity of reality, all reality is already quantity of force. There are nothing but quantities of force in mutual 'relations of tension' ... Every force is related to others and it either obeys or commands. What defines a body is this relationship between dominant and dominating forces. Every relationship of forces constitutes a body – whether it is chemical, biological, social or political. Any two forces, being unequal, constitute a body as soon as they enter into a relationship. (Deleuze, 1983, pp. 39–40)

What we call a body (whether subject or object) is already multiple, the outcome of relations between forces. When bodies come together these relations are multiplied and yet more bodies formed (e.g. the flash, car, passenger relationship). Hence agency can never be simply attributed to any body in particular, but must be continually indexed to whatever arrangement of forces is under consideration.

Actualisation expresses potential by configuring impersonal forces as a given state of affairs shared by distinct bodies of subjects and objects. Every such arrangement is a transformation in the relations between forces. As such, the actual folds back into the virtual. Bergson (1991) used the illustration of a cone to describe this notion, where the actual represents the most concentrated or focused point of an immense series of forces and processes. Whatever occurs at this point of focus feeds back directly into the entirety of the cone. The actual – the apex of the cone – remains part of the virtual (impersonal forces are immanent to bodies) whilst serving as a means of its expression. What both Deleuze and Bergson attempt to demonstrate is that plurality or multiplicity has a real existence as the virtual which is always immanent to every state of affairs and all bodies, but cannot be directly and consciously experienced as such without being rendered as actual:

> As Leibniz has shown, force is as much a virtual in the process of being actualized as the space through which it travels. The plane is therefore divided into a multiplicity of planes according to the cuts in the continuum, and to the divisions of force which mark the actualization of the virtual. But all the planes merge into one following the path which leads to the actual. The plane of immanence includes both the virtual and its actualization simultaneously,

without there being any assignable limit between the two. The actual is the complement or the product, the object of actualization, which has nothing but the virtual as its subject. Actualization belongs to the virtual. (Deleuze, 2002, p. 149)

The 'path that leads to the actual' is where multiplicity becomes individuated. Deleuze speaks of this tightly wired 'circuit' in which 'the actual and the virtual coexist' such that 'we are continually retracing from one to the other' (2002, p. 150). The virtual then seems to bleed into the actual. It is as though we can feel the present moment doubled with other possible moments. In the flash I can sense the other cars swerving, the imminent collision to come. I can feel my daughter's emerging anxiety even before she has spoken about the storm. These potential futures seem to be playing off one another even as I start to speak: 'virtuals communicate directly over the top of the actuals which separate them' (ibid., p. 151).

One source of this idea is in Bergson's description of duration, which we considered in Chapter 7. If lived experience is a continuous flow of actualisations, rather than a series of discrete instants, then the past is never really abolished. It is 'prolonged into the present'. Memory infuses our every act. However, not all of the past is made relevant at every moment, only selective aspects. If this is so then we never have a 'pure' experience of the present, since it is continuously refracted through those bits of the past which are currently being mobilised. The argument holds in the same way for the future. If, to use Whiteheadian terminology, there is only an ongoing flow of contemporary and consecutive actual occasions, then the present moment does not give way to a future which is about to transpire. Instead it appears oddly prefigured by the past which rushes up towards it, in the same way that the notes of a melody seem to already arrive before we actually hear them since their place is prepared in an unfolding pattern (much as we saw in Chapter 4 in Luhmann's notion of communication as an unfurling series of mutually recursive connections). The circuit between virtual and actual is then outside of 'clock time', since it seems to point forwards and backwards, relating the present moment to possible pasts and potential futures: 'The two aspects of time, the actual image of the present which passes and the virtual image of the past which is preserved, are unassignable limits, but exchange during crystallization to the extent that they become indiscernible, each relating to the role of the other' (2002, p. 151).

The value of all of this for psychology is that it gives a new image of experience – the lived moment as a 'crystal'. A classic metaphor in psychology is of subjective experience as a kind of mirror, in which a more or less accurate image of the external world is reflected (see Rorty, 1979, for an extended argument). What is reflected is the present moment, what is happening in the here and now. A crystal, by contrast, is formed by way of a *process* of crystallisation (i.e. actualisation). Also, it does not provide a clear image. It multiplies what it reflects and arranges them in strange juxtapositions. The images we see in a crystal do not appear to give a clear picture of the world, they produce an unsettling, vertiginous effect. Deleuze (1989) uses the phrase 'crystal image' to mark an experience of time where the divisions between past/present/future are not at all clear, but seem to break up into a multiplicity of potential images. If the lived moment is a crystal rather than a mirror, then what is this 'circuit' that actualises the virtual?

Desire and Pleasure

The long friendship between Deleuze and Michel Foucault is well documented (see, for example, Macey, 1993). It was Deleuze who read an extract from one of Foucault's last published works outside the hospital where he died, which served as a eulogy before his secular friends who had gathered there. And it was Foucault who coined the pithy phrase 'Perhaps one day this century will be known as Deleuzian', which has become a favourite by-line on many editions of Deleuziana. Foucault wrote the preface to *Anti-Oedipus*, and Deleuze in turn wrote several short pieces on Foucault's work. Many of these pieces were collected together and reworked as the book *Foucault*. The essay *Desire and pleasure* stands outside this. It was originally a letter sent by Deleuze to Foucault intended as a gesture of support when the latter 'suffered a crisis' following the mixed critical reception of *The history of sexuality I: The will to knowledge* (see translator's note, Deleuze 2006b, p. 402). In the last chapter we discussed the implications of this crisis for Foucault's later work. In this section we will outline the questions that Deleuze poses about Foucault's work and how it throws light on his own.

Desire and pleasure reviews the development of Foucault's 'micro-analysis' of power relations began in *Discipline and punish* and elaborated further in *The will to knowledge*. Deleuze praises the way in which Foucault moves beyond the study of discursive formations (see Foucault, 1972) and introduces 'power arrangements' as a distinct formation which stands in a complex relation to the discursive. The key achievement, for Deleuze, is that this analysis breaks with the notion of ideology and the corresponding idea of power as inherently repressive. As we saw in the last chapter, Foucault rejects what he terms the 'repressive hypothesis', where the role of power is to prohibit or forbid certain categories of acts (with sexual conduct being Foucault's primary concern). Power is considered instead in terms of its productivity – what it creates, what it makes possible. Power is not a 'thing' in itself, a force which is wielded by a sovereign or by an institution, but instead is shorthand for a whole set of strategies for intervening in relationships, for acting upon, steering and guiding the conduct of individuals. Power is not a force that comes from some external source which is then applied to the social field to 'dominate' or 'repress'. It is rather a 'multiplicity of force relations' that are 'immanent to the sphere in which they operate' (Foucault, 1979, pp. 92–93). As such, this theory of power is entirely cognate with Deleuze's Spinozist notion of the immanence of substance. The social is not distinct from some other set of entities (i.e. law, politics, nature) – there is simply one field of relations which continuously unfolds through 'ceaseless struggles'. This does not, however, mean that there is no place in this theory for the formal apparatus of the state (e.g. the police and the judicial system). Rather, these formal institutions are seen to emerge or 'crystallize' from the 'multiplicity of force relations' (ibid., pp. 92–93). The analysis of these institutions must then be done 'bottom-up' through tracing the particular ways in which they grow out of the social field through a consolidation or intensification of particular sets of force relations.

Despite his sympathy with this account of power, and the strong affinities with *Anti-Oedipus*, Deleuze wonders whether Foucault has adequately considered the relationship between the micro and the macro, and correspondingly between 'power' in the formal sense of the powers of the state, and 'power' as micro-level relations of force. The problem here is that without clarifying this relationship, the micro can look as though it is a 'miniaturization of a global conflict' (2006b, p. 124). The state then really is everywhere. But how could such a state of affairs actually be tolerated by citizens? Or as Deleuze puts it: 'How can power be desired?' (p. 125). Deleuze marks a difference between Foucault's use of the term *dispositif* (usually translated as 'apparatus') and his and Guattari's notion of *agencement*.

Apparatus was defined in the following way by Foucault:

> What I'm trying to pick out with this term is, firstly, a thoroughly heterogenous ensemble consisting of discourses, institutions, architectural forms, regulatory decisions, laws, administrative measures, scientific statements, philosophical, moral and philanthropic propositions–in short, the said as much as the unsaid. Such are the elements of the apparatus. The apparatus itself is the system of relations that can be established between these elements. Secondly, what I am trying to identify in this apparatus is precisely the nature of the connections that can exist between these heterogeneous elements. Thus, a particular discourse can figure at one time as the programme of an institution, and at another it can function as a means of justifying or masking a practice which itself remains silent, or as a secondary re-interpretation of this practice, opening out for it a new field of rationality. In short, between these elements, whether discursive or non-discursive, there is a sort of interplay of shifts of position and modifications of function which can also vary very widely. Thirdly, I understand by the term 'apparatus' a sort of – shall we say – formation which has as its major function at a given historical moment that of responding to an *urgent need*. The apparatus thus has a dominant strategic function. This may have been, for example, the assimilation of a floating population found to be burdensome for an essentially mercantilist economy: there was a strategic imperative acting here as the matrix for an apparatus which gradually undertook the control or subjection of madness, sexual illness and neurosis. (Foucault, 1977b, p. 214)

An apparatus is not the same thing as an institution or a state body, although it can include them within itself. It is a 'heterogeneous' collection of very different elements, ranging from formal laws and statements, through to less formalised sets of discourses, along with practices, norms and moral codes. Foucault is concerned with how these diverse elements hang together, with the shifting connections and relations that are established between them. These can be both 'discursive' and 'non-discursive'. Sometimes a code of rationality provides the link, at other times an architectural principle (for example, the common design of schools, hospitals and prisons as sites of surveillance within the disciplinary apparatus). In this way an apparatus is plugged into a field of power relations through which it operates and which is modified and transformed in the process. This includes the constitution of subjectivity – we discover the 'truth' of what we are through the rationalities established by an apparatus (for example, the prisoner is constituted as a 'criminal' in the truth-regime, discourse and practices of the penal apparatus). Finally, an apparatus is 'strategic' in that it constitutes itself as a response to a historically situated need (for example, the penal design as a solution to the problem of transient urban populations under industrial capitalism).

Deleuze's point is that whilst this is a sophisticated analytic tool, it does rather look as though the state has reduced itself to an all-encompassing engine of domination. What is missing for Deleuze is the concept of *desire*. In *Anti-Oedipus*, Deleuze and Guattari (1983) also emphasised the productivity of relations of force rather than their repressive effects. In particular they questioned the received wisdom that psychic repression (i.e. Freud's concept of the repression of threatening unconscious impulses by the ego) is directly related to social/political repression. This linkage, which originally stems from the work of Frankfurt School Critical Theorists such as Herbert Marcuse (e.g. 1991), was popularised in the heady brew of Freudianism and Marxism used to explain the social protests in France that reached a head in the 'éventments' of May 1968. The difficulty with this analysis, as Deleuze and Guattari see it, is that it stitches together two very different sorts of analysis which become entirely conflated. Social institutions become seen as massively overblown extensions of psychic repression (as Freud suggested in *Totem and taboo*), or, conversely, social law is internalised as the Oedipal complex. Revolution is then theorised as the liberation of desire from the Oedipal trap set up by bourgeois family relations, which is then doubled by the formal subsumption of the domestic within advanced capitalism (i.e. the entire fabric of the social is brought within the domain of capital). Deleuze and Guattari argue instead that at no point is desire ever fundamentally about 'mummy' and 'daddy', nor is the relationship of the 'worker' to the 'boss' another version of the Oedipal triangle. If there is a form of social repression extended to the psyche then this has no particular interest in the nature of what is being repressed; rather the object is solely to encourage and incite 'guilt' as a way of gaining a handle on the instincts and desires of individuals.

In psychoanalytic theory, desire is a contested term. It usually refers to an outgrowth of unconscious needs. In Jacques Lacan's work, desire is structured by a fundamental lack (see Lacan, 1977). Once a person acquires language, they experience a sense of self-estrangement, as though a fundamental wholeness has been lost. Desire is the 'impossible relation' to this unknowable 'lost object'. This becomes manifested in the imaginary identifications we have to the actual objects of our desires. Thus in principle desire can never be satisfied and will always be driven and intensified by an intrinsic sense of lack which is transferred to the desired object. Deleuze and Guattari (1983) reject the notion of desire as driven by lack. For them, the primary quality of desire is that it is *productive*. This productivity comes about because they view desire as a version of Spinoza's *conatus*, the endeavour to persist in being, or impersonal striving (indeed, as we saw in Chapter 6, for Spinoza desire was a variant of *conatus* accompanied by consciousness). Desire is the expression of this striving as a kind of will to connect, to forge relations. The productivity of desire arises through the impersonal striving to connect to other bodies, to constitute wider sets of relations that will allow for the expression of potential – 'desire constantly couples continuous flows and partial objects that are by nature fragmentary and fragmented. Desire causes the current to flow, itself flows in turn and breaks the flows' (Deleuze & Guattari, 1983, p. 5). *Desiring-production*, as Deleuze and Guattari call it, is then the driving force expressed by all bodies (human, animal, inorganic), which underpins particular needs and wants, along with all other forms of production (natural, social, industrial). In this way Deleuze & Guattari create a novel way of engaging with both the Freudian *libido* and Marxist *labour-power* from their Spinozist version of desire.

In *Anti-Oedipus*, Deleuze and Guattari use the terminology of machines to describe arrangements of bodies in relations which express desire. A machine is series of bodies which are connected together in such a way as to modify a flow of materials. For example, 'the breast is a machine that produces milk, and the mouth a machine coupled to it' (1983, p. 1). These arrangements are entirely heterogeneous and contingent. For example, Deleuze and Guattari describe a case of Melanie Klein in which she analyses the behaviour of a child called Dick playing with a train set. Klein sees the trains as symbols which stand for Dick and his parents: 'he picked up the train I called "Dick" and made it roll to the window and said "Station". *I explained* "The station is mummy; Dick is going into mummy"' (Klein, cited in Deleuze & Guattari, 1983, p. 45). By contrast, Deleuze and Guattari read this scene as a machine: Dick, the trains and the room constitute a machine which expresses desire, creating novel relations and affects. They refuse to symbolise desiring-production or codify it in the explanatory framework of Kleinian psychoanalysis – 'Say that it's Oedipus or you'll get a slap in the face. The psychoanalyst no longer says to the patient: "Tell me a little bit about your desiring-machines, won't you?" Instead he screams: "Answer daddy-and-mommy when I speak to you!"' (1983, p. 45).

By yoking together the terms desire-production-machine, Deleuze and Guattari emphasise that desire never exists in a raw or pure state. Desire is always immanent to the arrangement of bodies in which it is expressed: 'an assemblage of desire indicated that desire is never a natural or spontaneous determination' (Deleuze, 2006b, p. 124). In *A thousand plateaus*, Deleuze and Guattari substitute the word *agencement*, usually translated as *assemblage*. Whilst the term machine carries with it unfortunate resonances of functionalism and boundedness, assemblage has the various meanings of 'arrangement', 'laying out' or 'putting together' (see Wise, 2005, p. 77). It also connotes the process activity of arranging things together. An assemblage of desire is then, like Foucault's apparatus, a heterogeneous arrangement of elements that are contingently laid out together. The crucial difference, however, is that this arrangement is the expression of the impersonal striving of desire: 'desire is one with a determined assemblage, a co-function' (Deleuze, 2006b, p. 125).

An assemblage has two axes. Along one axis Deleuze and Guattari distinguish content from expression. By content (or its synonym *machinic assemblage*), Deleuze and Guattari mean the bodies which are arranged together and the relations between them – affects, forces, connections, flows. Expression (or *collective assemblage of enunciation*) names the formal and informal codes, statements and discourses which are threaded through these bodies. Deleuze illustrates these terms by using them to re-analyse Foucault's example of the Panopticon:

> The content has both a form and a substance: for example, the form is the prison and the substance is those who are locked up, the prisoners (who? why? how?). The expression also has a form and a substance: for example, the form is penal law and the substance is 'delinquency' in so far as it is the object of statements. Just as penal law as form of expression defines a field of sayability (the statements of delinquency), so prison as a form of content defines a place of visibility ('panopticism', that is to say a place where at any moment one can see everything without being seen). (Deleuze, 1988b, p. 47)

The content of the prison is the nondiscursive ordering of bodies, through a form of technology and administration (panopticism) which makes prisoners visible as distinct individualised criminals. This arrangement is expressed by discourses of penal law, which constitute a particular notion of delinquency, around which the whole penal system can turn. The relationship between content and expression is that between two distinct multiplicities which serve as 'limits and support' for one another. Without criminal bodies, there can be no discourse of delinquency. Without delinquency there is no formal programme upon which the effective division of mass criminality can be effected. But criminal bodies and delinquents are analytically distinct phenomena. Together, content and expression form a complete, if unstable, whole.

The notion of expression also allows Deleuze to offer a novel reading of how the discursive and the non-discursive are held together. Delinquency, the expressive element, is extracted *from* criminals rather than simply applied *to* them (e.g. 'aggression', 'rebelliousness', 'dishonesty'). Once extracted, the qualities are transformed within the discourse of penal law into a composite notion of delinquency. This notion is then reapplied back to the individual, who is henceforth a 'delinquent'. Deleuze calls the process of extraction and reapplication one of *territorialisation*. The key to this is that qualities are taken from their personal context and taken as expressions of a discursive phenomenon which is then fixed within the individual criminal through their insertion into the penal system. The convicted criminal will now have to admit to their own delinquency in order to seek release from confinement.

Territoriality constitutes the second axis of the assemblage. Power arrangements, in the Foucauldian sense, are seen as matters of territorialisation by Deleuze. Whilst Foucault opposes power with resistance, Deleuze and Guattari see *deterritorialisation*, or *lines of flight* on the other side of the axis. This is an opening out, a dissolution, a coming apart of relations as bodies leak from the assemblage into other kinds of relations. And just as territorialisation is an ongoing dynamic, so lines of flight are constantly being emitted from assemblages: 'a society, a social field does not contradict itself, but first and foremost it leaks out on all sides. The first thing it does is escape in every direction' (Deleuze, 2006b, p. 127). The concept of deterritorialisation allows Deleuze to analyse the ongoing modification and transformation of assemblages, as well as the ways these transformations become embedded in new kinds of power arrangements: 'flight lines are not necessarily revolutionary, on the contrary, they are what power arrangements are going to seal off and tie up' (2006b, p. 127).

In a key passage, Deleuze sums up what he takes to be the differences between his and Foucault's approach:

> Desire is wholly a part of the functioning heterogeneous assemblage. It is a process, as opposed to a structure or a genesis. It is an affect, as opposed to a feeling. It is a hecceity – the individual singularity of a day, a season, a life. Above all, it implies the constitution of a field of immanence or body-without-organs, which is only defined by zones of intensity, thresholds, degrees and fluxes. This body is as biological as it is collective and political. It is on this body that assemblages are made and come apart, and this body-without-organs is what bears the offshoots of deterritorialization of assemblages or flight lines. It varies (the body-without-organs of feudalism is not the same as that of capitalism). If I call it body-without-organs, it is because it opposes all strata of organization, the organism's organization as well as power organizations. It is precisely the whole group of body organizations that will smash the plane or the field of immanence, and will impose upon desire another type of plane, each time stratifying the body-without-organs. (Deleuze, 2006b, p. 130)

Foucault had suggested that the term 'pleasure' might serve as a corresponding term to what Deleuze calls 'desire'. As we saw in the last chapter, an exploration of the way the body and its pleasures was figured as the object of self-knowledge became important to Foucault in his final work. Pleasure is what grounds power relations, it is the field that they seize and articulate. However, for Deleuze the term pleasure seems to 'interrupt the immanent process of desire' (2006b, p. 131) since it implies a regulation, a 'zoning' of affect in an almost normalising fashion. Desire is depersonalised and deterritorialised in contrast to pleasure in the same way that, for Deleuze, affect differs from feeling. Deleuze explores this difference by opposing *strata* to *body-without-organs*. By strata, Deleuze means the formal articulation of elements around an organising principle (see Message, 2005). Legal language, for instance, is one form of stratum, but so is a knee-joint when it articulates the movement of a fibula and a tibia. The notion of strata resonates with the notion of 'organ', in the sense both of a formal organisation of functions and the routine application of a principle or plan for organising. Strata are the most territorialised limit of an assemblage's capacity for arranging.

We described in Chapter 5 how articulated language and articulated bodies were the object of attack by Artaud's Mômo thought. The body-without-organs, which Deleuze opposes to strata, is taken from Artaud's later work. Artaud sees 'organless living' as a process of resisting formal articulation, 'hidden judgement', putting up for evaluation and experimentation each and every relation which is possible between bodies:

> The time when man was a tree without organs or function, but possessed of will, and a tree of will which walks will return. It has been, and it will return. For the great lie has been to make man an organism, ingestion, assimilation, incubation, excretion, thus creating a whole order of hidden functions which are outside of the realm of deliberative will. (Artaud, 1988d, p. 515)

Deleuze elaborates body-without-organs as the limit to deterritorialisation – a kind of tendency towards absolute deterritorialisation where relations between bodies can only be grasped as 'zones of intensity, thresholds, degrees and fluxes'. The body-without-organs is not then a foundation for an assemblage, in the same way the virtual does not found the actual. It is the assemblage understood in the least formally organised, most open way, or the assemblage seen as pure potential, with every body connecting to every other such that their very difference becomes indiscernible. In the same way that Artaud takes the body-without-organs as the ultimate release from 'automatisms' and the source of 'true liberty', so Deleuze positions it as that which animates and impels lines of flight, which 'de-stratifies' formal organisation. For Artaud, it is possible for all of us to recall the time when we were 'trees without organs or functions' and to will its return. So for Deleuze and Guattari (1988) every body has the capacity to approach and create its body-without-organs through 'inevitable exercise and experimentation'. Indeed the capacity to de-stratify, to break and reformulate relations is already implied in the way an assemblage operates. Without the ability to break existing connections and create new kinds of relations, the assemblage would not be able to produce anything – hence 'desiring machines work only when they break down' (Deleuze & Guattari, 1983, p. 8). The body-without-organs as incitement towards pure immanence is then the 'place or agent of deterritorialization' (Deleuze, 2006b, p. 131).

In tracking the notion of life, we have moved from the impersonal force of pure immanence, through the circuit of virtual and actual, to the territorialising and deterritirialising of assemblages in the shadow of the body-without-organs. We have seen that subjectivity, the determination of our individual lives is caught up in these processes. In the final section we will see how in the final instance life becomes, for Deleuze, a matter of style.

He Stuttered

The work of the American poet ee cummings is noted for its stylistic invention. His poem *anyone lived in a pretty how town*, which was quoted at the beginning of the chapter, sets up rhythms and repetitions, marking the cycle of seasons. The lines create an intensely personal, lived space: 'children guessed (but only a few and down they forgot as up they grew autumn winter spring summer) that noone loved him more by more'. The juxtapositions, such as 'down they forgot as up they grew', create a sense of movement, without clarifying their meaning. The poem is alive with activity, bursting out on all sides. However, the odd use of personal markers and descriptions – 'he sang his didn't and danced his did' – creates ambiguities and indeterminacies. Just who is the subject? And what is the 'did' that is danced? In particular the blurring between the personal and indefinite pronouns (e.g. 'noone loved him more by more') seems to intensify the relations being described (e.g. loving, dancing, laughing, crying) without centring them on an individuated subject.

Cummings' poetry might be situated in the tradition of 'nonsense verse', of which Lewis Carroll is typically seen as the principal exponent. Deleuze's (1990a). *The logic of sense* explores Carroll's work at length, seeking to make the distinction between meaning and sense central to grasping the peculiar expressive effects that nonsense verse creates. Paradoxes, such as the changes in size amongst the characters that recur in *Alice in Wonderland* are treated as though they expressed impersonal becomings, which Deleuze links to stoic distinctions between the 'states of affairs' and 'incorporeal events'. A state of affairs corresponds to what we have been discussing as the actual. An incorporeal event is a virtual, an impersonal intensification of purely immanent relations. And yet, as we saw earlier, it is still possible to have an experience of such 'events' although that experience is not bounded by rational-consciousness. The sense of the event can strike us although the meaning eludes us. Deleuze proposes that nonsense verse opens up into sense through its use of the infinitive (e.g. 'the tree greens'). Thus in cummings' work 'he danced his did' acts as a kind of an event in that we become implicated in a set of relations that have expressive effects whilst appearing to deliberately withdraw their meaning.

In the short essay *He stuttered* Deleuze explores literary strategies of creating movement, for making language vibrate (e.g. 'he murmured', 'he sobbed', 'he stuttered'). Deleuze applies the distinction between content and expression to argue that literary experimentation goes furthest when it is not just the words, the text, that is full of stuttering, but when the bodies which are articulated by the verse or prose begin themselves to stutter: 'stuttering no longer affects pre-existing words, but itself introduces the words it affects; these words no longer exist independently of the stutter, which selects and links them together through itself. It is no longer the character who stutters in speech; it is the writer who becomes *a stutterer in language*' (Deleuze, 1998b, p. 107). For example, when Artaud begins to use nonsense and invented words in his late poetry – such as the verse 'klaver striva, cavour tavina, scaver kavina, okar triva' in *Artaud the Mômo* – the effect is not merely one of disrupting the expressive field. The sound and weight of the world, the roll of the vowels, all of which were care-fully chosen and well rehearsed by Artaud (see Barber, 1993), create a direct relationship to content, to Artaud's toothless mouth and wrecked body. As Deleuze puts it, 'the affects of language here become the object of an indirect effectuation, and yet they remain close to those that are made directly, when there are no other characters than the words themselves' (p. 108). We might say that we feel affectively engaged with Artaud despite there being nothing else before us than these strange lines of nonsense – an 'incorporeal event'.

To approach cummings' or Artaud's verses in this way is to make a distinc-tion between language, as a system of reference and meaning, and speech, as the utterances which take up and reorganise content (i.e. bodies) into patterns of expression. Deleuze points to a particular way in which this is done by some authors, notably Samuel Beckett, an Irishman writing in French, and Franz Kafka, a Czech writing in German. The peculiarity and the power of their writ-ing has its origins, for Deleuze, in this way that they are forced as writers into a system of expression which is not their own. In a small book they wrote between the two major volumes of *Capitalism and schizophrenia*, Deleuze and Guattari (1986) explore Kafka's work from this direction. They point to the problems Kafka faced as a German-speaking Jew in Prague, at that point a minority population in Bohemia. To speak in German is, for Kafka, to already distance oneself from a Czech identity. But he suffers the further difficulty of squaring his Jewish identity with speaking German. From his perspective German is the 'major language' in which he is forced to express the dilemmas of his own double estrangement. Deleuze and Guattari argue that this amounts to a 'minor use of a major language'. It is not the use of a major language by a minority group (i.e. Bohemian Jews) that is significant, but rather the uncanny effects that arise from being forced to make use of a system of expression which is and cannot be one's own – a minoritarian use of language. The 'minorising' of language is a particular kind of stuttering where writers 'make the language take flight ... send it racing along a witch's line, ceaselessly plac-ing it in a state of disequilibrium, making it bifurcate and vary in each of its terms, following an incessant modulation' (Deleuze, 1998b, p. 109). In listen-ing to minorised language, one is exposed to the 'booms' and 'busts' of a lan-guage that is strained way beyond its normative use or equilibrium point.

For example, Kurt Schwitters' *Sonata in Urlauten* is a tone poem consisting of repeated strings of vowel sounds and nonsense words which are meticulously strung together and repeated (see Fink, 1973 for a broader discussion). In audio recordings of Schwitters' performance of the poem, its character as a sonata becomes apparent, as Schwitters' voice swoops and expands through the various phrases which take on a strange kind of musicality and appear to almost become an entire orchestra unto themselves. Schwitters expands a new and strange kind of tonal language carved out within German. This is a language that seems to 'grow from the middle, like grass' (Deleuze, 1998b, p. 111). It is an illustration of what Deleuze and Guattari (1988) call a *rhizome*, a patterning of relations where any point is potentially connected to any others, without any privileging of any particular connections. Language as a rhizome seems to overspill at every turn, it 'tends towards a limit that is itself no longer either syntactical or grammatical' (1998b, p. 112). This limit is 'not external to language as a whole: it is the outside of language' (ibid., p. 112). The outside of language is rather like the underside of the canvas, the *subjectile*, sought by Artaud. Minorised language is a jet, a spurt that draws the speaker along with it. Kafka becomes the violin wail of the final pages of *Metamorphosis*, Schwitters becomes an entire orchestra in the *Sonata*.

In minorisation there is a passage beyond language, beyond expression, as part of a transformation in content, a becoming of she or he who minorises their speech. Deleuze sees this becoming as a matter of *style*, or the 'foreign element within language' (p. 113). Minorised language elevates style through its modesty or economy – only these vowels are repeated, only this tic marks speech, just this nonsense phrase here. Style is the marker, for Deleuze, of minoritarian literature, but it is also a more general description of a mode of living that pushes against the lures of familiar expression:

> Everyone can talk about his memories [sic], invent stories, state opinions in his language; sometimes he even acquires a beautiful style, which gives him adequate means and makes his an appreciated writer. But when it is a matter of digging under the stories, cracking open the opinions, and reaching regions without memories, when the self must be destroyed, it is certainly not enough to be a 'great' writer, and the means must remain forever inadequate. Style becomes nonstyle, and one's language lets an unknown foreign language escape from it, so that one can reach the limits of language itself and become something other than a writer, conquering fragmented visions that pass through the words of a poet, the colours of a painter, or the sounds of a musician. (Deleuze, 1998b, p. 113)

We usually call 'style' the expression of a recognisable aesthetic, a modus operandi, 'good taste'. Style seems to reinforce the character and subjectivity of the writer. Pushing beyond this, experimenting with novel forms of expression pushes style into forms of expression that 'do not yet exist' (p. 113). It is a becoming, an emergence of something different, an 'unknown foreign language' that escapes formal language and leads to a transformation of the speaker. Deleuze clearly means this style-as-nonstyle, or rather continuous experimentation and variation as style to be a matter of living per se, rather than of living as a writer. Style is what makes for singularisation rather than individuation in our lives. It is a way of seeing concrete individual lives as having their own particular patterns of unfolding that are outside of a notion of bounded subjectivity, of the person as the author of their own existence. Rather we are the stylists of our own existence. In this sense, Deleuze's notion of style is of a piece with Foucault's *techné tou biou*, or art of living. If *a life* is a matter of immanence, then *the life* is a matter of style.

We opened this chapter by remarking on how Roland Barthes' comments on the *Death of the author* have been taken as a prohibition on discussing the relation between the life of a given individual and the work they create, or even the talk they utter. The subject is dissolved in the undulating weave of discourse. Deleuze rescues us from this unfortunate limit on our thinking. Through the categories of life, style, assemblage, actual and virtual, Deleuze maps out complex relationships between the singular aspects of our lived experience without at any point seeking to reintroduce a bounded consciousness in which this is gathered together. There can be no Deleuzian psychology, but there can be a form of psychological enquiry which takes the astonishing creative world unfolded by Deleuze, with its affects and intensities, spurts of life and experiments with self-stylisation as its object.

TEN

Conclusion: On Losing Your Foundations and Finding Yourself Again

... [it] is always swinging between the surfaces that stratify it and the plane that sets it free. If you free it with too violent an action, if you blow apart the strata without taking precautions, then instead of drawing the plane you will be killed, plunged into a black hole, or even dragged towards catastrophe. Staying stratified – organized, signified, subjected – is not the worst that can happen; the worst that can happen is if you throw the strata into demented or suicidal collapse, which brings them back down on us heavier than ever. (Deleuze & Guattari, 1988, p. 161)

The Dimension of Vitality

In this book we have explored the possibilities of a 'second-order' psychology committed to the idea that we must reflexively create our own foundations. This reflexive foundationalism, however, goes 'all the way down'. That is to say, we must create our foundations in the context of an emotional, social, organic and material environment that is no less self-foundationing. We begin this conclusion by identifying a theme common to all of the thinkers and topics we have addressed in this book. This theme can be summarised as follows: whether one has consciously realised it or not, to live, to act, to think and to talk one must constantly negotiate a position between two impossible extremes of unrepeatable chaos and redundant order. These two extremes form the poles of what could be called a *dimension of vitality*. Any 'art of life' must find its way in the space/time of this dimension. If the creative (non) foundationalism that we have argued for in this book confronts the paradox that groundless being must create its own grounds, then it must do so as part of, and within the parameters of, the dimension of vitality.

Unrepeatable chaos

At one extreme, there is the chaotic and buzzing non-space of possibilities. Artists are well aware of this chaotic non-space since art, of all human endeavours, gets closest to it. Turner paints it in his masterpieces of tumultuous seas of light. In singing of Van Gogh, Joni Mitchell invokes the notion of *turbulent indigo*. Johnny Cash invokes a burning ring of fire. That most artistic of psychologists, William James, spoke of a 'blooming, buzzing confusion'. Patti Smith, the poet, sings of the 'sea of possibilities'. No life is possible in the buzzing confusion of the sea of possibilities, and yet life – nature itself – is born from the primordial soup of that turbulent sea of noise and fury. A complete return to that sea spells certain death: death by chaos. Or as Deleuze and Guattari (1988, p. 161) describe it in the opening quotation it results in the return of the strata as a form which is 'heavier than ever'. For this reason, as Whitehead points out (1927–8/1985, p. 96), Chaos has traditionally been associated with evil. In book II of *Paradise Lost*, for instance, Milton describes Satan's journey across Chaos in which he discovers,

> The secrets of the hoary deep; a dark
> Illimitable ocean, without bound,
> Without dimension, where length, breadth and highth,
> And time and place are lost; where eldest Night
> And Chaos, ancestors of Nature, hold
> Eternal anarchy amidst the noise
> Of endless wars, and by confusion stand.

But despite these negative, Satanic associations, we are also dimly aware that if we stray too far from this illimitable and anarchic ocean, our life loses its meaning and its creativity. Time, place and dimension may well be lost in it, but they are also born from it. It is our source: *ancestors of Nature*. In crossing Chaos, Satan left a permanent track. This track is a trace of order – a trail which might be followed by other demons in a preliminary gesture of repetition or pattern amongst the anarchy.

Redundant order

On the other hand, at the other extreme, there is the static total space of complete redundancy where nothing but the monotonous repetition of the same brute reality is possible. No life is possible in this frozen, stratified, nonmoving space of redundancy. The rule of the rule rules supreme. Creativity – the possibility of the new – is at a minimum, and then it is snuffed out altogether. The sense organ presented with repetition of the same ceases to sense.

This continuum of vitality has been felt in one form or another at least since the pronouncements of the pre-Socratic sages Heraclitus and Parmenides. Great thinkers have long been more or less dimly aware of it and many have particularised it in dualistic terms. Nietzsche distinguished the *Dionysian* from the *Apollonian*; Bergson distinguished *life* from *matter*; Freud distinguished the instinct of life from that of death. It seems that we risk destruction from two sides: from the side of *unrepeatable chaos*, and from the side of *redundant order*. Imagine a surfer who must constantly negotiate a position between zones too calm and still to carry the board, and zones so rough and unpredictable that no stability is possible. The becoming of the surfer is inseparable from the becoming of the wave. Perhaps we are all surfers in the dimension of vitality.

It is important to emphasise that, for any given individual, both extremes mean death. Amongst other things, death is: a) the one thing we can be certain of; and b) not something we can actually experience, since it marks the end of our experience. A corollary of the statement that both extremes of the continuum of vitality mean death can therefore be stated, quite emphatically: we can have no experience of these two extremes. We cannot know them empirically. They mark two limits of experience. It follows that we are always already in the middle of these possible non-experiences. We are thrown, as Heidegger put it, and then swim, in the *milieu* or medium of the dimension of vitality. Such is our destiny. But then death is not the end of the world.

In sum, we are creatures of a process of creation that did not begin with us and will not end with us. Each new phase of creation must take the results of the previous phase as its artistic medium. This is why we have placed such emphasis in the latter part of the book (particularly in the chapters on Foucault and Deleuze) on the notion of the *art of living*, a topic either ignored by psychology or consigned to the 'pop psychology' shelves. Aim and value are inescapable aspects of psychology once being is construed in relation to becoming, and ethics becomes a very real project of the coordination and harmonisation of personal and collective existence.

Interestingly enough, the theme of the *art of living* was also a significant concern for Whitehead, who took issue with the doctrine of evolution that seizes on the idea that life is essentially a struggle for existence in which the fittest eliminate the less fit (a doctrine that has risen to new prominence via 'evolutionary psychology'). For Whitehead (1929/1958, p. 4), the fallacy of such evolutionary thinking lies not in the belief of the 'survival of the fittest' (a fact that is 'obvious' and 'stares us in the face'), but in the belief that 'fitness for survival is identical with the best exemplification of the Art of Life'. 'Life', Whitehead points out, is quite deficient in survival value. The art of persistence, he states, 'is to be dead', since 'only inorganic things persist for great lengths of time'. The art of living, by contrast, concerns the active modification of one's environment, and the more sophisticated the organism, the more actively it transforms its surroundings. When it comes to us human beings, this transformation and creation of the environment becomes the most prominent fact in our existence. The *art of life* thus concerns this active relation to the environment, and it can be summarised as a three-fold urge:

(i) to live, (ii) to live well, (iii) to live better. In fact, the art of life is *first* to be alive, *secondly* to be alive in a satisfactory way, and *thirdly* to acquire an increase in satisfaction. (ibid., p. 8)

As we stressed in the previous chapter, this task must be distinguished from the narrowly individualistic dogma of the humanistic psychology movement in which we are invited to 'self-actualise'. The art of living ultimately cannot be dissociated from the social life of the collectivity, and here Spinoza and Deleuze's notion of impersonal beatitude becomes directly relevant. If we were pushed to sum up in a simple phrase what it is that we consider to be the point or aim of a second-order psychology, we might adapt Whitehead and say the following: the function of a psychology without foundations is the promotion of the art of life.

Pipe Dreams

This book is a response to what we think of as the pressing need to replace the dogma of reductionist materialism that still grips psychology with a radical alternative that better fits the facts and better satisfies our intuitions. It is often said that psychology is still a young science, and this is used as an excuse for the fact that it has not matured into a hard science that resembles the grown-ups such as physics, chemistry and biology. But for how many decades can we continue to tell this story of promising youth? Psychology is no longer a young science. On the contrary, it seems to us that psychology has grown old before its time, but without the maturity and wisdom that should accompany the ageing process. Psychology has been denied its phase of childish play, imagination and wonder. It has been denied this through a combination of two factors. On the one hand, there has been an idolisation and emulation of a positivistic image of those sciences which came before it and stimulated its development. On the other hand, there has been a socially imposed practical demand for knowledge and techniques that can be deployed in the never-ending quest for social control and progress. In our experience, any creativity not stifled by the dead hand of positivism is typically crushed by the premature responsibilities imposed by a short-term pragmatism. Psychology must rediscover its lost youth. It must, above all, expand its imagination, its creativity. We wish the discipline of psychology to fall in love once again with its subject matter. We encourage it to take some time out, to smoke a pipe, to dream. But what is its subject matter? What is the psyche? What is experience? How do these things relate to the human being more generally, and to our forms of activity? In our experience such questions are almost never to be heard uttered within departments of psychology.

In this book we have argued against the tendency to try to 'pin' the psyche down in some definitive manner. In place of this 'Ahab-function' we have introduced an 'Ishmael-function' the key note of which is to follow our subject matter wherever it appears to go, to note its unpredictable transformations and its complex relations. Instead of dismissing the complexities of process, relationality and mediation we have placed these centre stage and we have drawn upon theorists whose work can help us in this task. With Artaud and Spinoza, for example, we have seen that the psychic does not begin with biological embodiment and it does not end with biological embodiment, and yet it has a decisively important *relation* with physiology. With Bergson and Deleuze we have seen that perception, duration and life are bound up with the complex forms of temporality associated with relations between the virtual and the actual, the possible and the real. And with Luhmann and Foucault we have seen that the psychic does not begin with society and it does not end with society, and yet it has a relation with society from which it ought not to be entirely abstracted.

One difficulty with these kinds of ideas, of course, is that they are rather abstract and hence difficult to grasp into a convenient 'take-home-message'. One is left with what can sometimes feel like a cloud of smoke that drifts away, having subtly changed the smell, taste and appearance of the local atmosphere. What use is a cloud of smoke? What can be done with it? Without something more substantial, the prospect of making some difference to the discipline of psychology remains a mere pipe dream. If only there were something more solid, like the firm wooden pipe from which the smoke slowly rises. In English, when we wish to confront someone disagreeable with a brute fact of experience that cannot be wished away, we sometimes utter the phrase 'stick that in your pipe and smoke it!' If only the totality of the brute facts of our experience could be stuck into a pipe and smoked. If only the powers of affective existence and the images, tastes, scents, sounds and sensations of perceptual encounters and the propositions of cognitive processes and conceptual thought and the enunciations of discourse could be bound up in one memorable pipe! Perhaps it can. Surreal things can come in dreams.

This is a Pipe

In the 1920s Rene Magritte created his well-known painting *Ceci n'est pas une pipe*. This famous artwork shows a carefully rendered image of a pipe beneath which Magritte painted a sentence that in English would read 'this is not a pipe'. Much ink has been devoted to this rather tongue-in-cheek work, including an interesting little book by Michel Foucault (1982) in which the author ruminates over the difference between the 'visible' and the 'articulable'. But how are we to interpret the artwork's statement 'this is not a pipe' in the light of our book?

A first way of interpreting it is to diverge from Foucault (1982, p. 19) by drawing a distinction between what we call *power* and *image* (as should become clear, the actual words chosen are less relevant than the concepts they mark). That is to say, the *image* of the pipe that we see on Magritte's canvas is evidently not a pipe in the sense of something which we can fill with tobacco, light and smoke. There is, hence, a very easy commonsensical distinction to be drawn between the causally efficacious aspects of an entity (let us mark that causal efficacy with the word *power*) and an entity considered as an *image*.

Although this distinction, badly handled, might risk the recreation of a 'reality/representation' binary, we nevertheless think it is worth making. The point is not to deny that the image of a pipe has powers of its own (and hence is no less real than any real pipe), but to maintain a distinction which might then allow us to recognise that the powers of a painted image are not identical to those of the pipe that might have served as Magritte's model. In the light of Chapter 6 we leave it to the reader to list the affects both pipes might be capable of.

A second way of interpreting it is to add another distinction which we will mark with the word *proposition*. We wish to distinguish the pipe qua proposition from the pipe qua power and image. By the word proposition we wish to indicate a distinction between something actual and something potential. In the simplest terms, a proposition does not denote something that *is* but rather something that *might be*. It is what Whitehead described as a *lure* for feeling. A proposition is hence not first of all something linguistic (which is not to deny that language greatly amplifies the capacity to propose) but rather something conceptual. The pipe considered as a proposition is no more a pipe than the pipe considered as image. The painting, however, provokes those of us who have the patience to reflect upon the 'concept' of pipe and its possible meanings and relations. We thus have two distinct ways in which Magritte's phrase 'this is not a pipe' might be understood. The conceptual *proposition* of a pipe is distinct from the *image* of a pipe is distinct from the *causally efficacious* pipe that has the power to be filled with tobacco, lit and smoked.

A third way of interpreting it is to draw one last distinction by attending to the linguistic level of the actual words and punctuation that together form the sentence 'this is not a pipe'. Evidently the painted word 'this' is not something we might mistake for a pipe, and equally evidently the sentence *Ceci n'est pas une pipe* is not a pipe. It is as difficult to smoke those words as to smoke the conceptual proposition or the image. We now have three distinct ways in which *this* is not a pipe. The linguistic enunciation is distinct from the conceptual proposition is distinct from the image, and all are distinct from the causally efficacious pipe of power. We will mark this last distinction, which draws attention to the domain of communication, with the word *enunciation*.

Power, image, proposition and *enunciation* give us four initial letters that together do indeed sum to a pipe of sorts. Together, our four pipes give us the psyche stuffed in a pipe, or at least a mnemonic device for it. That is to say, we wish to suggest that, suitably understood, they cover the full domain of experience. Power and image can be considered as the two distinguishable modes of perception that Whitehead identifies in *Process and reality* as 'causal efficacy' and 'presentational immediacy'. In the first mode we perceive our thoroughly embodied and thoroughly temporal *affective* relation to the world, whilst the second deals with the predominantly spatial affair of sensory perception. It is important to stress that the word 'image' arbitrarily emphasises vision (since in our example we are dealing with a painting), but that this category should include all modes of sense perception. Proposition and enunciation, by contrast, can be considered conceptual modes that operate with meaning. We are affected, we sense, we think and we talk: affect, percept, concept, discourse.

These modes are also closely related in that they grow out of one another, and – developmentally and evolutionarily – as a new mode appears, it both inherits from and transforms its predecessor. As we suggested earlier, images too have their 'powers' in that they generate and are generated by real worldly activity – by real effects and affects. More specifically, the imagistic mode of sensory perception *presupposes* more primordial forms of affective power as a parasite presupposes its host. The eye is first of all a mediator by way of which an organism can affect its own body through being affected by changing patterns of light. Propositions and enunciations are likewise causally efficacious in their own domains of abstraction (hence the function of concepts and the pragmatics of discourse), which in turn presuppose the continued existence of the abstracted-from background provided by the two forms of perception. The boundaries between the four modes are thus ultimately far from distinct and exclusive. Power is applicable to each of the other modes, but in a manner that is increasingly abstract and refined (the powers of sensory experience, the powers of conceptual proposition, the powers of discourse). This is because the modes emerge from one another in a veritable parasitical cascade: image presupposes power; proposition presupposes both image and power and the difference between them; enunciation presupposes proposition, image and power, and the differences between these. Each time the newly emergent mode works back upon its inheritance, transforming it into an environment optimally conducive to its own continuance as a power in the universe.

To remain consistent with the Whiteheadian notion of concern outlined in Chapter 2, and with the Bergsonian notion of flow outlined in Chapter 7, this pipe of experience must be split down the middle. The split is made by way of a distinction between experience (subject) and expression (superject) that applies equally to each mode. On the one side, power, image, proposition and enunciation are forms of experience, on the other side, they are forms of expression. Together, experience and expression enable process. That is to say, experience (an occasion of experience considered from its own private internal 'subjective' perspective) concerns the reception of data from past expressions, and expression (an occasion of experience considered from the public external 'objective' perspective of a new occasion) passes on data for future experiences.

The experience side of power is the capacity to be affected by other entities.

The expression side of power points to the capacity to affect these other entities in turn.

Both aspects are essential to any definition of power. We are constituted by the ways in which others come into our experiences and, in turn, the ways in which we come into the experiences of others.

Turning to the next mode, the experience side of sensory perception concerns the reception of sense data or the objectification of the surrounding world in the form of sense perception (sounds, shapes and colours, sensations, tastes and smells).

The expression side of image, much as Bergson emphasised, concerns the 'motor' corollaries to sensation that make up the sensori-motor couple and that, in the organisms that possess these higher forms of perception, harness the capacity to affect to the capacity to be affected by sensory perception.

Both aspects are essential to any definition of sensory experience.

With respect to conceptual propositions the experience side concerns the forms of reception we call *understanding* in contrast to the expressive moment of active reasoning.

Finally, with respect to enunciation we can distinguish the experience of listening (or reading) with the expressions of speaking (or writing).

Let us systematise these four modes of experience/expression a little further.

Pipe 1: power

The pipe that we smoke affects us in various ways and likewise is affected by us when filled, lit, smoked, emptied, and so on. It is thus related to us via a field of power relations. It enters into our experience *affectively* as a causally efficacious aspect of our world.

We use the word power in a Whiteheadian/Deleuzian sense to capture a sense of the world as a field of functional activity in which things are what they are by virtue of their activity in that world. For Bergson (1911/1998, p. 302), this is the 'fluid continuity of the real'. The notion of power is thus integral to the idea of essential relationality (that things have *relational essences*). Things, in other words, are *definable* as their relevance to other things and in terms of the way other things are relevant to them. We noted that Spinoza defined power in this way in a two-fold manner as the capacity to affect other things and the capacity to be affected by other things. Likewise, Locke stated that power is to be conceived as a *relation* and as two-fold: 'viz. as able to make, or able to receive, any change: the one may be called "active," and the other "passive."' (Whitehead, 1927–8/1985, p. 57). This twofold aspect is important to emphasise, and it corresponds broadly to the experience/ expression distinction emphasised above whereby something is received or 'taken in' (experienced) and something is passed on (expressed). Following Whitehead's principle of relativity whereby 'it belongs to the nature of every "being" that it is a potential for every "becoming"' (ibid., p. 45), we can grasp that one occasion of experience is an experience of the expressions of others. An occasion of expression is likewise data for the experiences of new occasions, and so forth. This whole field of interrelated activity is a field of power relations in which entities are affected by and affect one another in manifold ways. It is in this context that Whitehead speaks of *causal efficacy* and Deleuze speaks of *affect* (as distinct from percept and concept). Power is the basic mode of experience and expression and it is irrelevant to no form of experience or expression, no matter how high-grade, rarefied and sophisticated.

Pipe 2: image

In Magritte's picture we merely *see* an image of the pipe as a collection of sense data (patterns of shape and colour) distributed spatially before us. Magritte's pipe is not a pipe since, via the medium of his artwork, he has abstracted all but a semblance of the visual impression of a pipe. Abstraction has been a key concept throughout our book, and it remains key here (in Chapter 7, for instance, we discussed Bergson's notion of the *image* as something 'cut out' from an ongoing 'flow'). Abstraction abstracts from something more complete and more complex. But that *from* which the abstraction is made is rendered temporarily irrelevant and is accorded no further attention. Let us mark this ideal notion of completeness with the traditional philosophical distinction between 'formal existence' and 'objective existence'. An entity can thus be considered as existing in its own 'formal' completeness (e.g. as an experience from its own point of view) but also as existing 'objectively' as an expression in the experience of another. From the complete formal existence of something, a reduced sample is abstracted. The entity in its *formal* existence is thus *objectified* into the experience of another entity. The objectified entity can now be described in terms of its 'objective existence' (its existence as an object for another) rather than its 'formal existence'. Abstraction thus abstracts something from out of a background. The background remains background and the abstraction alone is attended to and worked with. Abstraction is this process or gesture of isolating something from its background and attending to it or operating with it. Of all the ways that a pipe can affect us and be affected by us, we retain in Magritte's picture only what we might call its 'visual aspect'. We lose its feel in our hand, its smell and its taste, the way it might soothe or repulse us. In the same way, when we merely look at a pipe (even one we could pick up and smoke), we entertain that pipe only in so far as it is 'objectified' for us in visual form as something *seeable*. When we touch it or smell it, we objectify it in other distinctive ways.

But let us not forget that Magritte gives us a very detailed and realistic image of a pipe. It is not a piece of abstract art, like Matisse's snail, which abstracts an absolute minimum of visual 'snailness' and leaves practically all of the visual details, let alone the rest, in the background. Via his 'realism', Magritte draws our attention to the fact that even if we were looking at a 'real' pipe, we would, in merely looking, still be dealing only with sensa or 'percepts' from the visual modality. That is to say, we would be dealing only with those objective aspects abstracted via the complex organic pathways of our visual system. Whether we are looking at a real pipe or at Magritte's picture, we are dealing in our experience with nothing more than a spatially arranged pattern of colours. There is nothing in what we are given that warrants the claim to have seen a *pipe*. We are in the domain of what Deleuze called *percepts* and with the mode of perception that Whitehead called *presentational immediacy*. In presentational immediacy the world is given in sense-presentation. Clearly, this way of objectifying the world is limited to sophisticated forms of animal life. The experience of lower organisms, in contrast, is dominated by the affective sense of causal efficacy that we are calling power. Perception in the mode of power is thus primordially dominant, and only secondarily does the world come to be objectified via sense data. As we touched upon in Chapter 7, Bergson (1911/1998, p. 204) articulates the difference between image and power in terms of a distinction between 'surface' and 'depth': 'motionless on the surface, in its very depth it lives and vibrates'. Image is the comparatively superficial product of great complexity. It nevertheless dominates our consciousness with its definiteness and precision. And yet it is obviously a 'show' generated by our own bodily activity. All we need do is close our eyes and the image of the pipe disappears. But the clarity and distinctness of the image is always accompanied by a haunting sense of a deeper affective power to things, vague and imprecise and yet, somehow, indescribably important.

Imagine for a moment that the picture were so well crafted that we actually take it for a pipe, reach out for it, and find our hand bumping into the surface of the picture, disappointed, perhaps, that we will not be able to smoke. Power and image would here be out of sync. We would be confronted by what we described earlier as the difference between power and image. We would be like the fabled dog that dropped his meat through grasping at its tempting reflection in the still water of a lake. The dog too failed to coordinate image and power, and was confronted with their difference. The germ of consciousness is to be found in the confrontation with this difference.

Pipe 3: proposition

There is nothing in the play of colours arrayed before us in their immediacy that warrants our claim to have seen a *pipe*. Whether the image is a painting, a photograph, a mirror image of a pipe or a pipe in front of us may be entirely irrelevant to the question of the facticity of the sense perceptions arrayed before us during a given moment. What we see is not yet a 'pipe' but this array of colour and shape. That is to say, to see a 'pipe' is already to have taken the sense-presentation of the image as something else: i.e. not as an array of 'sensa' but as *a pipe*. To take something *as* something else is to engage in symbolism. More specifically, it is to take the image as a *proposition*. It is to think something like: 'this *might be* a pipe', or 'these are not merely interesting colours dominating my field of vision: this is a pipe!' Of course, such a move is not necessarily something we are consciously aware of having made. On the contrary, as Husserl made clear, it can be extremely difficult not to automatically adopt the 'natural attitude' according to which our sense perceptions are routinely taken to be things in the world. Nevertheless, to *take* one thing *as* something else is to open up the possibility of a mis*take*. Unlike the pure facticity of the image (or of power), a proposition takes a risk and hence admits of error.

More specifically, a proposition plays precisely with the difference between the actual and the possible that is expressed in the phrase 'this *might be* a pipe!' Aesop's dog took the risk of such a proposition, and paid the price of error. However, although he lost his piece of meat for one that could not satisfy his hunger, he gained the possibility of a quantum leap in imagination (Whitehead, 1927, p. 19). That is to say, he gained the possibility of an intensification of the contrast that is the difference between the possible and the actual. A proposition thus plays the difference between what is given to us in the mode of causal efficacy and what is given to us in the imagistic mode of presentational immediacy. The most primitive conceptual symbol is the taking of an image as something with the power to otherwise affect and be affected by us (as something that can be eaten, for example). To return to what Magritte shows us, the most primitive conceptual symbol (pipe 3: proposition) is taking the pipe given in presentational immediacy (pipe 2: image) as the causally efficacious pipe that can be smoked (pipe 1: power). Pipe 3 thus literally links the difference between pipes 1 and 2. The first glimmers of consciousness and high-level conceptual thought are born in this difference between image and power. The difference is also the germ of value, and hence the primary issue involved in the art of life. To put it in Spinozist and Deleuzian terms, we take the risk of articulating power and image into a proposition in order to increase our powers (to eat, to think, to love). To put it in Whiteheadian terms, the basic expression of value embodied in a proposition is: 'Have a care, here is something that matters! Yes – that is the best phrase – the primary glimmering of consciousness reveals, something that matters' (Whitehead, 1938/1966, p. 116). 'Importance' is thus decisive to propositions. More specifically, image derives its importance from its relation with power. The coordination of power and image must take place within the flow of process. Sometimes it matters that 'this is a pipe', and sometimes it matters that '*ceci n'est pas une pipe*'.

Pipe 4: enunciation

A word is clearly not the same kind of thing as an image. However, as with each of our distinctions, it is important to recognise the mutual implication of power, image, proposition and enunciation. As an artist, Magritte amplifies both the similarities and differences between word and image. As Magritte himself put it, 'Between words and objects one can create new relations and specify characteristics of language and objects generally ignored in everyday life' (Foucault, 1982, p. 38). For example, the words *Ceci n'est pas une pipe* are not written on the canvas but *painted* on it so as to *resemble* writing. We are thus not dealing here with natural handwriting but with a meticulously executed painterly rendition of a natural hand. As such, the sentence is, of course, in the realm of the image. But the writing-image does not resemble a pipe. It is worth further quoting the artist here: 'In a painting, words are of the same cloth as images. Rather one sees images and words differently in a painting.' Enunciation thus has an image-aspect (when the spoken word is used it has its perceptual aspect objectified as sound, of course), and it also has a power-aspect. Its most profound links and disjunctures, however, are with the proposition-aspect.

The *word* pipe is both closest to, and furthest away from the *concept* pipe. It is closest to it, since once we have learned the meaning of the word, we can take the tight coupling of word and concept for granted. But, nevertheless, word and concept share with image and power the fact that they are connected only via the intermediary of symbolism. In fact, the enunciation (pipe 4) is *not* the proposition (pipe 3) just as the image (pipe 2) is not the causally efficacious power (pipe 1). As Artaud teaches us so profoundly, the risk that one takes in putting propositions into words is equivalent to the risk entailed in taking an image for the important thing it might stand in place of. But perhaps the risks are worth taking. Certainly once enunciation is possible in a form of life, propositions are forever transformed:

> The mentality of mankind and the language of mankind created each other. If we like to assume the rise of language as a given fact, then it is not going too far to say that the souls of men are the gift from language to mankind. The account of the sixth day should be written, He gave them speech, and they became souls. (Whitehead, 1938/1966, p. 41)

Wonder and Wander

We do not wish our pipe mnemonic to be mistaken for an essentialist scheme such that any experience can be boiled down to one of four modes, or such that they are taken as static, clear and distinct categories of experience/expression. It is less a model than an adventure to be had. As we stressed in Chapter 2, reductionist materialism makes a number of problematic assumptions: that some form of stuff or 'matter' is the basic foundation of the universe and hence the ultimate 'reality'; that ultimate reality is meaningless and value free; that there exists a temporally static material base for which development is irrelevant; that real things are ultimately context independent; that creativity is therefore irrelevant to a mechanistic nature, and so forth. We have posited instead that there is nothing more fundamental than *activity, events,* or *actual occasions of experience*; that value is of the essence; that the universal is relational and interconnected; that process is the prior concept; and that the universe is a process of creative advance.

One implication of this is that we must contrast reduction downwards with creative evolution upwards. This requires that we be struck with wonder. A pipe, despite certain health risks, can be an impressive aid to adventures of thought, memory and feeling. With a pipe in hand it might be easier to imagine, not a process of moving downwards through epiphenomenal illusion towards an increasingly real and factual base (from communication to consciousness to physiology to physicality, for instance) but rather a move upwards from a scene of pure unactualised potential to scenes of increasingly vivid forms of real experience and expression. One might imagine, for instance, that enunciation, and discourse more generally, presupposes and builds upon proposition, image and power and it 'contains' the other modes as an essential aspect of its forms of order. The physical world concerns modifications of *energy*, and this world thus involves a pure form of power which has nothing to do with image, proposition or enunciation. But it remains a stubborn fact that forms of imagery, conceptual proposition and symbolic communication came into this universe of energy. Basic organic life was able to self-organise in a manner that diverted the flow of that energy, converting it into what might be called the *vitality* of that which lives, for instance, and living things evolved imagery, and the capacity to propose and to communicate symbolically, presumably through further diversions. We live routinely with the fact of this improbable state of affairs, and yet we rarely *wonder* at it. Physical worlds of energy, biological worlds of vitality, psychic worlds of 'personality' and cultural worlds of communication co-exist with each and every occasion of human existence, and the future awaits us. What potentials can we actualise?

Another implication is that we must wander: we must follow the white whale where it goes. Yes, it is important to conduct controlled research in laboratories, but 'psychology' can never be pinned and mounted like a butterfly. If we are to be equal to our subject matter, we must wander as it does, and we must adapt to diverse circumstances as it does. The last thing we need is to live our lives in the laboratories and classrooms of a university psychology department, specialising increasingly on smaller and smaller sub-topics, reading only specialist journals maintained by those who devote their lives to that one narrow area. Too many of our colleagues have ceased to wonder and have ceased to wander. If the discipline of psychology is to grow up then it must shed some of its methodological weapons and some of its disciplinary armour, and it must climb the specialist walls and breathe fresh air. If a naked and vulnerable ape that has wandered the surface of the earth could triumph over the 'armour plated monsters' (Whitehead, 1926/2005, p. 258) of prehistory, then there is a glimmer of hope that an undefended second-order psychology might have a future. A tower block needs foundations. Psychology needs a backpack, a pair of good boots, and, of course, a pipe.

References

Adlam, D., Henriques, J., Rose, N., Salfield, A., Venn, C., & Walkerdine, V. (1977). Psychology, ideology and the human subject. *Ideology and Consciousness*, *1*, 5–56.

Agamben, G. (1998). *Homo Sacer: sovereign power and bare life*. Stanford: Stanford University Press.

Agamben, G. (2004). Absolute immanence. In J. Khalfa (Ed.), *An introduction to the philosophy of Gilles Deleuze*. London: Continuum.

Althusser, L. (2001). *Lenin and philosophy*. New York: Monthly Review Press.

Ansell-Pearson, K. (2002) *Philosophy and the adventure of the virtual*. London: Routledge.

Antaki, C., Biazzi, M., Nissen, A. & Wagner, J. (2008). Managing moral accountability in scholarly talk: the case of a Conversation Analysis data session. *Text and Talk*, *28*, 1–30.

Artaud, A. (1965a). Van Gogh: the man suicided by society. In J. Hirschman (Ed.), *Artaud anthology*. San Francisco: City Lights.

Artaud, A. (1965b). All writing is pigshit. In J. Hirschman (Ed.), *Artaud anthology*. San Francisco: City Lights.

Artaud, A. (1968a). Correspondence with Jacques Rivière. *Collected works: volume one*. (V. Corti, Trans.). London: Calder & Boyars.

Artaud, A. (1968b). Letter to the chancellors of the European universities. *Collected works: volume one* (V. Corti, Trans.). London: Calder & Boyars.

Artaud, A. (1968c). The situation of the flesh. *Collected works: volume one* (V. Corti, Trans.). London: Calder & Boyars.

Artaud, A. (1968d). Address to the Pope. *Collected works: volume one* (V. Corti, Trans.). London: Calder & Boyars.

Artaud, A. (1968e). On suicide. *Collected works: volume one* (V. Corti, Trans.). London: Calder & Boyars.

Artaud, A. (1974). The theatre and its double. *Collected works: volume four* (V. Corti, Trans.). London: Calder & Boyars.

Artaud, A. (1988a). Letter to the Buddhist Schools. In S. Sontag (Ed.), *Antonin Artaud: selected writings*. Berkeley: University of California Press.

Artaud, A. (1988b). What I came to Mexico to do. In S. Sontag (Ed.), *Antonin Artaud: selected writings*. Berkeley: University of California Press.

Artaud, A. (1988c). A voyage to the land of the Tarahumara. In S. Sontag (Ed.), *Antonin Artaud: selected writings*. Berkeley: University of California Press.

Artaud, A. (1988d). Letter to Pierre Loeb (April 23, 1947). In S. Sontag (Ed.), *Antonin Artaud: selected writings*. Berkeley: University of California Press.

Artaud, A. (1988e). Fragments of a diary from hell. In S. Sontag (Ed.), *Antonin Artaud: selected writings*. Berkeley: University of California Press.

Artaud, A. (1995a). Artaud the Mômo. In *Watchfiends and rack screams: works from the final period* (C. Eshleman & B. Bador, Trans.). Boston: Exact Change 91–177.

Artaud, A. (1995b). Here lies. In *Watchfiends and rack screams: works from the final period* (C. Eshleman & B. Bador, Trans.). Boston: Exact Change.

Artaud, A. (1995c). The human face. *Watchfiends and rack screams: works from the final period* (C. Eshleman & B. Bador, Trans.). Boston: Exact Change.

Artaud, A. (1995d). To have done with the judgement of God. *Watchfiends and rack screams: works from the final period* (C. Eshleman & B. Bador, Trans.). Boston: Exact Change.

Artaud, A. (1995e). The theatre of cruelty. *Watchfiends and rack screams: works from the final period* (C. Eshleman & B. Bador. Trans.). Boston: Exact Exchange.

Artaud, A. (2003). *The monk*. London: Creation Books.

Artaud, A. (2006). *Heliogabalus, or the crowned anarchist: a blood history*. London: Creation Books.

Artaud, A. (2008). *50 drawings to murder magic*. London: Seagull Books.

Ashmore, M., Brown, S.D., & MacMillan, K. (2005). Lost in the mall with Mesmer and Wundt: demarcation and demonstration in the psychologies. *Science, Technology & Human Values. 30* (1), 76–110.

Ashmore, M., MacMillan, K., & Brown, S.D. (2004). It's a scream: professional hearing and tape fetishism. *Journal of Pragmatics*, 36, 349–374.

Atkinson, J.M. & Heritage, J. (1984). (Eds.). *Structures of social action: studies in conversation analysis*. Cambridge: Cambridge University Press.

Atlan, H. (1981). Hierarchical self-organization in living systems: noise and meaning. In M. Zeleny (Ed.), *Autopoiesis, a theory of living organizations*. New York: North Holland.

Auer, P. (2005). Projection in interaction and projection in grammar. *Text, 25* (1), 7–36.

Austin, J.L. (1962). *How to do things with words*. Clarendon Press: Oxford.

Averill, J.R. (1980). A constructivist view of emotion. In R. Plutchik and H. Kellerman (Eds.), *Theories of emotion*. New York: Academic Press.

Bachelard, G. (1934/1962). *The new scientific spirit*. New York: Beacon.

Banister, P., Burman, E., Parker, I., Taylor, M., & Tindall, C. (1989). *Qualitative methods in psychology: a research guide*. Buckingham: Open University Press.

Barber, S. (1993/2005). *Antonin Artaud: bombs and blows*. London: Fontana.

Barber, S. (2004). *The screaming body. Antonin Artaud: film projects, drawings and sound recordings*. London: Creation Books.

Barber, S. (2006). Introduction. In A. Artaud, *Heliogabalus, or the crowned anarchist: a blood history*. London: Creation Books.

Barthes, R. (1977). The death of the author. In *Image–music–text*. London: Fontana.

Bass, E. & Davis, L. (1988). *The courage to heal: a guide for women survivors of child sexual abuse* (3rd ed.). New York: Harper Perennial.

Bentall, R.P. (2003). *Madness explained: psychosis and human nature*. London: Penguin Books.

Bentall, R., Cromby, J., Harper, D., and Reavey, P. (2009). *Understanding mental health and distress: beyond abnormal psychology*. Basingstoke: Palgrave.

Bergson, H. (1908/1991). *Matter and memory* (N.M. Paul & W.S. Palmer, Trans.). New York: Zone.

Bergson, H. (1911/1998). *Creative evolution* (A. Mitchell, Trans.). Mineola, New York: Dover.

Bergson, H. (1913/2001). *Time and free will: an essay on the immediate data of consciousness* (F.L. Pogson, Trans.). Mineola, New York: Dover.

Bergson, H. (1922/1999). *Duration and simultaneity*. (R. Durie, Ed.). Manchester: Clinamen.

Bergson, H. (1933/1992). *The creative mind: an introduction to metaphysics* (M.L. Andison, Trans.). New York: Citadel.

Blanchot, M. (1959/2004). Artaud. In E. Scheer (Ed.). *Antonin Artaud: a critical reader*. London: Routledge.

Boyle, M. (2002). Schizophrenia: A scientific delusion? (2nd ed.). London: Routledge.

Bradley, B.S. (2005). *Psychology and experience*. Cambridge: Cambridge University Press.

Brannigan, A. (1997). The postmodern experiment: Science and ontology in experimental social psychology. *British Journal of Sociology, 48* (4), 594–610.

Brown, S.D. (2001). Psychology and the art of living. *Theory & Psychology, 11* (2), 171–192.

Brown, S.D. (2002a). 'Psychology without foundations'. *History & Philosophy of Psychology, 4* (1), 69–83.

Brown, S.D. (2002b). 'Michel Serres: science, translation and the logic of the parasite'. *Theory, Culture & Society, 19* (3), 1–27.

Brown, S.D. (2003). Natural writing: the case of Serres. *Interdisciplinary Science Review, 28* (3), 184–192.

Brown, S.D. (2004). Parasite logic. *Journal of Organisational Change Management, 17* (4), 383–395.

Brown, S.D. (2005). Collective emotions: Artaud's nerves. *Culture & Organization, 11* (4), 235–246.

Brown, S.D. (2006a). The determination of life. *Theory, Culture & Society, 23* (2/3), 331–332.

Brown, S.D. (2006b). Bonga, tromba and the organizational impetus: evolution and vitalism in Bergson. *Culure & Organization, 12* (4), 307–319.

Brown, S.D. (2007). After power: Artaud and the theatre of cruelty. In C. Jones & R. ten Bos (Eds.), *Philosophy and organization*. London: Routledge.

Brown, S.D. (2008). The quotation marks have a certain importance: prospects for a 'memory studies'. *Memory Studies, 1* (3), 261–271.

Brown, S.D. & Lunt, P. (2002). A genealogy of the social identity tradition: Deleuze & Guattari and social psychology. *British Journal of Social Psychology, 41* (1), 1–23.

Brown, S.D. & Stenner, P. (2001). Being affected: Spinoza and the psychology of emotion. *International Journal of Group Tensions, 30* (1), 81–105.

Brown, S.D. & Tucker, I. (2009). Eff the ineffable: affect, somatic management and mental health service users. In G. Seigworth & M. Gregson (Eds.), *The affect reader*. Durham, NC: Duke University Press.

Buckley, K.W. (1989) *Mechanical man: John B. Watson and the beginnings of behaviorism*. New Tork: Guilford Press.

Burman, E. (2007). *Deconstructing developmental psychology* (2nd ed.). London: Routledge.

Cameron, D. (2000). *Good to talk?* London: Sage.

Campbell, S. (2003). *Relational remembering: rethinking the memory wars*. Oxford: Rowman & Littlefield.

Canguilhem, G. (1980). What is psychology? *Ideology and consciousness, 7*, 37–50.

Canguilhem, G. (1991). *The normal and the pathological*. New York: Zone.

Canguilhem, G. (1994). Normality and normativity. In F. Delaporte (Ed.), *A vital rationalist: selected writings from Georges Canguilhem*. New York: Zone.

Chertok, L. & Stengers, I. (1992). *A critique of psychoanalytic reason: hypnosis as a scientific problem from Lavoisier to Lacan*. Stanford: Stanford University Press.

Clam, J. (2000). System's sole constituent, the operation: clarifying a central concept of Luhmannian theory. *Acta Sociologica, 43*, 63–79.

Clough, P. (2007). The affective turn: introduction. In P. Clough & J. Halley (Eds.), *The affective turn: theorizing the social*. Durham, NC: Duke University Press.

Comte, A. (1903). *Discourse on the positive spirit*. London: William Reeves.

Cooper, D. (1978). *The language of madness*. London: Pelican.

Cooper, R. (1990). Organization/disorganization. In J.S. Hassard & D. Pym (Eds.), *The theory and philosophy of organizations*. London: Routledge.

Cummings, E.E. (1960). *Selected poems 1923–1958*. London: Faber.

Cummings, E.E. (1994). *Complete poems 1904–1962*. New York: W.W. Norton.

Curt, B. (1994). *Textuality and tectonics: troubling social and psychological science*. Buckingham: Open University Press.

Damasio, A. (2000). *The feeling of what happens*. London: Vintage.

Damasio, A. (2004). *Looking for Spinoza*. London: Vintage.

Damasio, A. (2006). *Descartes' error: emotion, reason and the human brain*. Harmondsworth: Viking Penguin.

Danziger, K. (1990). *Constructing the subject.* Cambridge: Cambridge University Press.

Deleuze, G. (1972/2000). *Proust and signs* (complete text) (R. Howard Trans.). London: Continuum.

Deleuze, G. (1983). *Nietzsche and philosophy.* London: Athlone Press.

Deleuze, G. (1986). *Cinema 1: the movement-image.* London: Athlone Press.

Deleuze, G. (1988a). *Spinoza: practical philosophy* (R. Hurley, Trans.). San Francisco, CA: City Lights.

Deleuze, G. (1988b). *Foucault* (S. Hand, Trans.). Minneapolis: University of Minnesota Press.

Deleuze, G. (1989). *Cinema 2: the time-image.* London: Athlone Press.

Deleuze, G. (1990a). *The logic of sense* (M. Lester, Trans.). New York: Columbia University Press.

Deleuze, G. (1990b). On *A thousand plateaus.* In *Negotiations.* New York: Columbia University Press.

Deleuze, G. (1991). *Bergsonism.* New York: Zone.

Deleuze, G. (1992). *Expressionism in philosophy: Spinoza* (M. Joughin, Trans.). New York: Zone.

Deleuze, G. (1993). *The fold: Leibniz and the baroque.* London: The Athlone Press.

Deleuze, G. (1994). *Difference and repetition* (P. Patton, Trans.). London: The Athlone Press.

Deleuze, G. (1998a). To have done with judgement. In *Essays critical and clinical* (D.W. Smith & M.A. Greco, Trans.). London: Verso.

Deleuze, G. (1998b). He stuttered. In *Essays critical and clinical* (D.W. Smith & M.A. Greco, Trans.). London: Verso.

Deleuze, G. (2001). *Empiricism and subjectivity: an essay on Hume's theory of human nature.* New York: Columbia University Press.

Deleuze, G. (2002). The actual and the virtual. In G. Deleuze & C. Parnet, *Dialogues II.* London: Athlone Press.

Deleuze, G. (2005). Spinoza and us. In M. Fraser & M. Greco (Eds.), *The body: a reader.* London: Routledge.

Deleuze, G. (2006a). Immanence: a life.... in *Two regimes of madness: texts and interviews 1975–1995.* New York: Semiotext(e).

Deleuze, G. (2006b). Desire and pleasure. In *Two regimes of madness: texts and interviews 1975–1995.* New York: Semiotext(e).

Deleuze, G. & Guattari, F. (1983). *Anti-Oedipus: capitalism and schizophrenia* (R. Hurley, M. Seem & H. Lane, Trans.). Minneapolis: University of Minnesota Press.

Deleuze, G. & Guattari, F. (1986). *Kafka: Towards a minor literature.* Minneapolis: University of Minnesota Press.

Deleuze, G. & Guattari, F. (1988). *A thousand plateaus: capitalism and schizophrenia* (B. Massumi, Trans.). London: Athlone Press.

Deleuze, G. & Guattari, F. (1994). *What is philosophy?* (H. Tomlinson and G. Burchill, Trans.). London: Verso.

Deleuze, G. & Parnet, C. (1987/2002). *Dialogues* (H. Tomlinson and B. Habberjam, Trans.). London: Athlone Press and Continuum Press.

Derrida, J. (1978a). La parole soufflée. In *Writing and difference.* London: Routledge.

Derrida, J. (1978b). The theatre of cruelty and the closure of representation. In *Writing and difference.* London: Routledge.

Derrida, J. & Thévenin, P. (1998). *The secret art of Antonin Artaud* (M.A. Caws, Trans.). Cambridge, MA: MIT Press.

Dewey, J. (1950). *John Dewey to Joseph Ratner 1950.08.05: The correspondence of John Dewey* [Electronic resource http://dewey.pragmatism.org/#deweywebsites]. Accessed December 2008.

Dilthey, W. (1883/1989). *Introduction to the human sciences: an attempt to lay a foundation for the study of society and history.* Detroit, MI: Wayne State University.

Dixon, T. (2004). *From passions to emotions: the creation of a secular psychological category.* Cambridge: Cambridge University Press.

Doroshow, D.B. (2007). Performing a cure for schizophrenia: Insulin Coma Therapy on the wards. *Journal of the History of Medicine and Allied Sciences, 62* (2), 213–243.

Dumoncel, J.C. (2003). Whitehead's faculty psychology. In F. Riffert, & M. Weber (Eds.), *Searching for new contrasts: Whiteheadian contributions to contemporary challenges in neurophysiology, psychology, psychotherapy and the philosophy of mind.* Franfurt am Main:Peter Lang.

Durkheim, E. (1912/2001). *The elementary forms of religious life* (M. Cladis, Ed., C. Cosman, Trans.). Oxford: Oxford University Press.

Edwards, D. (1997). *Discourse and cognition.* London: Sage.

Edwards, D. (2007). Managing subjectivity in talk. In A. Hepburn & S. Wiggins (Eds.), *Discursive research in practice: new approaches to psychology and interaction* (pp. 31–49). Cambridge: Cambridge University Press.

Edwards, D. & Potter, J. (1992). *Discursive psychology.* London: Sage.

Engel, S. (2000). *Context is everything: The nature of memory.* New York: W.H. Freeman.

Esslin, M. (1976). *Artaud.* London: John Calder.

Etain, B. & Roubaud, L. (2002). Jean Delay, M.D. 1907–1987. *American Journal of Psychiatry, 159*, 9.

Fink, U. (1973). Kurt Schwitters' contribution to concrete art and poetry. *Forum for Modern Language Studies, IX* (1): 75–85.

Foerster, H. von. (1960). On self-organising systems and their environment. In M.C. Yovits & S. Cameron (Eds.), *Self-organising systems.* New York: Pergamon Press.

Foerster, H. von. (1993). *Understanding understanding: essays on cybernetics and cognition.* New York: Springer.

Forrester, M. (1996). *Psychology of language.* London: Sage.

Foucault, M. (1961/2005). *History of madness* (J. Murphy, Trans.). London: Routledge.

Foucault, M. (1972). *The archaeology of knowledge* (A. Sheridan, Trans.). London: Routledge.

Foucault, M. (1977a). *Discipline and punish: the birth of the prison* (A. Sheridan, Trans.). Harmondsworth: Penguin.

Foucault, M. (1977b). *The confessions of the flesh. Power/knowledge: selected interviews and other writings.* London: Longman.

Foucault, M. (1978). What is an author? *Language. Counter-Memory, Practice.* Ithaca, New York: Cornell University Press.

Foucault, M. (1979). *The will to knowledge: The history of sexuality, volume 1* (R. Hurley, Trans.). Harmondsworth: Penguin.

Foucault, M. (1982). *This is not a pipe.* California: University of California Press.

Foucault, M. (1984). On the genealogy of ethics: an overview of work in progress. In P. Rabinow (Ed.), *The Foucault reader: an introduction to Foucault's thought.* Harmondsworth: Penguin.

Foucault, M. (1987). *The use of pleasure: The history of sexuality, volume 2.* (R. Hurley, Trans.). Harmondsworth: Penguin.

Foucault, M. (1988). *The care of the self: The history of sexuality, volume 3.* (R. Hurley, Trans.). Harmondsworth: Penguin.

Foucault, M. (1989a). *Maurice Blanchot: the thought from outside.* New York: Zone.

Foucault, M. (1989b). An aesthetics of existence. In S. Lotringer (Ed.), *Foucault live (Interviews 1966–84).* New York: Semiotext(e).

Foucault, M. (1995). Madness, the absence of work. *Critical Inquiry, 21*, 290–298.

Foucault, M. (2000a). Technologies of the self. In *Ethics: Essential works of Foucault 1954–1984, Vol. 1.* Harmondsworth: Penguin.

Foucault, M. (2000b). On the government of the living. In *Ethics: Essential works of Foucault 1954–1984, Vol. 1.* Harmondsworth: Penguin.

Foucault, M. (2000c). Subjectivity and truth. In *Ethics: Essential works of Foucault 1954–1984, Vol. 1.* Harmondsworth: Penguin.

Foucault, M. (2000d). On the genealogy of ethics: an overview of work in progress. In *Ethics: Essential works of Foucault 1954–1984, Vol. 1.* Harmondsworth: Penguin.

Foucault, M. (2000e). Self writing. In *Ethics: Essential works of Foucault 1954–1984, Vol. 1.* Harmondsworth: Penguin.

Foucault, M. (2000f).The ethics of concern for self as a practice of freedom. In *Ethics: Essential works of Foucault 1954–1984, Vol. 1.* Harmondsworth: Penguin.

Foucault, M. (2002). The subject and power. In *Power: Essential works of Foucault 1954–1984, Vol. 3.* Harmondsworth: Penguin.

Foucault, M. (2004a). *Society must be defended: lectures at the Collège de France 1975–1976.* Harmondsworth: Penguin.

Foucault, M. (2004b). *Sécurité, territoire, population: Cours au Collège de France 1977–1978.* Paris: Seuil.

Foucault, M. (2004c). *Naissance de la biopolitique: Cours au Collège de France 1978–1979.* Paris: Seuil.

Freud, S. (2001). *Totem and Taboo.* London: Routledge.

Freyd, J. (1998). *Betrayal trauma: the logic of forgetting childhook abuse.* Cambridge, MA: Harvard University Press.

Froggett, L (2002). *Love, hate and welfare: psychosocial approaches to policy and practice.* Bristol: Policy Press.

Frosh, S. (2003). Psychosocial studies and psychology: is a critical approach emerging? *Human Relations, 56,* 1547–1567.

Gadamer, H.G. (1993). *Truth and method.* London: Continuum.

Gergen, K.J. (l973). Social psychology as history. *Journal of Personality and Social Psychology, 26,* 309–320.

Gergen, K.J. (1982/1994). *Towards transformation in social knowledge.* London: Sage.

Gibson, J.J. (1966). *The senses considered as perceptual systems.* Boston: Houghton Mifflin.

Gilbert, D.T. (1991). How mental systems believe. *American Psychologist, 26* (2), 107–119.

Girard, R. (1987). *Things hidden since the foundation of the world.* Stanford, California: Stanford University Press.

Girard, R. (1988). *Violence and the sacred.* London: Continuum.

Girard, R. (1989). *The scapegoat.* Baltimore: Johns Hopkins University Press.

González Rey, F.L. (2007). Social and individual subjectivity from an historical cultural standpoint. *Outlines: Critical Social Studies, 2,* 3–13.

Greco, M. (2004). The politics of indeterminacy and the right to health. *Theory, Culture & Society, 21* (6), 1–22.

Greco, M. (2005). On the vitality of vitalism. *Theory, Culture & Society, 22* (1), 15–27.

Greco, M. (2009). On the art of life: a vital reading of medical humanities. In J. Latimer and M. Schillmeier (Eds.). *Un/Knowing bodies.* Oxford: Blackwell.

Greco, M. and Stenner, P. (Eds.). (2008). *The emotions: a social science reader.* London: Routledge.

Green, A. (1977). Conceptions of affect. *International Journal of Psycho-Analysis, 58,* 129–156.

Guattari, F. (1984). *Molecular revolution: psychiatry and politics.* London: Penguin.

Haaken, J. (1998). *Pillar of salt: gender, memory, and the perils of looking back.* New Brunswick, NJ: Rutgers University Press.

Haaken, J. and Reavey, P. (Eds.). (2009). *Memory matters: contexts for understanding recollection of child sexual abuse.* London: Routledge.

Habermas, J. (1988). *Legitimation crisis.* Cambridge: Polity.

Hacking, I. (2000). *The social construction of what?* Cambridge, MA: Harvard University Press.

Hadot, P. (1995). *Philosophy as a way of life: spiritual exercises from Socrates to Foucault.* Oxford: Blackwell.

Hamlin, J.K., Wynn, K. & Bloom, P. (2007). Social evaluation by preverbal infants. *Nature, 450,* 557–560.

Hampshire, S. (1988). *Spinoza: an introduction to his philosophical thought.* Harmondsworth: Penguin.

Haraway, D. (1991). *Simians, cyborgs and women: the reinvention of nature.* New York: Routledge.

Hardt, M. & Negri, A. (2000). *Empire.* Cambridge, MA: Harvard University Press.

Hardt, M. & Negri, A. (2004). *Multitude: war and democracy in the age of empire.* Harmondsworth: Penguin.

Harré, R. (1983/4). *Personal being.* Blackwell: Oxford.

Harré, R. (1991). *Physical being: a theory for a corporeal psychology.* Oxford: Blackwell.

Harré, R. & Parrott, W. G. (1996). *The emotions: social, cultural and biological dimensions.* London: Sage

Harré, R. & Secord, P.F. (1972). *The explanation of social behaviour.* Oxford: Blackwell.

Hartshorne, C. (1934). *The philosophy and psychology of sensation.* Chicago: University of Chicago Press.

Healy, D. (2002). *The creation of psychopharmacology.* Cambridge, MA: Harvard University Press.

Heidegger, M. (1977). The question concerning technology. In *The question concerning technology and other essays* (W. Lovitt, Trans.). New York: Harper & Row.

Heidegger, M. (1982). *The basic problems of phenomenology* (A. Hofstadter, Trans.). Bloomington/Indianapolis: Indiana University Press.

Heidegger, M. (1990). *Being and time.* Oxford: Blackwell.

Henriques, J., Hollway, W., Urwin, C., Venn, C. & Walkerdine, V. (1984). *Changing the subject: psychology, social regulation and subjectivity.* Methuen: London.

Hetherington, K. & Munro, R. (Eds.). (1997). *Ideas of difference: social spaces and the labour of division.* Oxford: Blackwell.

Ho, C. (1997). Antonin Artaud: from center to periphery, periphery to center. *Performing Arts Journal, 19* (2), 6–22.

Hollway, W. (Ed.). (2004). Psycho-social methods. Special issue of the *International Journal of Critical Psychology,* 10.

Hollway, W. & Jefferson, T. (2000). *Doing qualitative research differently: free association, narrative and the interview method.* London: Sage.

Honneth, A. (1995). *The struggle for recognition.* Cambridge: Polity.

Hopper, P.J. (1992). Times of the sign: on temporality in recent linguistics. *Time and Society, 1* (2), 223–238.

Hyman, I.E., Husband, T.H. & Billings, J.F. (1995). False memories of childhood experiences. *Applied Cognitive Psychology,* 9, 1–17.

Israel, J. & Tajfel, H. (Eds.). (1972). *The context of social psychology: a critical assessment.* London: Academic Press.

Jacob, F. (1976). *The logic of life: a history of heredity.* New York: Vintage Books.

James, H. (Ed.). (1926). *The letters of William James.* Boston: Little, Brown.

James, W. (1910/2003). *The meaning of truth.* Mineola, NY: Dover Publications.

James, W. (1911/1996). *Some problems of philosophy: a beginning of an introduction to philosophy.* Nebraska, USA: University of Nebraska Press.

Johnson, A.H. (1945). The psychology of Alfred North Whitehead. *Journal of General Psychology, 32,* 175–212.

Lacan, J. (1977). *Ecrits.* London: Routledge.

Langer, S. (1988). *Mind: an essay on human feeling.* Baltimore, MD: Johns Hopkins University Press.

Lansdale, M. (2004). When nothing is 'off the record': exploring the theoretical implications of the continuous recording of cognitive process in memory. *Memory, 13* (1): 31–50.

Lapoujade, D. (2000). From transcendental empiricism to worker nomadism: William James. *Pli, 9,* 190–199.

Latour, B. (2005). *Reassembling the social: an introduction to actor-network theory.* Oxford: Oxford University Press.

Law, J. (2002). *Aircraft stories: decentring the object in technoscience*. Durham: Durham University Press.

Lawlor, L. (2003). *The challenge of Bergsonism: phenomenology, ontology, ethics*. London: Continuum.

Levinson, S.C. (1983). *Pragmatics*. Cambridge: Cambridge University Press.

Little, W., Fowler, H. & Coulson, J. (1978) *The shorter Oxford English dictionary on historical principles*, prepared by, revised and edited by C.T. Onions, 3rd edition revised by G.W.S. Friedrichsen. Oxford: Oxford University Press.

Loftus, E.F., Coan, J.A. & Pickrell, J.E. (1996). Manufacturing false memories using bits of reality. In L.M. Reader (Ed.), *Implicit memory and metacognition* (pp. 195–220). Mahwah, NJ: Lawrence Erlbaum Associates.

Loftus, E.F. & Ketcham, K. (1994). *The myth of repressed memory: false memories and allegations of sexual abuse*. New York: St Martin's Press.

Loftus, E.F. & Palmer, J.C. (1974). Reconstruction of automobile destruction: an example of the interaction between memory and language. *Journal of Verbal Learning and Verbal Behaviour*, *13*, 585–589.

Loftus, E. & Pickrell, J.E. (1995) The formation of false memories. *Psychiatric Annals*, *25*: 720–725.

Lotringer, S. (2004). Interview with Jacques Latrémolière. In E. Scheer (Ed.), *Antonin Artaud: a critical reader*. London: Routledge.

Lowenthal, D. (1985). *The past is a foreign country*. Cambridge: Cambridge University Press.

Luhmann, N. (1981). Subjektive Rechte: Zum Umbau des Rechtsbewußtseins für die moderne Gesellschaft. In: *Gesellschaftsstruktur und Semantik Bd. 2*, Frankfurt: Suhrkamp.

Luhmann, N. (1982). *Trust and power*. London: John Wiley & Sons.

Luhmann, N. (1995). *Social systems*. Stanford: Stanford University Press.

Luhmann, N. (1998a). *Love as passion: the codification of intimacy*. Stanford: Stanford University Press.

Luhmann, N. (1998b). *Observations on modernity*. Stanford: Stanford University Press.

Luhmann, N. (1999). *Die Wirtschaft der Gesellschaft*. Frankfurt am Main: Suhrkamp.

Luhmann, N. (2000a). *Art as a social system*. Stanford: Stanford University Press.

Luhmann, N. (2000b). *The reality of the mass media*. Stanford: Stanford University Press.

Luhmann, N. (2004). *Law as a social system*. Oxford: Oxford University Press.

Luria, A. (1962). *The mind of a mnemonist*. Harmondsworth: Penguin.

Lyons, H. (1968). *The Royal Society: 1660–1940*. New York: Greenwood Press.

Lyotard, J.-F. (1979/1984). *The postmodern condition: a report on knowledge*. Manchester: Manchester University Press.

Macey, D. (1993). *The lives of Michel Foucault*. London: Vintage.

MacKay, D.M. (1972). Formal analysis of communicative processes In R.A. Hinde (Ed.), *Non-verbal communication*. Cambridge: Cambridge University Press.

Mannheim, K. (1952/1985). *Ideology and Utopia: an introduction to the sociology of knowledge*. San Diego: Harcourt.

Marcuse, H. (1991). *One dimensional man: studies in the ideology of advanced industrial society*. Boston: Beacon Press.

Marks, J. (2000). Foucault, Franks, Gauls: Il fait defendre la société: the 1976 lectures at the Collège de France. *Theory, Culture & Society*, *17* (5), 127–147.

Marowitz, C. (1977). *Artaud at Rodez*. London: Marion Boyars.

Marres, N. (2008). *The object turn changes register?: green living experiments, material practices of engagement, or how to handle entanglement in public*. Presented at 'A Turn to Ontology?', Said Business School, Oxford, June 2008.

Maslow, A. (1962/1998). *Towards a psychology of being*, 3rd edn. London: Wiley.

Mason, P. (1995). Editorial: False memory syndrome vs. lying perpetrator syndrome: the big lie. *Post-Traumatic Gazette*, *4* (November–December 1995). Available online http://www.patiencepress.com/samples/4thIssue.html. Accessed 3 October 1998.

Massumi, B. (1996). The autonomy of affect. In P. Patton (Ed.), *Deleuze: a critical reader*. Oxford: Blackwell.

Massumi, B. (2002). *Parables for the virtual: movement, affect, sensation*. Durham, NC: Duke University Press.

Matthis, I. (2000). Sketch for a metapsychology of affect. *International Journal of Psycho-Analysis, 81*, 215–227.

Maturana, H.R. & Varela, F. (1975). Autopoietic systems. In Biological Computer Laboratory, Report No. 9.4. Urbana, Ill: University of Illinois.

Maturana, H. & Varela, F.J. (1987). *The tree of knowledge: the biological roots of human understanding*. Boston: New Science Library.

McCormack, D. P. (2003). An event of geographical ethics inspaces of affect. *Transactions of the Institute of British Geographers, 26*, 488–507.

Melville, H. (1851/2003). *Moby Dick: Or the Whale*. Revised edition. Harmondsworth: Penguin.

Message, K. (2005) Strata. In A. Parr (Ed.), *The Deleuze dictionary*. Edinburgh: Edinburgh university Press.

Middleton, D. (2002). Succession and change in the socio-cultural use of memory: building-in the past in communicative action. *Culture & Psychology, 8* (1), 79–95.

Middleton, D. & Brown, S.D. (2005). *The social psychology of experience: studies in remembering and forgetting*. London: Sage.

Morss, J. (1995). *Growing critical: alternatives to developmental psychology*. London: Routledge.

Motzkau, J. (2007). *Cross-examining suggestibility: memory, childhood, expertise*. PhD thesis, Loughborough University.

Mullarkey, J. (1999). *Bergson and philosophy*. Edinburgh: Edinburgh University Press.

Neu, J. (1977). *Emotion, thought and therapy*. Berkeley, CA: University of California Press.

Newnes, C., Dunn, S., & Holmes, G. (Eds.). (1999). *This is madness: a critical look at psychiatry and the future of mental health services*. Ross-on-Wye: PCCS Books.

Newnes, C., Holmes, G. & Dunn, S. (Eds.). (2001). *This is madness too: critical perspective on mental health services*. Ross-on-Wye: PCCS Books.

Nicolescu, B. (2002). *Manifesto of transdisciplinarity*. Albany: State University of New York Press.

Ofshe, R. (1995). *Making monsters: false memories, psychotherapy and sexual hysteria*. New York: André Deutsch.

O'Leary, T. (2002). *Foucault and the art of ethics*. London: Continuum.

Parker, I., Georgaca, E., Harper, D., McLaughlin, T., & Stowell-Smith, M. (1995). *Deconstructing psychopathology*. London: Sage.

Pezdek, K., Finger, K. & Hodge, D. (1997). Planting false childhood memories: the role of event plausibility. *Psychological Science, 8*, 437–441.

Pope, K.S. (1995). What psychologists better know about recovered memories, research, lawsuits, and the pivotal experiment. *Clinical Psychology: Science and Practice*, Fall, 2/3, 304–315.

Pope, K.S. (1996). Memory, abuse and science: questioning claims about the false memory syndrome epidemic. *American Psychologist, 51* (9), 957–974.

Pope, K.S. and Brown, L.S. (1996). *Recovered memories of abuse: assessment, therapy, forensics*. Washington, DC: American Psychological Association.

Porter, R. (1990). *Mind-forg'd manacles: history of madness in England from the restoration to the regency*, (2nd ed.). London: Penguin.

Potter, J. (1996). *Representing reality*. London: Sage.

Proust, M. (2003). *In search of lost time, volume 1: the way by Swann's* (J. Grieve, Trans.). Harmondsworth: Penguin.

Quattrone, P. (2004). Accounting for God. Accounting and accountability practices in the Society of Jesus (Italy, 16th–17th centuries). *Accounting, Organizations and Society, 29* (7), 647–683.

Rathbun, C. (1934). On certain similarities between Spinoza and psychoanalysis, *Psychoanalytic Review, XXI*, 1–14.

Reavey, P. & Brown, S.D. (2006). Transforming agency and action in the past, into present time: adult memories and child sexual abuse. *Theory and Psychology*, *16* (2), 179–202.

Reavey, P. and Brown, S.D. (2007). The embodiment and spaces of memory: child sexual abuse and the construction of agency, *Journal of Social Work Practice*, *21* (4): 213–229.

Reavey, P. and Brown, S.D. (2009). The mediating role of objects in recollections of adult women survivors of child sexual abuse. *Culture and Psychology*, in press.

Redding, P. (1999). *The logic of affect*. Ithaca: Cornell University Press.

Richards, G. (1995). *Putting psychology in its place*. London: Routledge.

Riffert, F. & Weber, M. (Eds.). (2003). *Searching for new contrasts: Whiteheadian contributions to contemporary challenges in neurophysiology, psychology, psychotherapy and the philosophy of mind*. Franfurt am Main: Peter Lang.

Rorty, R. (1979). *Philosophy and the mirror of nature*. Oxford: Blackwell.

Rose, N. (1985). *The psychological complex*. London: Routledge.

Rose, N. (1989). *Governing the soul: the shaping of the private self*. London: Routledge.

Rose, N. (1996). *Inventing our selves*. Cambridge: Cambridge University Press.

Rose, N. (2001). The politics of life itself. *Theory, Culture and Society*, *18* (6), 1–30.

Rose, N. & Miller, P. (Eds.). (1986). *The power of psychiatry*. Oxford: Polity.

Rowell, M. (Ed.) (1996). *Antonin Artaud: works on paper*. New York: Museum of Modern Art.

Rustin, M. (2002). Introduction: ways of thinking about human emotions, *European Journal of Psychotherapy, Counselling and Health*, 5 (3), 197–203.

Ryle, G. (1975). *Concept of mind*. New York: Barnes & Noble.

Sacks, H. (1992). *Lectures on conservation*, Oxford: Blackwell.

Said, E. (1978). *Orientalism*. New York: Vintage Books.

Schacter, D.L. (1996). *Searching for memory: the brain, the mind, and the past*. New York: Basic Books.

Scheer, E. (Ed.). (2002). *One hundred years of cruelty: essays on Artaud*. Sydney: Power Publications.

Scheer, E. (Ed.). (2004). *Antonin Artaud: a critical reader*, London: Routledge.

Sedgwick, E.K. (2003). *Touching feeling: affect, pedagogy, performativity*. Durham, NC: Duke University Press.

Sedgwick, P. (1982). *Psychopolitics*. London: Pluto Press.

Serres, M. (1980/1982). *The parasite*. Baltimore: Johns Hopkins University Press.

Serres, M. (1990/1995). *The natural contract* (E. MacArthur & W. Paulson, Trans.). Ann Arbor: University of Michigan Press.

Serres, M. (1991). *Rome: the book of foundations* (Felicia McCarren, Trans.). Stanford, CA: Stanford University Press.

Serres, M. (1992). *Hermes: literature, science, philosophy* (J.V. Harari & D.F. Bell, Eds.). Baltimore: Johns Hopkins University Press.

Serres, M. (1995). *Angels: a modern myth*. Paris: Editions Flammarion.

Serres, M. (1997). *The troubadour of knowledge*. Ann Arbor: University of Michigan Press.

Serres, M. (1998). *Genesis*. Michigan: Michigan University Press.

Serres, M. with Latour, B. (1995). *Conversations on science, culture and time*. (R. Lapidus, Trans.). Ann Arbor: University of Michigan Press.

Shannon, C. & Weaver, W. (1949). *The mathematical theory of communication*. Urbana: University of Illinois Press.

Shaughnessy, P. (2000). Into the deep end. In T. Curtis, R. Dellar, E. Leslie & B. Watson (Eds.), *Mad pride – a celebration of mad culture*. London: Spare Change Books.

Shorter, E. (2000). Review: Jean Thullier, Ten years that changed the world. *Journal of Psychopharmacology*, *14* (1), 89.

Shotter, J. (1994). *Conversational realities*. London: Sage.

Silverman, H.J. (Ed.). (1993). *Questioning foundations: truth/subjectivity/culture*. London: Routledge.

Snow, C.P. (1959/2003). *The two cultures*. Cambridge: Cambridge University Press.

Sontag, S. (Ed.). (1988). *Antonin Artaud: selected writings*. Berkeley CA: University of California Press.

Speer, S.A. (2005). *Gender talk: feminism, discourse and conversation analysis*. London: Routledge.

Spencer-Brown, G. (1969/1994). *Laws of forms*. Portland, OR: Cognizer Connection.

Spinoza, B. (1677/1993). *Ethics and treatise on the correction of the intellect*. (A. Boyle, Trans.). London: J.M. Dent.

Stainton Rogers, R. & Stainton Rogers, W. (1992). *Stories of childhood: shifting agendas of child concern*. Hemel Hempstead: Harvester Wheatsheaf.

Stainton Rogers, R., Stenner, P., Gleeson, K. & Stainton Rogers, W. (1995, reprinted 1996). *Social psychology: a critical agenda*. Cambridge: Polity Press.

Stam, H.J. (1997). *The body and psychology*. London: Sage.

Stengers, I. (1997). *Power and invention*, Minneapolis: University of Minnesota Press.

Stengers, I. (2000). *The invention of modern science*. (D.W. Smith, Trans.). Minneapolis: University of Minnesota Press.

Stengers, I. (2002). *Penser avec Whitehead: une libre et sauvage création de concepts*. Paris: Gallimard.

Stenner, P. (1998). Heidegger and the Subject: questioning concerning psychology. *Theory and Psychology, 8* (1), 59–77.

Stenner, P. (2002). Social psychology and Babel. *History and Philosophy of Psychology, 4* (1), 45–57.

Stenner, P. (2003). Dostoevsky and the spirit of critical psychology. *International Journal of Critical Psychology, 8*, 96–128.

Stenner, P. (2004). Psychology and the political: on the psychology of natural right and the political origins of modern psychology. *International Journal of Critical Psychology, 12*, 14–37.

Stenner, P. (2006). An outline of an autopoietic systems approach to emotion. *Cybernetics and Human Knowing, 12* (4): 8–22.

Stenner, P. (2007a). Non-foundational criticality? On the need for a process ontology of the psychosocial. *Outlines, Critical Social Studies, 9* (2), 44–55.

Stenner, P. (2007b). The adventure of psychosocial studies: re-visioning the space between the psychic and the social. Inaugural Lecture, University of Brighton, at: http://www.brighton.ac.uk/sass/contact/staffprofiles/stenner/inaugural_lecture.pdf (Accessed December 2008).

Stenner, P. (2008). A.N. Whitehead and subjectivity. *Subjectivity, 22*, 90–109.

Stenner, P. and Eccleston, C. (1994). On the textuality of being. *Theory and Psychology, 4* (1), 85–103.

Terr, L. (1994). *Unchained memories: true stories of traumatic memories, lost and found*. New York: Basic Books.

Thien, D. (2005). After or beyond feeling? A consideration of affect and emotion in geography, *Area, 37* (4), 450–456.

Thrift, N. (2008). *Non-representational theory: space/politics/affect*. London: Routledge.

Thullier, J. (1999). *Ten years that changed the face of mental illness*. London: Martin Dunitz.

Tucker, I. (2006). *Deterritorializing mental health: unfolding service user experience*. PhD, Loughborough University.

Venn, C. (1984). The subject of psychology. In J. Henriques, W. Hollway, C. Urwin, C. Venn, & V. Walkerdine (1984). *Changing the subject: psychology, social regulation and subjectivity*. London: Methuen.

Verschraegen, G. (2002). Human rights and modern society: a sociological analysis from the perspective of systems theory. *Journal of Law and Society, 29*, 258–281.

Volosinov, V.N. (1987). *Freudianism: a critical sketch*. Bloomington and Indianapolis: Indiana University Press.

Vygotsky, L. (1934/1987). *Thought and language.* Cambridge, MA: Harvard University Press.

Vygotsky, L.S. (1982). Vosprijatie i ego razvitije v detskom vozraste. In L.S. Vygotsky, *Collected works.* In 6 volumes. Vol. 2 (pp. 363–381). Moscow: Pedagogica.

Wallerstein, I., Jumas, C., Fox Keller, E., Kocka, J., Lecourt, D. Mudimbe, V.Y., Mushakoji, K. Prigogine, I., Taylor, P.J., Trouillot, M.R. (1996). *Open the social sciences: report of the Gulbenkian Commission on the Restructuring of the Social Sciences.* Stanford, CA: Stanford University Press.

Weber, S. (2000). The greatest thing of all: the virtuality of theatre. In E. Scheer (Ed.), *One hundred years of cruelty: essays on Artaud.* Sydney: Power Publications.

Wertsch, J.V. (2002). *Voices of collective remembering.* Cambridge: Cambridge University Press.

Whitehead, A.N. (1920/2004). *The concept of nature.* New York: Prometheus Books.

Whitehead, A.N. (1926/1985). *Science and the modern world.* London: Free Association Books.

Whitehead, A.N. (1926/2005). *Religion in the making.* New York: Fordham University Press.

Whitehead, A.N. (1927). *Symbolism: its meaning and effect.* Virginia: University of Virginia Press.

Whitehead, A.N. (1927–8/1985). *Process and reality.* New York: Free Press.

Whitehead, A.N. (1929/1958). *The function of reason.* Boston: Beacon Press.

Whitehead, A.N.(1933/1935). *Adventures in ideas.* London: Cambridge University Press.

Whitehead, A.N. (1934). *Nature and life.* Cambridge: Cambridge University Press.

Whitehead, A.N. (1938/1966). *Modes of thought.* New York: Free Press.

Willig, C. (2001). *Introducing qualitative research in psychology.* Buckingham: Open University Press.

Wilson, M.D. (1996). Spinoza's theory of knowledge. In D. Garrett (Ed.), *The Cambridge companion to Spinoza.* Cambridge: Cambridge University Press.

Windelband, W. (1894/1998). History and natural science. *Theory & Psychology, 8* (1), 5–22.

Wise, J.M. (2005). Assemblage. In C.J. Stivale (Ed.), *Gilles Deleuze: key concept.* Chesham, Bucks: Acumen.

Wittgenstein, L. (1921/1981). *Tractatus logico-philosophicus.* London: Routledge.

Wittgenstein, L. (1958). *Philosophical investigations.* London: Macmillan.

Wolf, G. (1981). Psychological physiology from the standpoint of a physiological psychologist. *Process Studies, 11* (4): 274–291.

Woolgar, S. (1988). *Science: the very idea?* London: Routledge.

Zeleny, M. (1981). What is autopoiesis? In M. Zeleny (Ed.), *Autopoiesis: a theory of living organization.* New York: Elsevier.

Zizek, S. (2003). *Organs without bodies: on Deleuze and consequences.* London: Routledge.

Index

communication *cont.*
    as mediation 66–70
    and money 73
    nonverbal 79
    open 41
    performative culture of 41
    reality of 81
    real-time, unfolding in 70
    self-referentiality 81
    socially structured communicative activity 69
    third selection of understanding 77–8
    transmission model of 83–4
    utterance and information 78–82
communicational utopia (Habermas) 40, 41
communicative events 70
communicative understanding 80
complexity theory 82
complexity-from-noise principle 40, 51
Comte, Auguste 17, 18
conatus 180, 181, 183
    and desire 124, 191
    Spinozism, subject 119
The concept of nature (Whitehead) 25
concrescence 27, 34, 35, 58
confession 157, 161, 162, 164, 166
confidence 126
conjunctive synthesis 27, 35, 182, 184
connectivity principle 54
consciousness 53, 54
    Artaudian 92–3, 94
    Bergson on 139
    and communication 85
    and duration *see* duration
    and embodiment 103
constructionism 142
constructivism 12
content analysis techniques 64
continuity, and actual occasions 28
Conversation Analysis 63, 72
Cooper, Robert 173
cosmology, Whiteheadian 12, 25, 29, 31
Creative evolution (Bergson) 150–1
creative foundationalism 3, 6, 32, 113
creativity
    bottom up creative evolution 31
    and conjunctive synthesis process 27
    foundations as product of creative effort 32
    principle of 27, 33, 34
    self-creative 34
The Creative Mind (Bergson) 143
Cromby 110
cruel thought 97–100
    interpretation of 'cruelty' 99
Cummings, ee 195
Curt, Beryl 59
cybermetics, second order 5

Damasio, Antonio 9
    and Artaud 111
    on decision-making 110

Damasio, Antonio *cont.*
    on Descartes 109–10, 131
    error of 127–32
    on feelings 123, 127
    neuroscientific approaches 138
    somatic marker hypothesis of 110
    stories of 111
Danziger, K. 19
das Ge-stell (Enframing) 163
The death of the author (Barthes) 175, 198
deconstruction 24
deep empiricism 12, 35, 37
Delay, Jean 153, 155–6
Deleuze, Giles 7, 106, 169–70, 175–98, 203
    actual and virtual 183–8
    and Artaud 101
    desire and pleasure 188–95
    on emotions 112, 123
    and Foucault 188, 193
    on ideas 122
    Immanence: a life 177–83
    post-structuralism 112
    and Proust 148
    and Serres 183–4
    and Whitehead 12, 179
delinquency 192, 193
Deniker, Pierre 153, 154
dermatological psychology 173
Derrida, Jacques 92–3, 103, 173
Descartes, R. 14
    critique by Spinoza 114–18, 138
    on experience 13
    mind/body relation 94, 95, 114, 115,
        127, 138
Descartes' Error (Damasio) 109–10
desire
    affects of 124
    and conatus 124, 191
    lack 191
    mimetic desire theory 60
    and pleasure 193–194
        see also Desire and pleasure (essay)
        188–95
    psychoanalysis 190
Desire and pleasure (essay) 188–95
desire-production-machine 191
despair 125–6
determinism, mechanistic 112
deterritorialisation 193, 194
developmental psychology 107
Dewey, John 12, 20
dialectics of nature 69
Dickens, Charles 182–3
Dilthey, Wilhem 24
direct perception 140
disappointment 126
Discipline and punish (Foucault) 164, 188
discourse
    'assumed' of 73
    and communication 69

discourse *cont.*
  incomprehensibility to outside observers 76
  phenomenology 84
  and terminology issues 68
Discourse Analysis 157, 158
discursive psychology 7, 62, 65, 72, 90–1
  discursive turn 66–8
disequilibrium 39
disjunctive diversity 27
dispersed multiplicity 56
displacement, foundation through 3
dispositif 189
Drew, 72
drive theory, Freudian 111–12
dualism 16
  see also mind/body relation
  Cartesian 25, 94, 95, 114, 127
  and triads 70
Dulac, Germaine 105
duration
  actual and virtual 187
  and Foucault 168
  memory as 144–9
  pure 178
Durkheim, Emile 55, 56

education system, two cultures of 16
Edwards, D. 62, 63, 64
Electro-Convulsive Therapy (ECT) 153, 154
embodiment, Artaud on 94, 102, 103
emergent reality, communication as 70, 81
emotions
  see also feelings
  and affect/affective turn 111, 112, 119
  antipathy 124
  confidence 126
  and Deleuze 112, 123
  despair 125–6
  disappointment 126
  and encounters 120
  execution 'switch' 130, 131
  fear 126
  hate 124
  hope 126
  and individuals 112
  jealousy 125
  love 124–5
  Spinoza on 124–6
  transitory feelings of 146
empiricism 177
  deep 12, 35, 37
  radical 65
empty space, notion of 23
encounters 120–4
endurance 21, 22, 33, 145
  and occurrence 28, 34
enframing 163
Ensembles and multiplicities (Deleuze) 184
enterprise culture 41
entities, actual *see* actual occasions/entities

enunciation 204, 209–10
epimeleisthai sautou (to take care of
  yourself) 164
essence of a thing 118, 119
  relational essences 206
Ethics (Spinoza) 114, 117, 127, 132
euphoria 124, 126
events, as activities of realisation 25
evolutionary theory, Darwinian 19
exagoreusis 162
excluded middle, law of 43–50
excluded third, role of 38
existential hermeneutics 67
exomologēsis 162
experience
  impersonal, pure immanence as 180
  of language 66
  and physiology 13
  and psychology 11
  pure 179
  subject of 15
experimental psychology 63, 147
extension
  causality 120
  and thought 114, 115, 116
extraverbal pragmatic situations 71, 73
extreme case formulation (ECF) 63
eyewitness testimony 133–4

false memory syndrome 7
False Memory Syndrome Foundation
  (FMSF) 135
faultline 155
fear 126
feelings 27, 111–12, 123, 127
  see also emotions
Ferdière, Gaston 100–1
flow, foundation based on 38
FMSF (False Memory Syndrome Foundation) 135
Foerster, H. von 5, 40, 51
forgetfulness, language of 91
The formation of false memories (Loftus and
  Pickrell) 133
Foucault, Michel 4, 203
  on absence of work 94
  on ancient Greeks 163, 164, 165
  on Artaud 169
  and Deleuze 188, 193
  Discourse Analysis 157, 158
  and language 93
  psychology of 156–61
  on self 168
  on sensuality 164
  on subjectivity 8, 9, 154–74
  on thought 91
foundation
  defined 21
  by exclusion 18, 48–50
  flow, based on 38
  as product of creative effort 32

Lacan, Jacques 91, 104, 155, 190
Laing, R.D. 154
Langer, Susanne 12
language
　and Artaud 93, 94
　and communication 53–4, 66, 71
　definitions 99–100
　Deleuze on 182
　and Foucault 93
　mental processes mediated by 68–9
　minorizing of 196
　sign 99
　and thought 90, 91
Lapoujade, David 178–9
law, and subjectivism 13
Le Parole Soufflée (Derrida) 92
life
　art of living 164, 170, 201
　as impersonal striving/of given
　　individual 181
　and imminence 177–83
life-work 94, 169
light, transmission theory for 15
LIM *see* Lost in shopping mall (LIM) procedure
linguistic imperialism 7
literary criticism 93–4
Locke, J. 206
Loftus, Elizabeth 133, 134, 135, 136
logic, classical 43
Logic of sense (Deleuze) 195
logos 142
Lost in shopping mall (LIM) procedure 150, 151
　aims of 135
　criticism of 135
　description of 133
　importance for psychology of memory 152
　limitations of 137
　strategies exposed by 136
　as suitable analogue 134
Lot and his daughters (painting by van
　Leyden) 97
love 124–5
Lowenthal, David 3
Luhmann, Niklas 5, 7, 8
　and Artaud 8
　on communication 70–6, 82, 89
　on third selection of understanding 77–8
lungs, mediation of 53
Lyotard, J.-F. 41, 67

machinic assemblage 192
Mackay, D.M. 79
MacMillan, K. 64
madness, Foucault on 155, 157
Magritte, Rene 203, 204, 207, 209
Making monsters (Ofshe) 135
Mannheim, Karl 167
Marcus Aurelius (Roman) 165–6, 173
Marcuse, Herbert 190

Marres, Nortjes 142
Marseilles, bubonic plague in (1720) 97–8
Massumi, Brian 112, 184
master narratives 149
materialism, scientific *see* scientific materialism
materialist monism 15
matter, location of particles in space and time
　14, 15, 23
Matter and Memory (Bergson) 137–8, 139,
　142, 144
Maturana, H. 22, 163
McCormack 112
mechanistic materialism *see* scientific
　materialism
mediation
　ambulatory relations between mediators 65
　audio-tape transmission and mediators 64–5
　communication as 66–70
　concept of (Serres) 6, 37–61
　excluded middle, law of 43–50
　forms of media, between 52
　foundation by exclusion, and paradoxical
　　ambivalence 48–50
　identity of parasite 44–8
　and intermediaries 38, 43, 45, 46
　of lungs 53
　parasite as 45
Melville, Herman 1–2, 4
memory
　as duration *see* duration
　false memory syndrome 7
　and Foucault 174
　recovered 7, 134
　representation and action 137–41
　virtual and actual 141–4
memory aids 173
memory wars 7, 149, 152
mental health 155
mental health service users, daily routines 170–2
message transmission, and exclusion
　of parasite 44
metacommunication, real-time 75
metaphors 21, 22, 33
metaphysics 67, 93, 177, 178
micro and macro 189
Milgram, Stanley 135–6
milieu 38
Mill, John Stuart 17
mimetic desire theory 60
mind, science of as anti-science 18
mind/body relation
　and Bergson 139
　and Descartes 94, 95, 114, 115, 127, 138
　and Spinoza 116, 117, 138
misplaced concreteness, fallacy of 34
Mitteilung (utterance) 70, 77, 79, 81
　see also utterances
mittel 38
Moby-Dick (Melville) 1–2, 4

positive prehension 27
positivism 17, 23
post-crisis writing, in social psychology 3
postmodern condition of knowledge 67
post-structuralism 67, 112
potentialities 27, 34
Potter, J. 72
power
    Fouault on 158, 188, 189
    PIPE mnemonic 203, 206–7
power-knowledge, inseparability of 162
pragmatism 7, 19
prefrontal regions of brain, dorsal/medial 130
prehension 27, 179
presentational immediacy 208
presiding occasions 32
Prigogine, Ilya 11
primary and secondary qualities 15
Principia Mathematica (Whitehead and Russell) 11
Principles of Psychology (James) 20
process
    concept of (Whitehead) 6, 11–36
    concrescence, process of 27
    of conjunctive synthesis 27
    definition of 'process' 26
    and integration 56
    as reality 34
    and relationality 38, 43
    and stasis 33
    unification 27
Process and reality (Whitehead) 11–12, 26, 204
professional hearing 65
proper names 182
proposition 204, 208–9
Proust, M. 143, 148, 149
psychiatry/anti-psychiatry debate 154
psychic causality 19, 22
psychic existence 31
psychic processes, and communication 69, 85
psychoanalysis 136, 156, 162, 176, 190
psychological complex (psy-complex) 157–8,
    158–9, 160
psychological theatre 107–8
psychology
    as branch of medicine 18, 19
    dermatological 173
    developmental 107
    discipline of 18–19, 22
    discursive see discursive psychology
    and experience 11
    experimental 147
    foundational paradox of 18–20, 23, 25
    North American 20
    physiological 11
    qualitative developments in 84
    second order 5
    social see social psychology
    and social sciences 18
    sociocultural 147

psychometric tradition 19
psychophysiological parallelism 138
psychosocial research 176
The psychology of Alfred North Whitehead
    (Johnson) 12
pure immanence 178, 180, 195

quantum theory 23, 44
quasi-objects 56–8

radical empiricism 65
realisation, concept 26
realism 140, 141
reconstruction 147, 149
recovered memory 7, 134
reflexive foundationalism 3, 6, 9, 176
re-foundationalism 20, 21, 24, 25, 32
relational process approach 12–13, 32, 37, 38
relativity theory 11, 23, 34, 206
reminiscence 173–4
representation
    and action 137–41
    and image 142
    notion of 139
repression/repressive hypothesis 134, 135, 188
resistance 158
    and subjectivity 167–74
rhizome 197
Richards, Barry 111
Riemann, Georg 186
Rivière, Jacques 89, 90
Rose, Nikolas 157, 158–9, 161
Rousseau, Jean Jacques 46, 88
Royal Society statutes 16
Russell, Bertrand 11

Sacks, Harvey 76
sacrifice 61
Said, Edward 95
scapegoat mechanism 59, 60
Schwitters, Kurt 197
Science and the modern world (Whitehead) 25–6
scientific materialism
    efficiency of 16
    and foundational paradox of psychological
        science 18–20, 23, 25
    objectivism of 14
second order psychology 5
self (auto) creation 8
self-actualisation 181
self-care 167, 168, 172, 173
self-knowledge 167
self-mastery 165
self-realisation 27, 32, 34, 35
self-referential systems 22
semiotics 122
sensation 139
sense-awareness 71
sensuality 164

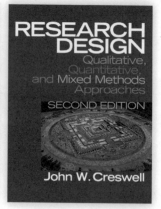

The Qualitative Research Kit

Edited by Uwe Flick

Read sample chapters online now!

Doing Ethnographic and Observational Research — Michael Angrosino — The SAGE Qualitative Research Kit — Edited by Uwe Flick

Using Visual Data in Qualitative Research — Marcus Banks — The SAGE Qualitative Research Kit — Edited by Uwe Flick

Doing Focus Groups — Rosaline Barbour — The SAGE Qualitative Research Kit

Designing Qualitative Research — Uwe Flick — The SAGE Qualitative Research Kit — Edited by Uwe Flick

Managing Quality in Qualitative Research — Uwe Flick — The SAGE Qualitative Research Kit — Edited by Uwe Flick

Analyzing Qualitative Data — Graham Gibbs — The SAGE Qualitative Research Kit — Edited by Uwe Flick

Doing Interviews — Steinar Kvale — The SAGE Qualitative Research Kit — Edited by Uwe Flick

Doing Conversation, Discourse and Document Analysis — Tim Rapley — The SAGE Qualitative Research Kit — Edited by Uwe Flick

www.sagepub.co.uk

Supporting researchers for more than forty years

Research methods have always been at the core of SAGE's publishing. Sara Miller McCune founded SAGE in 1965 and soon after, she published SAGE's first methods book, *Public Policy Evaluation*. A few years later, she launched the Quantitative Applications in the Social Sciences series – affectionately known as the 'little green books'.

Always at the forefront of developing and supporting new approaches in methods, SAGE published early groundbreaking texts and journals in the fields of qualitative methods and evaluation.

Today, more than forty years and two million little green books later, SAGE continues to push the boundaries with a growing list of more than 1,200 research methods books, journals, and reference works across the social, behavioural, and health sciences.

From qualitative, quantitative and mixed methods to evaluation, SAGE is the essential resource for academics and practitioners looking for the latest in methods by leading scholars.

www.sagepublications.com